The Daily Life of
The Queen

TO
VIOLET

May You
Enjoy
Many Years
Of Leisure

FLO

2002

The Daily Life of
The Queen

An Artist's Diary by
MICHAEL & VIVIEN NOAKES

EBURY
PRESS

DEDICATION

To Vida Box

First published in Great Britain in 2000

1 3 5 7 9 10 8 6 4 2

Ebury Press

Random House, 20 Vauxhall Bridge Road, London SW1V 2SA

Random House Australia Pty Limited

20 Alfred Street, Milsons Point, Sydney, New South Wales 2061, Australia

Random House New Zealand Limited

18 Poland Road, Glenfield, Auckland 10, New Zealand

Random House (Pty) Limited

Endulini, 5A Jubilee Road, Parktown 2193, South Africa

The Random House Group Limited Reg. No. 954009

www.randomhouse.co.uk

Papers used by Ebury Press are natural, recyclable products made from wood grown in sustainable forests.

A CIP catalogue record for this book is available from the British Library.

Edited by Alison Wormleighton

Designed by David Fordham

ISBN 0 091 86982 X

Typeset by MATS, Southend-on-Sea, Essex

Printed and bound in Italy by Graphicom

ACKNOWLEDGEMENTS

OUR FIRST THANKS must go to Her Majesty The Queen, for approving and encouraging this project and for her co-operation throughout. From the beginning it was made clear to us that there would be Palace support but no censorship of either illustrations or text, a rare privilege which has given us the maximum freedom to be with The Queen as she went about her working life, combined with the opportunity to observe and interpret what we saw in our own way. For this we are most grateful.

We owe a debt of gratitude to Lord Fellowes who, as Sir Robert Fellowes, was Private Secretary to The Queen at the time the project was proposed, and who encouraged and supported the book from the beginning. To his successor, Sir Robin Janvrin, we extend our thanks for the help he subsequently gave us. Penny Russell-Smith, Deputy Press Secretary to The Queen, was involved in the project from its inception, and her imagination, enthusiasm and support have been invaluable. We also wish to thank Dickie Arbiter, and those in the Press Office who had the imagination to understand the unusual aspect of what we were trying to do and the courtesy to help us do it.

Many members of The Queen's Household have been patient with our enquiries and generous with their time, in particular the Communications Secretary, Simon Lewis; Tim Hitchins and Andrew Dent of The Private Office; The Master of the Household, Major-General Sir Simon Cooper and his deputy, Sir Guy Acland, Bt; The Crown Equerry, Lieutenant-Colonel Seymour Gilbart-Denham and The Superintendent of The Royal Mews, Major Ian Kelly; The Equerry-in-waiting to The Queen, Squadron Leader Simon Brailsford; and The Queen's Personal Protection Officers, David Robinson and Ken Atmore. For their interest and help we wish to thank Joe Grimwade, Manager of The Royal Studs; Bill Meldrum of the Sandringham kennels; Gill Pattinson of the Sandringham Estate Office; Peter Ord, Resident Factor at Balmoral; Pat Pentney, the Florist; and Bob Turvey, the Assistant Sawmill Manager at Sandringham. For the welcome they extended to us we are grateful to Lady Grove, Diana Hall, Jean Lee and members of the West Newton Women's Institute.

Many have given their time in arranging visits, showing us their establishments and answering endless queries. In particular we would like to acknowledge the help of Irene Allen of LEPRA; Emma Armstrong of The Joint Commonwealth Societies' Council; Captain Anthony Brumwell, Adjutant of the RHA; Anne Cohen of the Parkside Health Trust; Cheryll Dorall and Mischa Manderson Mills of the Commonwealth Secretariat; Brigadier Hedley Duncan, Yeoman Usher of the Black Rod, and Joanne Fuller of Black Rod's Department; Colonel Iain Ferguson, Director of The Royal Tournament; Didy Grahame, Secretary of The Victoria Cross and George Cross Association; Ted Johns and Dr Michael Barraclough of Mudchute Farm; David Le Breton, Secretary of the Overseas Service Pensioners' Association; Barrie Matterson, Regeneration Manager of CityVision, Hull; Sue Minter, Curator of the Chelsea Physic Garden; Captain Rupert Phelps, The Life Guards; and Louise Ward, Headmistress of The King George VI School, Great Bircham.

Our visits to Scotland were made both enjoyable and memorable by the unflappable and generous professionalism of Sandy Sutherland, and his assistant Karen Crawford. We would also like to thank Jane Ferguson and Barbara Fraser of Historic Scotland. For help during out visit to Wales we are grateful to Alan Thomas of the Welsh Office, and the staff of Quadrant Public Relations and BBC Wales. For their assistance at various venues we are grateful to Lorraine Coulton, Eileen Jones and Jane Neale of the Central Office of Information.

During and after our visit to the Republic of Korea we received much courtesy from His Excellency Mr Choi Sung-hong, Ambassador of the Republic of Korea to the Court of St James's, and from the staff of the British Embassy in Seoul especially Colin Crooks, Ros Sparrow, Jonathan Dart, Anne Marie Graham and Kim Jeong-oh. During our visit to Africa we were helped in Ghana by Mike Nithavrianakis, in South Africa by Mike Doig and Samantha Hyde, and in Mozambique by Andrew Bowes.

We have spoken to a number of people who have been, at one time or another, closely involved in The Queen's working life, and whose ideas and suggestions have given us valuable insights. In particular we are grateful to the late Lord Charteris of Amisfield, Sir William Heseltine, Sir Edmund Grove and Dr Michael Shea.

A number of people kindly read parts of the text and commented on them for accuracy, including The Lady Airlie, Philip Everett, Brian Hanson, Sir William Heseltine, Peter Ord, Professor Jack Scarisbrick, Daniel Woolford and William Tallon. We alone are responsible for any remaining errors.

During the year we have made many friends among the press, who shared their thoughts, expertise and stories with us. We thank Peter Archer, Arthur Edwards, Terry Chambers, Fiona Hanson, Ian Jones, Dorinda McCann, Mark Stewart, Judy Wade and Peter Wilkinson. The ideas expressed in the section on The Queen and the Press are ours alone, gleaned from our observation of many situations during the year.

We are grateful to Dr Frank Prochaska for suggesting we might read his *Royal Bounty: The Making of a Welfare Monarchy*, which was invaluable in our discussion of this subject, to Michael Pitel for his incomparable knowledge of wines, to Fay Hewett for matters equestrian and to Ben Noakes for his many ideas. Finally, for their quiet and unfailing support we owe a debt of gratitude to Mr and Mrs Richard Devine, Sheila Watson, Julian Shuckburgh, David Fordham and Alison Wormleighton.

INTRODUCTION

THE ORIGINAL SEED from which this book has grown was sown nearly twenty years ago with an invitation to observe and sketch the Prince of Wales at work. From these drawings – done on the only paper available and headed *Memorandum from HRH The Prince of Wales* – grew an idea which led to a proposal that we might record the Queen's working life in pictures and text.

It was inconceivable even a few years ago that the Queen would have agreed that two outsiders should be with her throughout a whole year, recording her working life at Buckingham Palace, Windsor, Sandringham and Balmoral, at many other venues through-out Great Britain and during her travels abroad. But in those years things have changed. It is a different world, and the monarchy has become more vulnerable, more answerable and more open.

In fact, the moves to openness were already underway. There has been no sudden modernisation of the monarchy, but there has been a speeding up. It is not new for the Queen to visit a pub, or to travel on an ordinary train, although when these things happen they are often reported as the Royal Family anxiously seeking answers to their perceived dilemma of being old-fashioned, elitist and out of touch. As long ago as 1967, in the TV film *Royal Family,* the public saw behind-the-scenes images of the Queen at work and at play. This was followed in the Jubilee year of 1992 by a second film, *Elizabeth R*, with an accompanying book written by Antony Jay.

In preparing the two films, television crews were given access to the Queen over a year, but their access was to selected events which were chosen so as to give a rounded picture of royal life. Never before has anyone been with the Queen for all her public, and many of her official but non-public, engagements over such a long period. We were being given an opportunity to build up a comprehensive picture of her working life, to see it in all its scope, its variety, its fascination and its relentless repetitiousness.

The timing of our book was fortuitous, for few other years can have offered more fascinating opportunities. There has been no

year like it in the recent past, and neither 2000 nor 2001 will have so many important royal events. The Golden Jubilee year of 2002 will be full and exciting but it will not be typical, and after that the Queen will inevitably wind down her public engagements, for by then she will be seventy-six and the Duke of Edinburgh will be eighty-one.

The year 1999 saw the making of history in Scottish devolution and the opening of the Welsh Assembly. It saw also the fiftieth anniversary of the Commonwealth; the biennial Commonwealth Heads of Government Meeting; a three-country tour of Africa including a visit to Mozambique, the first country to enter the Commonwealth that was not previously part of the British Empire; a State Visit to Korea, where so many British, Commonwealth and US forces fought and died; a contentious State Visit by the President of the most populous country on earth; the fiftieth anniversary of the Council of Europe; the final Royal Tournament; the granting of a Royal Charter to The Prince's Trust; a World Cricket Cup and a World Rugby Cup, both competed for in the UK; a royal wedding; the reopening of the Royal Opera House, Covent Garden; the cen-tenary of the appointment of the first Court Correspondent; a deputation of Aboriginal leaders (the Queen rarely sees any deputation, however important); a new Poet Laureate; a change of Private Secretary; and the end of a millennium, as well as the usual full timetable of private audiences, receptions, away days and celebrations typical of any year. When we talked to the Palace about the proposal in the summer of 1998 we had no idea what a vintage year 1999 would be.

We went into the year with open minds. We were not setting out to prove or demonstrate anything. Instead we wanted to discover what went on as the Queen went about her daily working life and to see just how hard she worked, what that work really was and how important, or not, it was to the people of this and other countries. For us, as much as for our readers, it was going to be an exploration.

We were not, though, unused to royal events. Any artist painting the Queen will spend many hours alone with her – in this case between twenty and thirty hours since 1972. For various reasons we had, over the years, had contact with many other members of the Royal Family. A number of now retired people from the Royal Household have been long-standing personal friends. Yet we were not committed royalists. At the beginning of the year we assessed how we felt, and concluded that we were sixty per cent in favour of the monarchy and forty per cent questioning its value. Like others, we had watched the unravelling of respect that had surrounded the unhappy events involving the younger generation. We thought that the Queen was unwise not to have paid tax earlier than she did. At a time of deep recession and financial worry for so many, we believed it to be a public relations disaster that the taxpayer should have been expected to meet the bill for the restoration of Windsor Castle; in the event this did not happen, but in the public mind the damage was done. Our royal year would be a time to discover, to question and to analyse what we saw. We had no idea at the beginning how we were going to feel at the end.

Of immense importance was the proposal – which came not from us but from the Palace – that we should be free agents in interpreting what we saw. The Palace would supply the opportunities and check facts, but there would be no censorship. Of course, it would have been of value to neither them nor us if we had been Palace poodles carrying out a public relations exercise on their behalf, but it was an indication of the trust they put in us – for which we are grateful – and of their belief in the value of what we would be witnessing during the year, that they felt able to enter into such an open arrangement with us. It was both a freedom and a responsibility.

We decided from the beginning that we would list, in a form resembling the *Court Circular*, every engagement carried out by the Queen, even though we could neither illustrate nor comment on all of these. We would not list each day her routine meetings with her private secretaries or her reading of the State papers which come in the famous red boxes, nor would we set down the work-related but in the end personal appointments with her hairdresser or her dressmaker. Everything else would be listed, and this would give a chance for us to see just how many things the Queen does of which the public is unaware. The Wednesday List, giving the public engagements of all the Royal Family, is available to journalists and others who are interested; it is now published on the Palace web site. One of the privileges the Palace extended to us was allowing us to see the Queen's Weekly Card, a confidential timetable published for the information of the Royal Household only. This is issued each Monday morning and lists every engagement and every official arrival and departure from the Palace. It forms the basis of the listings we have given. Timings seemed both interesting and important, and many of these have been incorporated so that readers might have an idea of how precise and exact the Queen's arrangements are.

The book is arranged chronologically. At the beginning of each month there is a section dealing with some particular aspect of the Queen's work. In planning the book the publishers decided to incorporate eight triple- and four quadruple-page spreads. Given the chronological arrangement, we needed to arrive at these spreads – which, for technical reasons, can only come at the end of sixteen-page sections – at the right time, for only a few events could justify such expansive treatment. This we have done, but in each of the groupings of panoramas for Korea in April, Windsor in June and Edinburgh in July, one gatefold has been moved slightly forward out of sequence, since the Queen did not conveniently attend three panoramic occasions one after another. In each case it has been clearly dated.

In many ways the monarchy is under siege. Follies have fed a relentless public appetite for scandal and trivia on which many people base their ideas of the value and purpose of the Royal Family. But there is a limit to the appeal of speculation; the public also likes to know real facts. These facts in words and pictures, alongside our personal – and sometimes critical – diary of the year, are what this book offers.

JANUARY
THE QUEEN AS LANDOWNER

THE QUEEN ONCE SAID that, had she not been monarch, she would have enjoyed living in the country surrounded by dogs and horses. That cannot be her way of life, but she is able to spend several months each year away from London in one of her two privately owned estates, at Sandringham in Norfolk and Balmoral in the Scottish Highlands. Both are owned and funded by the Queen personally rather than as sovereign, and although each is under the supervision of an estate manager – or factor as he is called in Scotland – overall control of the estates rests with the Duke of Edinburgh as head of the family, and with the Queen and the Prince of Wales. A third estate, at Windsor, where the Queen goes for most weekends when she is in London, belongs to the Crown rather than to the Queen personally, but it too comes under the supervision of the Royal Family, with decisions about the management of all three being made at the twice-yearly Forward Planning Meetings for the Royal Estates.

Sandringham has nearly 20,000 acres of land, and Balmoral 45,000, but they are very different from one another. The land at Balmoral is poor, mostly lying 1,000 feet above sea-level and with seven mountains above 3,000 feet. Only about 450 acres are suitable for farming, and of this about half is let to tenant farmers. The rest of the estate is forest and moorland. The Queen has a small, prize-winning herd of Highland cattle, and a number of Highland, Fell and Haflinger ponies which are used for trekking and for bringing deer down from the hills during the stalking season. The rest of the estate is given over to forestry and to raising grouse and red deer.

In all the Royal Estates there has been a long-standing emphasis on conservation and environmental husbandry. It is a sign of the success of the conservation programme, which began before conservation was fashionable, that 6,000 acres of woodland, moorland and hilltop at Lochnagar and Ballochbuie on the Balmoral estate are designated Special Protection Areas under the European Birds Directive, with 4,000 acres of this at Ballochbuie

also recommended as a Special Area of Conservation under the European Habitats Directive. Much of the Balmoral estate is freely open to the more than 180,000 hill walkers and other visitors who come to explore the hills and countryside each year, with conducted walks to sites of natural heritage interest and a continuing programme of footpath repair and maintenance. In addition the estate contains one of the last surviving and largest remnants of native Caledonian pine forest. This type of forest – a mixture of birch, pine, rowan and juniper – goes back to the last Ice Age and was widespread over Scotland until it was felled for wood and to make way for grazing. Ballochbuie Forest was bought by Queen Victoria in 1878 to prevent its being sold to a local timber merchant, and for more than twenty-five years has been undergoing systematic regeneration overseen by the Duke of Edinburgh and monitored by the Institute of Terrestrial Ecology. Deer management is carefully controlled to guarantee the restoration of the heather habitat and the health of the herd. Although income is generated by farming, forestry, grouse and venison sales, and from visitors to the castle, this does not cover the expenses of the estate, which are borne privately by the Queen.

Edward VIII described Sandringham as 'a voracious white elephant', but during the Queen's reign it has been turned into a profitable estate. The Estate Office of Sandringham is in York Cottage, the modest house which was the preferred home for many years of King George V and Queen Mary, and where the Queen's father, King George VI, was born. The estate is a designated Area of Outstanding Natural Beauty and is a mixture of arable land, forest and country park. Of its 20,600 acres, about 12,000 are sublet to tenant farmers. There are 600 acres of woodland which make up the Sandringham Country Park and nearly 2,000 acres of forest, with the rest given over to livestock, wheat, barley, sugar beet, peas and beans, and fruit-farming. There are also twelve Highland cattle. Whereas in Balmoral felled trees are sold to commercial mills, Sandringham has its own sawmills selling a wide range of

wood products, from stakes and fencing to sheds, bird tables and garden furniture. Some of the wheat is stone-ground at a local watermill, and sold in the Visitors' Centre. The blackcurrant crop becomes Ribena, and strawberries, raspberries and English apples (Cox, Laxton, Howgate Wonder, Discovery, Bramleys and Worcester Pearmain) are sold to 'Pick Your Own' customers and at the Centre. During the apple season up to 3,000 people each weekend come to pick the fruit. Glasshouses provide cut flowers for the house and for a flower and pot-plant stall adjacent to the shop, which, with the restaurant, tea-room and ice-cream kiosk, is an important source of income; more (locally made) ice cream is sold at Sandringham than on Norfolk's Great Yarmouth beach. In addition to the farm there is the 600-acre Sandringham Country Park of woodland, rich in birdlife and with two established nature trails open to the public.

Pheasant is shot during the October to February season, but these shoots are private, low-key affairs involving only the Royal Family and their friends, quite unlike those of Edward VII when hundreds of birds might be shot in a single day. Also at Sandringham the Queen has kennels for the breeding and training of working dogs, and two studs – one at Sandringham and one nearby at Wolferton – where she breeds racehorses. The Queen's own riding horses are stabled at Sandringham while she is there, and she begins each day with a ride of an hour or so within the estate.

When the Queen returns to London, monthly reports are sent to her outlining what is happening at both Sandringham and Balmoral. As well as six weeks at the start of the year, she generally manages a short stay in Sandringham in April, and sometimes another at the end of July, and she returns to Craigowan, a stone-built house on the Balmoral estate (not to the Castle, which would have to be opened specially for her) as often as she can.

Unlike the other two estates, Windsor is owned by the Crown Estate Commissioners; here the Queen is a tenant farmer rather than a landowner. Her forebear George III, known affectionately as 'Farmer George', brought modern farming methods to Windsor. In the Great Park he laid out Norfolk Farm, so called because it followed the revolutionary new system of circulation of crops invented by 'Turnip' Townshend (the 2nd Viscount Townshend) on his estate at Holkham in Norfolk; and Flemish Farm, a replica of a model farm in Flanders. After the King became ill the farms declined, but they, and three further farms on the estate, were revived by Prince Albert to become model farms once more. They comprise nearly 2,000 acres, part dairy farm with herds of Jersey and Ayrshire cows, and part arable land planted with cereal. The herd supplies the Queen with her milk. There is also a herd of pigs and a small herd of single suckler beef cattle running on an organic system.

Although she has so little time to give to it, the Queen knows all about responsible stewardship and realises at first hand the problems modern farmers have to face.

SANDRINGHAM
SANDRINGHAM HOUSE

SUNDAY 3RD JANUARY. *After Church. The Queen presented The Queen's Gold Medal for Academic Excellence to Bridget Davies.*

SUNDAY 10TH JANUARY. *After Church. Mr David Senior is received by the Queen.*

MONDAY. *Meeting of the Privy Council.*

THURSDAY. *The Queen visited King George VI School, Great Bircham, Norfolk.*

Wherever she is, the 'red boxes' are delivered to the Queen each day. The Cabinet papers and Foreign and Commonwealth communications which they contain have been selected and marked for her by her Private Secretary.

A LTHOUGH THE SIX WEEKS that the Queen spends at Sandringham at the beginning of the year is a time when she can fulfil her other role as landowner away from matters of State, many of her duties continue. She spends one to two hours each day working on official papers, which are delivered to her in the 'red boxes'.

An unexpected meeting of the Privy Council has been called because of a resignation from the Cabinet. All members of the Cabinet must be Privy Counsellors, and the new Minister comes to Sandringham to go through the formalities of reception into the Privy Council and to receive his Seals of Office.

GREAT BIRCHAM

KING GEORGE VI SCHOOL, Great Bircham, near Sandringham, was built on land given to the village by the King. As he was driving through Great Bircham one day in 1948, a group of children playing football kicked the ball into the street and hit his passing car. He stopped and talked to the boys, and when he discovered they had nowhere to play he decided to donate land on the Sandringham estate for playing fields and a primary school.

The Queen Mother has continued to take a particular interest in the school. Last January she came here to commemorate the fiftieth anniversary of the gift of land, but this year she is unwell and the Queen has come in her place. She takes part in the children's assembly, in which the theme is community and the children's part in it, and they give her two framed photographs of the whole school in their newly designed uniforms – one for her and one for their planned guest. They then show her their paintings and drawings and, before she leaves, one of the children, Annie Smith, presents her with a posy to take home for the Queen Mother. 'It was the greatest moment in my life so far,' Annie says later.

SANDRINGHAM

KING'S LYNN

SUNDAY 17TH JANUARY. *After Church. Mr Stephen Pockington, Headteacher of Sandringham and West Newton Voluntary Aided Primary School, was received by The Queen when Her Majesty presented a Bible to Master Joshua Harrison for proficiency in Religious Instruction.*

MONDAY. *10.30 a.m. The Queen visited Campbell's Foods, King's Lynn. 11.30 a.m. The Queen opened the new Day Surgery Centre at The Queen Elizabeth Hospital, King's Lynn. 6.30 p.m. The Queen gave a cocktail party for neighbours of the Sandringham Estate.*

Campbell's Soup, invented in 1897 in America, is now manufactured world-wide. In Norfolk they employ more than 700 local people. Each year 7,000 tons of locally grown vegetables are used to produce 288 million of the cans made famous by the artist Andy Warhol.

IN BOTH NORFOLK AND SCOTLAND the Queen makes a point of being involved in the surrounding community, and each year during her time in Sandringham she visits a number of local enterprises. She has come to Campbell's Soup factory to mark the fortieth anniversary of the opening of the factory in King's Lynn. The press are hoping she will wear a white coat and a muslin hair-veil when she tours the production line, examining the steaming soup kettles, each of which contains 600 gallons. She duly dons the coat, but disappoints them by keeping her hat.

The Queen goes from there to open a new day-surgery centre at the local hospital. Queen Elizabeth the Queen Mother was brought here a few months ago after falling and breaking her hip. The day-surgery centre is part of a growing country-wide network of short-stay treatment centres, specialising in keyhole surgery and treating outpatients who a few years ago would have had general anaesthetics and been in hospital for several days. The Queen talks to some of those who have had cataract operations this morning, and watches a demonstration of the new operating techniques.

On our first mini away day it is interesting to watch the last-minute polishing and hoovering, the careful but not too pervasive security, the mounting anticipation and buzz, and then the outright enjoyment of everyone involved. We also have our first brush with petty officials, who decide we shouldn't be here. There will be more of these to come.

SANDRINGHAM

Sandringham was bought for Edward VII, then Prince of Wales, in 1862, and the Ballroom was added in 1883. Sandringham has always been a favourite home of the Royal Family.

IN THE EVENING the Queen and the Duke of Edinburgh give a party in the Ballroom at Sandringham for some of their neighbours – tenant farmers, local landowners, businessmen, schoolteachers . . . Some have known her for years, but others aren't sure how they have come to be invited. The Queen and the Duke greet each guest at the door of the Ballroom and then she moves easily and informally round the room, insisting that old people don't stand up for her and catching some of the guests by surprise as she joins their group.

SANDRINGHAM
WEST NEWTON WOMEN'S INSTITUTE

SUNDAY 24TH JANUARY. *After Church. Mr Gwynne Jones was received by The Queen when Her Majesty decorated him with the 30 year clasp to Long and Faithful Service Medal. Mr Raymond Eridges was received by The Queen when Her Majesty decorated him with the Royal Victorian Medal (Gold).*

MONDAY. *1.00 p.m. The Prime Minister of New Zealand, accompanied by Mr Burton Shipley, was invited to Luncheon.*

WEDNESDAY. *Forward Planning Meeting for the Royal Estates.*

THURSDAY. *2.45 p.m. The Queen attended the January Meeting of the West Newton Women's Institute. Queen Elizabeth The Queen Mother, President, also attended.*

WEST NEWTON WOMEN'S INSTITUTE was founded in 1919 by Queen Alexandra and was one of the first in the country. The Queen has been coming here with her mother each year since she was a young woman. Queen Elizabeth the Queen Mother is the President of this branch and, apart from us, only members are allowed into the meeting.

This is the first time that Queen Elizabeth has been out since a recent illness, so there is a clutch of photographers and well-wishers outside to see her when she and the Queen arrive. As they come into the hall, the members sing the National Anthem, and the meeting opens with the WI hymn 'Jerusalem'. Then, as with any WI gathering, comes business. The minutes are read, and signed by Queen Elizabeth who speaks briefly about her pleasure at being with them. She and the Queen present some awards, and then comes a half-hour talk about Crown Derby china given by a lecturer from the pottery. Suddenly the lecturer's throat goes dry and she begins to cough. Queen Elizabeth digs into her handbag and finds a lozenge for her. 'I shan't want to suck this. I'll want to keep it,' says the lecturer. 'Go on,' says Queen Elizabeth, 'you suck it.' After the talk three of the members act a playlet, and before sitting down to a tea of home-made scones and cakes the Queen and Queen Elizabeth look at a display of members' craftwork. As the Queen observes to us, we are certainly getting varied material. As they come away after two hours the small crowd outside has grown, and they climb into their car holding bouquets of flowers for the short drive back to Sandringham.

SANDRINGHAM
THE KENNELS

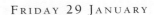

WHEN THE QUEEN INHERITED Sandringham the kennels had been neglected. They were turned around in the 1950s and '60s, but they had not yet had a Field Trial Champion. We are here to see Bill Meldrum, who has run the kennels and trained the Queen's dogs since 1964. She had watched him working his dogs, and in 1963 he won the British Retriever Championship. The Queen invited him to see the kennels, and asked him if he would take over their running. From then until the early 1980s they competed seriously and had six champions. Now, however, the competition side has been wound down and there are fewer dogs, used only for private shooting on the estate and at Balmoral. Meldrum says that as the Queen's car approaches the gate at Sandringham about half a mile from the kennels, the dogs begin to bark. 'We don't know how they can tell. They don't do it with anyone else.' The corgis and dorgis – dachshund/corgi cross – which are house-dogs and pets rather than working dogs, are bred at Windsor.

The Queen, driving herself in a Land Rover, meets us at the kennels in the late afternoon, in wet and muddy waterproofs after a day's shooting. She shows us her dogs and talks about

their parentage and personalities. She herself has three working cockers – Oxo, Bisto and Flash – and two puppies, Spick and Span, who will start working at about eight months. When there is shooting she collects them herself in the morning and brings them back at the end of the day. Bill Meldrum, a cautious Scot, describes her without sycophancy as one of the best dog-handlers he has ever watched; talking to him we observe what we are to see more than once – a respect for her achievement combined with an unspoken but obvious affection for her personally.

The Queen is coming to the end of her holiday in Sandringham, and as we leave she warns us that the pace of things will change when she gets back to London.

16

SANDRINGHAM
THE ROYAL STUDS

SUNDAY 31ST JANUARY. *After Church. The Reverend Canon George Hall was received by The Queen when Her Majesty invested him with the Insignia of Lieutenant of the Royal Victorian Order.*

WEDNESDAY. *Visit to the Sea Defences, Norfolk.*

RACING IS ONE OF THE QUEEN'S great interests. Unlike the Queen Mother, she owns only flat-racing horses. Her racing colours of purple body with gold braid, scarlet sleeves and black velvet cap, date back to George IV. As with everything at Sandringham, the studs are a private enterprise – horses for official purposes are bred at Hampton Court or Windsor. In front of the stables is a statue of Persimmon, who in 1896 won both the St Leger and the Derby for the then Prince of Wales, later Edward VII.

We go to see Joe Grimwade, the Stud Manager, and some of his staff. At any time the Queen owns about twenty-five brood mares and two or three stallions, with fifteen to twenty foals. At six or eight months the weanlings go to Polhampton near Newbury, and then on to Highclere to be broken. At about eighteen months the trainer, the Earl of Carnarvon, takes over. Between the Queen's visits to Sandringham, she is sent videos and photographs so that she can see the progress of the foals. She has a real, practical understanding of horses and years of accumulated knowledge of bloodlines, and with some suggestions from others it is she who chooses the matings. The Queen has been to visit studs in Kentucky, and since the 1970s a number of her broodmares have been sent there to be covered. Some of her stallions are managed commercially, but the Queen breeds to race and not to sell. Her horses have won more than six hundred races, but the jewel in the racing crown, the Derby, still eludes her.

While we are at the studs, the Queen's Farrier is re-shoeing some of the Duke of
Edinburgh's driving horses. The newest foal that we saw was two weeks old, born by
'Zafonic' out of 'Trying for Gold'. The Queen names her horses when they are about
eighteen months old.

FEBRUARY
THE ROYAL HOUSEHOLD

THE ROYAL HOUSEHOLD assists the Queen in carrying out her official duties, and is made up of between six and seven hundred full-time employees, with others who are called upon from time to time.

The senior member of the Household is the Lord Chamberlain. He is responsible for coordinating all the Household departments, which come under the direction of the Private Secretary, the Keeper of the Privy Purse, the Comptroller, Lord Chamberlain's Office, the Master of the Household, the Crown Equerry, and the Director of the Royal Collection. He presides at monthly meetings of the heads of department and is the link between the Sovereign and the House of Lords.

Although answerable to the Lord Chamberlain, the Private Secretary is in practice the one who works most closely with the Queen. Apart from the Sovereign herself, it is he – working in conjunction with the Press Office, which is part of his department – who has most influence on the public perception of the monarchy. Together with his Deputy and Assistant, the Private Secretary organises the Queen's official programme both at home and overseas, selecting and coordinating its various elements and establishing that they are acceptable to the government of the day. He is the channel of communication between the Queen and her government, both within the United Kingdom and in the sixteen Commonwealth countries of which she is Sovereign, advising her on constitutional, governmental and political matters. He liaises with the armed forces and with the Church, deals with her official correspondence and drafts many of her speeches. He is also Keeper of the Royal Archives.

The Keeper of the Privy Purse (the Privy Purse is an actual embroidered bag carried by the Keeper at a coronation) oversees the management of the Civil List. – money voted by Parliament which finances the Queen's duties as Head of State – and the revenues from the Duchy of Lancaster. He administers the Grants-in-Aid made by government departments for specific use in royal travel and the maintenance of the Royal Palaces, and he supervises the financial aspects of the Queen's private estates.

It is the Comptroller, rather than the Lord Chamberlain, who runs the Lord Chamberlain's Office. This is the centre of ceremonial organisation within the Palace, responsible for inward State Visits, the State Opening of Parliament, Investitures, Garter ceremonies, Garden Parties, weddings and funerals. It oversees the Central Chancery of the Orders of Knighthood, the Honourable Corps of Gentlemen at Arms, the Royal Body Guard of the Yeoman of the Guard, and the Royal Company of Archers, as well as the Crown Jewels. It also monitors the number and condition of the Queen's swans on the River Thames during the annual ceremony of Swan Upping.

The Master of the Household heads the largest and most complex department in the Household. He is responsible for all domestic arrangements and entertaining, not only within the royal palaces but also when the Queen travels abroad on State Visits. He draws up guest lists, sends out invitations, arranges seating plans and oversees the kitchens. Through the Chief Housekeeper he supervises cleaning by housemaids and dailies and is responsible for the maintenance of furnishings by craftsmen such as gilders and cabinetmakers, and for the distribution of pages (who greet guests and escort them within the palaces), footmen (who look after those who are staying, act as messengers and help to serve formal meals) and porters. His department is also in charge of the Queen's travel and baggage arrangements and of the Court Post Office. The titular head of the Master of the Household's Department is the Lord Steward.

The Crown Equerry controls the Royal Mews, with its horses, carriages and cars. He is responsible for chauffeurs, grooms and coachmen, and for the maintenance of their transport. The titular head of the Royal Mews is the Master of the Horse.

The Director of the Royal Collection coordinates the work of the Surveyor of the Queen's Pictures, the Surveyor of the Queen's

Works of Art and the Librarian. It is his responsibility to make the Royal Collection accessible to the public in The Queen's Gallery and the State Apartments, and by loans to exhibitions.

In addition to these departments there is the Queen's personal staff, whose appointments are made directly by her. The Mistress of the Robes is in attendance on State occasions, and organises the rota of Ladies and Women of the Bedchamber, the Ladies-in-waiting. The Ladies-in-waiting are there to support the Queen, both daily in the Palace and when she is out on engagements. A more senior Lady of the Bedchamber accompanies the Queen when she and the Duke of Edinburgh are together on engagements and a Woman of the Bedchamber is with her when the Queen is by herself. They are close behind her on walkabouts, taking flowers, cards and presents from her and passing them to the chauffeur, and accompanying her in the car if she is otherwise alone. Their work is people-orientated, ensuring that those who meet the Queen are looked after. They also do shopping for the Queen and help with correspondence, replying to many of the letters sent by the public, particularly those from children. Although the Mistress of the Robes is historically responsible for the Queen's jewellery and clothes, this is now the task of the Queen's Dresser and her two

assistants. One is always with the Queen on her travels abroad, packing, ironing and overseeing her wardrobe. There is also the Queen's Hairdresser.

The Junior Equerry, or Equerry-in-waiting to the Queen, is seconded for three years from one of the armed services. During his appointment he becomes part of the Queen's innermost circle, supporting her on official engagements and when she is off-duty. Also in constant attendance is a Personal Protection Officer, a member of the Royalty Protection Division (S.O.14) of the Royal and Diplomatic Protection Department of the Metropolitan Police.

The Medical Household is drawn from eminent members of the profession on whom the Queen can call as required. The Ecclesiastical Household is made up of the College of Chaplains, domestic chaplains and chaplains of the Chapels Royal.

Finally, there are the Political Members of the Household, appointments made by the Queen on ministerial advice from Westminster with political duties. The Comptroller of the Household is one of these, as also are the Lords and Baronesses in Waiting, who may be deputed by the Queen to meet and bid goodbye to important overseas visitors on her behalf, or to represent her at funerals and memorial services.

Police outriders waiting at Buckingham Palace. Security, and the need for accurate timing, mean that the Queen travels with outriders to give her uninterrupted passage. She is insistent, however, that traffic disruption should be kept to a minimum. The Queen generally travels in a maroon Rolls-Royce Phantom VI, adapted so she can be seen. The Queen's official cars are the only ones in the country without number plates.

The Queen attended the West Newton Sunday School Prizegiving and gave a lunch for the children.

MONDAY. *The Queen returned to London.*

TUESDAY. *12 noon. His Excellency Mr Vuong Thua Pong was received in audience by The Queen and presented the Letters of Recall of his predecessor and his own Letters of Credence as Ambassador of Vietnam to the Court of St James's.*

12.20 p.m. His Excellency Dr Richard Grant was received in farewell audience by The Queen and took leave upon His Excellency relinquishing his appointment as High Commissioner for New Zealand in London.

12.40 p.m. The Dean of Westminster was received by The Queen.

12.55 p.m. The Lord Camoys, Lord Chamberlain, had an audience of The Queen and presented an Address from the House of Lords to which Her Majesty was graciously pleased to make reply.

3.00 p.m. The Queen recorded the Commonwealth message.

6.30 p.m. The Rt Hon Tony Blair, MP, Prime Minister and First Lord of the Treasury, had an audience of the Queen.

LONDON

THE QUEEN'S WORKING DAY

O N HER RETURN TO LONDON, the Queen resumes her full working timetable. She gets up at about 8 o'clock, and over breakfast looks through the daily newspapers, reads her personal letters and checks the Royal Menu Book. Each morning at 9 o'clock the Queen's Piper plays outside her window. Between two and three hundred letters addressed to the Queen arrive each day at the Palace, and from these she takes twenty or thirty, unopened, so that she can see a random selection of what has arrived. Almost all the letters are answered, by either her Private Secretaries or her Ladies-in-waiting. Some are passed to government departments to be dealt with. After reading her selected letters, the Queen sees first one, and then a second of her Private Secretaries. They go through outstanding paperwork, and discuss the day's appointments and arrangements for forthcoming engagements. There may be speeches to go over, Parliamentary Bills requiring Royal Assent, signings of appointments or new stamps or coins to approve.

On some days at about noon the Queen begins a succession of audiences with newly appointed or retiring Ambassadors, High Commissioners, senior members of the armed forces, judges or bishops. Sometimes she gives honours, such as the Order of Merit, or

The Queen with her new Private Secretary, Sir Robin Janvrin.

receives people who have won awards and prizes. The audiences are private, and each lasts for ten or twenty minutes; there can be up to six in a morning. Every few weeks she will meet with members of the Privy Council. More than twenty times a year she holds Investitures, beginning at 11 o'clock and lasting about an hour and a half. At the end of the morning she lunches privately, although once every two months she holds a small lunch party for a cross-section of people who have made important contributions to public life.

In the afternoon she may go out on public engagements in London, and every two or three weeks will spend an entire away day visiting projects across the country, often leaving London the evening before and travelling overnight in the Royal Train so that she is ready for her first engagement at about 10 o'clock. Throughout these days, for which she will have been carefully briefed, she must think of questions to ask and observations to make. Sometimes there will be evening engagements, either as part of an away day or in London. These might be receptions in the Palace, dinners, visits to the theatre or concerts, or events like the annual Festival of Remembrance.

Every day at about 7.30 p.m. a report of the proceedings in Parliament is delivered to the Palace, and the Queen generally reads this the same evening. At some point during the day she must also go through the red boxes prepared by her Private Secretaries. These contain Cabinet documents, letters, telegrams and State papers from her own ministers and from abroad. She has to prepare for her engagements by preliminary reading and briefing sessions, to have discussions and fittings with her dressmaker, and to sit for portraits and official photographs.

ROBERT FELLOWES, who in 1978 married Lady Jane Spencer, the elder sister of the late Princess of Wales, took over from Sir William Heseltine as Private Secretary in 1990. His successor, Sir Robin Janvrin, spent thirteen years in the Royal Navy before moving to the Diplomatic Service. He joined the Royal Household as Press Secretary in 1987.

Sir Robert Fellowes, the Queen's retiring Private Secretary.

LONDON
WESTMINSTER ABBEY

The western front of Westminster Abbey. Just inside, in the centre of the aisle so that everyone, even the Queen, must walk round it, is the Tomb of the Unknown Warrior.

THIS YEAR IS THE FIFTIETH ANNIVERSARY of the Commonwealth, and during the second week of February we go to Westminster Abbey to observe a recce for the annual Commonwealth Day Service to be held there in March. Such recces are routine before any visit by the Queen. There are two people from the Abbey, two from the Commonwealth organisations staging the event, and from the Palace an assistant Private Secretary to advise on its smooth running, and a Press Secretary to see what might interest the press. During the hour and a half we are there, problems and solutions, possibilities and suggestions are tossed backwards and forwards as the Queen's movements are paced out and precise timings calculated.

The theme for Commonwealth Day this year is music. A stage will be erected in the Abbey forecourt for a performance which will begin an hour or so before the Queen arrives; there will be an atmosphere of happy celebration as she steps from her car. There is a long-established format for her reception at the West Door by the Dean and Chapter, but this time it will be slightly different as the King of Swaziland will also be here to greet her. As she goes into the Abbey the music outside will stop and the service will begin.

The Order of Service is gone through, and television opportunities within the Abbey discussed; Sky News plans to cover the event which will also be broadcast on the BBC World Service. After the service, the Queen and the Secretary General will lead the procession back down the aisle, followed by the Duke of Edinburgh with the Secretary-General's wife, and the Prime Minister. The leading figures will pause at the West Door, and the Dean will then bid them goodbye at the iron gate where, technically, his territory ends. Photographers need to be placed so that they can record these two moments, and also the Queen receiving a posy against a background of Commonwealth flags. It's important that they are not in a position where only the Queen's back can be seen or where she is separated from them by railings. She will then move out to watch the musicians. At this point the music needs to be continuous, and loud enough to drown the noise of nearby traffic – a thumping good steel band will be better than a delicate harp.

Before she leaves there is to be a walkabout, so a place for the public is chosen that is safe and not too cramped. The normal departure point for the Queen's car will be occupied by the stage, and another position has to be found so that as she reaches the end of her walkabout she can make a seamless departure.

ON 11TH FEBRUARY, the Queen was represented by Sir Richard Hanbury-Tenison, Lord Lieutenant of Gwent, at the Service of Thanksgiving for the life of Colonel Roderick Hill, an ex-Lord Lieutenant and racing friend of the Queen. It is not possible for the Queen to go to the Memorial Services of all the people whom she has known during her reign, although she does attend those for family and close friends.

BUCKINGHAM PALACE

THURSDAY 11ᵀᴴ FEBRUARY. *11.00 a.m. The Queen, accompanied by The Duke of Edinburgh, presented The Queen's Anniversary Prizes for Higher and Further Education, and afterwards Her Majesty and His Royal Highness gave a Reception.*

FRIDAY. *Afternoon. To Windsor.*

THE HIGHER AND FURTHER EDUCATION CEREMONY is held in the Ballroom of Buckingham Palace, which these days is more often used for State Banquets and Investitures than for dancing. At one end is a balcony where an orchestra from one of the regiments of the Household Division plays, and at the other a dais with the two Chairs of Estate used at the 1902 Coronation of Edward VII and Queen Alexandra. They are overhung by a crimson canopy designed by Sir Edwin Lutyens for the 1911 Coronation Durbar in India.

Among the Chancellors are the Princess Royal and the Duchess of Kent in academic robes. The prizewinners with their sponsors sit in two long rows, one down each side of the room. They stand for the Queen's arrival, and then she works her way slowly down first one side and then the other, presenting medals and talking briefly to each winner. Behind her comes the Duke of Edinburgh, who presents them with scrolls.

The Prizes were set up in 1992 to celebrate the Fortieth Anniversary of the Queen's Accession. Donations were made by commercial and professional bodies wanting to support enterprise and excellence in higher education. This year they went to schemes as varied as applied mathematics, training for voluntary work, and the Globe Theatre.

LONDON
INTERCONTINENTAL HOTEL

MONDAY 15TH FEBRUARY. *Return to London.*

TUESDAY. *11.00 a.m. The Queen held an Investiture.*

6.30 p.m. Prime Minister's audience.

WEDNESDAY. *12 noon. His Excellency Mr Roy Warren Blackbeard was received in audience by The Queen and presented the Letters of Recall of his predecessor and his own Letters of Commission as High Commissioner for Botswana in London.*

12.20 p.m. Mr Justice Jackson was received by The Queen upon his appointment as a Justice of the High Court when Her Majesty conferred upon him the honour of Knighthood and invested him with the Insignia of Knight Bachelor.

12.30 p.m. Sir Ivan Callan (Muscat), Mr Anthony Layden (Rabat) and Mr Peter Ford (Bahrain) were received in audience by The Queen and kissed hands upon their appointment as Her Majesty's Ambassadors. Mr Peter Smith was received in audience by The Queen and kissed hands upon his appointment as Governor to the Cayman Islands.

THURSDAY. *11.00 a.m. The Queen held an Investiture.*

FRIDAY. *12 noon. The Queen and The Duke of Edinburgh attended a reception given by the American Chamber of Commerce at the Hotel Intercontinental, London.*

Afternoon. To Windsor.

THE RECEPTION FOR the American Chamber of Commerce is being held in the Grand Ballroom at the Hotel Intercontinental, Hyde Park Corner. The guests represent a range of American business, from financial services and information technology to hotels and cosmetics. Behind a small stage, the Stars and Stripes and the Union Jack hang in front of a wall projected with brilliant aquamarine colour, and the huge room is set out with two rows of small, numbered tables around which the five hundred or so guests have gathered in groups of about twenty. This arrangement is often used at royal receptions, for it creates a feeling of informality while giving the Queen a chance to speak easily to as many people as possible.

She and the Duke go separately, one down each side of the room, so that every table is visited by one or the other. Before they come together on the platform there is a crafty bit of footwork. All the guests have been given self-adhesive labels with their names, and one of these has stuck conspicuously to the sole of the Queen's shoe. We watch as her Equerry-in-waiting goes over to join the Queen, standing with his foot close to hers. Does she realise, as she walks away from the group onto the platform, that she has left a large sticky label attached to Simon Brailsford's shoe?

On the platform the Queen and the Duke are welcomed by the US Ambassador before signing photographs. In his speech Ambassador Lader speaks of the strong commercial links that exist between the two countries: forty per cent of US investment in Europe is in the UK, more than in the whole of Asia.

After the royal party has left we talk to some of the guests to find out what they think of their visitors, and of the whole idea of the Royal Family. Some see it as quaint, interesting but irrelevant, but others are fascinated by an institution which has survived so long and which they feel still justifies its existence.

ON FRIDAY MORNING the Marshal of the Diplomatic Corps, who acts as a link between the Queen and the foreign diplomatic missions, calls on the Greek Ambassador to bid him farewell. His Excellency Mr Vassilis S Zatiropoulos has come to the end of his appointment and is about to return to Greece. Shortly after his arrival his successor will go to Buckingham Palace to present his own Credentials, or Letters of Credence, to the Queen. At the same time he will present the Letters of Recall of his predecessor, who has earlier been to the Palace to bid the Queen goodbye.

All Ambassadors are accredited to the Court of St James's. Since 1702, when Queen Anne moved there from the Palace of Whitehall, St James's Palace has been the monarch's official residence, although no monarch has lived there since Queen Victoria moved to Buckingham Palace in 1837. Following the death of a monarch, the Accession Council still meets in St James's Palace.

LONDON
BUCKINGHAM PALACE

As soon as we arrive for our first Investiture we sense the atmosphere of celebration and welcome. Some events at the Palace can disappoint, but never an Investiture. Everything is done to make this a very special day. 'Congratulations!' says the policeman at the gate. We thank him, but have to admit that we are only here to make drawings and observe.

There are twenty Investitures in London each year, and one each in Edinburgh and Cardiff, although as more honours are given this number will increase. At Buckingham Palace, the guests drive – or walk – across the forecourt and disappear through the central arch into the Quadrangle. Once inside the Palace, they move up the Grand Staircase to the first floor with its State Rooms. Those to be invested are taken to the Green Drawing Room or the Picture Gallery to be briefed, and their guests are shown into the scarlet and gold Ballroom. While they wait they are entertained with a selection of light music played by the Orchestra of The Irish Guards. On the dais, beside the Chairs of Estate, stand five members of the Yeomen of the Guard in their scarlet uniforms and white ruffs. This is the most ancient Royal Body Guard in the world, created by Henry VII in 1485 after victory at the Battle of Bosworth Field.

The actor Nigel Hawthorne (right) signing autographs after receiving a knighthood from the Queen. 'Scipio' (below), the Slow March of the Grenadier Guards.

SUNDAY 21ST FEBRUARY. *After Church. Mr Barry Ambrose and Mr Richard Cottrell were received by The Queen when Her Majesty presented them with the Royal Victorian Medal (Silver).*

MONDAY. *Return to London. 6.00 p.m. Sir Michael Oswold's leaving party.*

TUESDAY. *11.00 a.m. The Queen held an Investiture.*

As 11 o'clock approaches, the Lord Chamberlain welcomes the guests and explains what will be happening, and as the hour strikes the Queen arrives with members of her Household, and two Gurkha Orderly Officers in a tradition begun by Queen Victoria in 1876. The National Anthem is played, then the Queen says, 'Please be seated', and the Investiture begins.

The badge of the Royal Victorian Order. The Order was established by Queen Victoria to acknowledge personal service to the Sovereign.

Years of public or previously unsung work are being acknowledged as the recipients, brought in small groups to the wide corridor outside, move into the Ballroom one by one. Most are becoming members of one of the Orders of Chivalry, but a few of the awards may be for gallantry. As the orchestra plays quietly, the Lord Chamberlain reads out the names and accolades: 'For services to Theatre, Film, and Television', 'For services to the Families of Sufferers of Creutzfeldt-Jakob Disease', 'For services to the War Widows' Association' . . . The insignia have been laid out in meticulous order, checked and rechecked, and are passed one by one on a velvet cushion to the Queen. Those receiving a knighthood kneel on a velvet stool, while others lean forward so that the Queen can slip their insignia over their heads, or wait as she hooks it onto a small loop that has been earlier fixed to their lapel or dress. She then speaks to each one for a few moments before shaking their hand, the signal that their time with her is over. Outside the Ballroom once more, the insignia is taken from them, placed in a box and returned, again with congratulations. They then go back to the Ballroom, into one of the empty chairs waiting there for them. Today, 130 people are being honoured.

As the ceremony draws to a close the orchestra turns from its published programme to 'Scipio', the Slow March of the Grenadier Guards, which can be stopped within a few bars. The National Anthem is played once more, the Queen leaves and the recipients return down the Grand Staircase and out into the Quadrangle where photographers, reporters and television cameras are waiting.

LONDON

BUCKINGHAM PALACE

WHEN PARLIAMENT IS IN SESSION, each Tuesday evening at 6.30 the Prime Minister goes to Buckingham Palace for his weekly audience with the Queen. Following police outriders, his car is driven straight into the inner courtyard, and he is received by the Private Secretary at the King's Door. They then go straight upstairs (at speed, for the Prime Minister likes to move fast), where he and the Queen meet alone in the Audience Room. Meanwhile their two Private Secretaries have their own meeting in the Private Secretary's office. Here, at the end of the audience and if he has time, the Prime Minister joins them for a drink and a chat. However, since Tony Blair likes to spend time each evening with his children, this part of the weekly ritual is somewhat shorter now than it has been with other Prime Ministers. Early in her reign the Queen had changed the time of the audience from late afternoon to early evening, so that she could be with her children before they went to bed.

The Queen's first Prime Minister's Audience, in 1952, was with Winston Churchill. Since then she has seen ten Prime Ministers, the youngest of whom, Tony Blair, was born a year after she came to the throne.

THE ROYAL GEOGRAPHICAL SOCIETY

'QUEST FOR DIGNITY', a competition open to young artists from the UK, India, Africa and Brazil, was set up to promote positive images of leprosy. The works submitted needed to express something of the inherent dignity of human beings. The Queen sees the leading entries and presents prizes to the winners.

The Royal Family has supported the work of the Leprosy Relief Association (LEPRA) since its creation in 1924. It is one of the more than 670 charities of which the Queen is Patron. In 1947, as Princess Elizabeth, she became a sponsor of their Child Adoption Scheme, and between then and 1975 sponsored the treatment of ten children. As each was discharged, a new child was taken on. During the evening she is shown photographs of a visit she paid in 1956 to the Oji River Settlement in a part of eastern Nigeria heavily infected with the disease. She was the first sovereign to visit a leper settlement, and she recalls meeting and talking to the child patients in the largely self-supporting community as they did weaving and carpentry, and watching adults working as blacksmiths and shoemakers, or pressing palm oil which they sell for oil and soap.

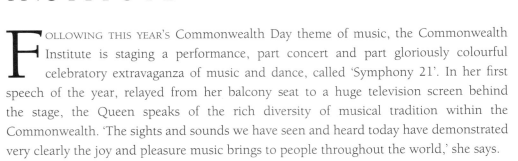

LONDON
THE COMMONWEALTH INSTITUTE

FOLLOWING THIS YEAR'S Commonwealth Day theme of music, the Commonwealth Institute is staging a performance, part concert and part gloriously colourful celebratory extravaganza of music and dance, called 'Symphony 21'. In her first speech of the year, relayed from her balcony seat to a huge television screen behind the stage, the Queen speaks of the rich diversity of musical tradition within the Commonwealth. 'The sights and sounds we have seen and heard today have demonstrated very clearly the joy and pleasure music brings to people throughout the world,' she says.

WEDNESDAY 24TH FEBRUARY. *12 noon. His Excellency Mr César B Bautista was received in audience by The Queen and presented the Letters of Recall of his predecessor and his own Letters of Credence as Ambassador of the Philippines to the Court of St James's.*
12.20 p.m. The Prime Minister of Tuvalu was received by The Queen.
1.00 p.m. The Queen and The Duke of Edinburgh held a Luncheon Party at Buckingham Palace.
3.00 p.m. The Queen, accompanied by The Duke of Edinburgh, attended 'Symphony 21' – a celebration in music and dance of the Institute's vision for the twenty-first century at the Commonwealth Institute, London. Evening: Army Equerries Dinner.

THURSDAY. *11.40 a.m. The Queen received His Excellency Chief Emeka Anyaoku, Commonwealth Secretary-General.*
12 noon. His Excellency Dr George Gonello du Puis was received in audience by The Queen and presented the Letters of Recall of his predecessor and his own Letters of Commission as High Commissioner for Malta in London.
12.20 p.m. The Hon Mr Justice Bodey was received by The Queen upon his appointment as a Justice of the High Court when Her Majesty conferred upon him the honour of Knighthood and invested him with the Insignia of Knight Bachelor.

TULSE HILL

THERE ARE FLOWERS FOR US ALL, buttonholes to celebrate the royal visit. In the hall three pupils self-consciously stand wearing the school's original seventeenth-century dress, for this is St Martin-in-the-Fields High School's tercentenary. It was founded in 1699, in the parish of St Martin-in-the-Fields, by forward-thinkers who believed that some of the effects of poverty might be countered by education. It now serves a multicultural community, and still offers quality education for inner-city girls.

The school in Tulse Hill is famed for its gospel choirs. Perhaps it is unfortunate that while they are singing for the Queen a bench collapses and rather a lot of the choir disappears, but they cope wonderfully well and it means that the visit makes the television news that night. Certainly the Queen enjoys herself; two weeks later she is singing the school's praises to some of her Chaplains.

12.30 p.m. Mr David Lyscom (Bratislava), Mr Chris Ingham (Tashkent) and Mr Richard Muir (Kuwait) were received in audience by The Queen and kissed hands upon their appointment as Her Majesty's Ambassadors. Mr David Hollamby was received in audience by The Queen upon his appointment as Governor to St Helena.

FRIDAY. 11.00 a.m. The Queen visited St Martin-in-the-Fields High School, Tulse Hill, London. Her Majesty toured the school and attended a musical concert performed by the school choirs. Afternoon. To Windsor.

MARCH
AWAY DAYS

THE QUEEN HAS ABOUT fifteen or sixteen away days each year, when she visits towns or cities in different parts of the United Kingdom. During them she can meet people from all over the country, and they give more of the public a chance to see her in person. Generally the Duke of Edinburgh accompanies her, their timetables often dividing for at least part of the day.

An away day will usually begin about a year before with an invitation to some special event, perhaps an important anniversary or the opening of a new building. Before accepting, the Palace checks how recently the Queen or another member of the Royal Family has visited that area, so that all parts of the country have the opportunity of a royal visit. They will also establish that the invitation carries no political overtones or possibilities of unwelcome commercial exploitation. They will then work closely with the Queen's representative in the county, the Lord Lieutenant, in creating a programme for the rest of the day. Sometimes these are theme days devoted to something like the emergency services, but more often the venues are varied, reflecting particular local needs or achievements.

There are three fixed points in the day – arrival, lunch and departure. The Queen will arrive by car, train or helicopter. Because of distances travel by car is not always practicable, and the helicopter is only suitable if there is a convenient landing place. More often she will arrive by Royal Train from London, having left one of the mainline stations at about 11 o'clock the night before. The train will draw into its destination at about 10 o'clock the next morning, after spending some of the night in a quiet siding. A railway station is a good starting point for a visit, with plenty of space on the concourse for groups of local people to gather under cover, often to play welcoming music. Having arrived by train into the city centre, the Queen may leave by helicopter from the final venue further outside.

If the away day coincides with a civic anniversary there will generally be a lunch at the Town Hall. Otherwise this will be arranged at one of the places she is visiting, wherever possible involving students from a local catering college. A choice of three possible lunch menus will have been sent in advance to the Palace.

When an outline plan has been drawn up, the Lord Lieutenant will meet with a Palace representative so that suggestions and possible changes can be made. Timing is vital. The Queen's Rolls-Royce, driven up the day before, will be waiting to take her between venues. Local police will be involved from an early stage, calculating how long it takes to drive between locations and establishing that there will be no problems manoeuvring the Queen's car. Is there an opportunity for a walkabout, an important part of away days, either before she leaves somewhere by car or as she walks from one venue to another?

With the broad pattern agreed, the Lord Lieutenant and those advising him will draw up detailed suggestions of what the Queen might like to see within each place she visits. The time here is blocked out in five or ten minute slots. If she is going to a school she may be shown some new method of teaching or information technology, talk to children in a painting class and be invited to watch a dance or theatrical performance. The Duke meanwhile may be at a separate location such as a factory, or possibly elsewhere in the school seeing science or technology classes before joining her for the performance. In the gym or sports hall, representatives of local voluntary organisations will set up displays and have a chance to talk to the Queen about their work.

The detailed plan is sent to the Palace for the Queen's approval, and then a recce party will go to discuss everything in detail on the spot. This gathering will be chaired by the Lord Lieutenant, and will include staff from the venues concerned, one of the Queen's Assistant Private Secretaries, someone from the Press Office, possibly a representative of the Central Office of Information who will coordinate the final arrangements including dealing with the press, and members of the local police – a separate detailed security recce involving Palace security and the local police will be carried

out later. The recce generally lasts a whole day and covers every aspect of the visit, concentrating particularly on problems that were not apparent on paper. The occasional days when, it is said, a man in the Palace party had to put on a skirt in order to pace out the route up and down stairs, and in and out of lifts, are over. The Queen now employs a number of women in her Press Office. Often the recce is carried out in wellington boots and hard hats as the party steps across electric cables and holes in the ground, although it is difficult to work out precise timings when the staircase has not yet been built. Occasionally the building is not finished in time and the visit has to be cancelled, but this happened only once during our year.

A more usual problem may be the number of people in the line-up – there are just too many. Perhaps some of them could be presented to the Queen later in the visit, possibly when she joins everyone for coffee? Or here she is walking straight past too many things without stopping; she will want to pause and look and talk, which means that something else will have to go. Perhaps the answer could be for the Queen and the Duke to divide this part of the tour between them so that no one will be disappointed, but their movements must be planned so that the two parties don't overlap. And that splendid sauna in the new sports centre – it has

a narrow walkway that will be difficult to negotiate. The Queen will have to go round another way, and no, it doesn't matter at all if that means that she goes through the changing rooms – after all, no one will be using them. How many people can get into the lift? Is there a staircase nearby which the rest of the party can use? And this area where tea is to be served – it's very big and empty, so let's bring in extra tables and chairs and invite lots more people so it will buzz with a relaxed, social atmosphere – she actually *likes* the clattering of cups. Since it might rain, are there plans to lay a temporary pathway across the muddy football pitch to the helicopter?

The organisers have questions too: what do the children call the Queen if she speaks to them, and is it necessary to bow or curtsey? The message from the Palace is that you call her Ma'am to rhyme with Sam, that deep curtseys are out and that she prefers a relaxed approach, with everyone enjoying themselves – an atmosphere of bustle rather than anxious silence – but the Lord Lieutenant will go through those points with them again nearer the time. Meanwhile the recce has satisfied the Palace that all is well, and has helped the organisers to iron out glitches. And to complete it all, someone has been able to do a special deal in Union Jacks (made in China) to hand out to the schoolchildren who will be lining the roads.

MONDAY 1ST MARCH. *Return to London.*
6.00 p.m. The Queen and The Duke of
Edinburgh gave a Reception for the
winners of the Queen's Award for Export,
Technological and Environmental
Achievement in 1998.

TUESDAY. *11.00 a.m. The Queen held an*
Investiture.

WEDNESDAY. *12 noon. His Excellency*
Baron Oswald Bentinck van Schoonheten
was received in audience by The Queen
and presented the Letters of Recall of his
predecessor and his own Letters of
Credence as Ambassador of The
Netherlands to the Court of St James's.
12.20 p.m. The Hon Mr Justice Gillen
was received by The Queen upon his
appointment as a Justice of the High
Court of Northern Ireland when Her
Majesty conferred upon him the honour
of Knighthood and invested him with the
Insignia of Knight Bachelor.
12.30 p.m. His Excellency Choi Dong-Jin
was received in farewell audience by The
Queen and took leave upon relinquishing
his appointment as Ambassador of the
Republic of Korea to the Court of St
James's.
6.30 p.m. Prime Minister's audience.

LONDON

BUCKINGHAM PALACE

THE FIRST PALACE RECEPTION we attend is being given for representatives of companies who have achieved outstanding results in export and industry during the previous year. Shortly before 6 o'clock we go up into the White Drawing Room, one of a series of intercommunicating reception rooms on the first floor overlooking the gardens. It leads into the Music Room with its huge bow windows, the Blue Drawing Room and the long, thin Picture Gallery.

As the guests arrive they wait for the door to the White Drawing Room to open, and then each is announced by the Master of the Household and greeted by the Queen and the Duke of Edinburgh. They go through into the Music Room where they are offered a drink from a selection of red or white wine, whisky, gin and tonic, orange juice and mineral water, and are encouraged to move on into the Blue Drawing Room to leave room for others coming through. The guests are to be distributed evenly between the rooms so that no one is too crowded, and as they go they are unobtrusively counted on a clicker. When there are about 120 in the Blue Drawing Room, the door is closed and those behind are invited to go into the Picture Gallery. Footmen with trays of canapés and drinks circulate among the guests.

It takes rather a long time to welcome three hundred guests, but other members of the Royal Family are here to talk to those who have already been greeted. Then, as the Queen and the Duke come to the end of the long line of arrivals, they go through into the Music Room. Here a few people have been asked to wait so that the Queen can talk to them at greater length. They are gathered into small groups, and before she reaches each one the Master of the Household speaks to them, finding a point of interest with which he can brief the Queen. As she moves on to the next group, a Lady-in-waiting joins those she has just left, continuing the conversation.

These State Rooms, designed by John Nash, were built onto the existing Buckingham House in the early nineteenth century. Although the new building was commissioned by George IV while Prince Regent, it was not ready for use until Victoria's reign. The furnishings were almost all acquired by the Prince Regent, for as well as the fine English furniture of his time he had the choice of many beautiful older pieces that came onto the market after the French Revolution and the defeat of Napoleon. He bought them originally for Carlton House, which stood at the eastern end of the Mall. This was later demolished and the site developed to raise funds to pay for his increasingly ambitious schemes at Buckingham House, plans that he never saw completed.

Since 1993 the State Rooms have been open to the public between August and October when the Queen is at Balmoral. It has become one of the most popular tourist attractions in London but has received a mixed press. Money from entrance tickets, which helped to fund the restoration of Windsor Castle after the fire, is now being used for the redevelopment of The Queen's Gallery at Buckingham Palace.

LONDON
THEATRELAND

THURSDAY 4TH MARCH. *10.10 a.m. The Queen visited the Young Vic Theatre, London SE1, met teachers and children from the Sacred Heart School, Southwark, and attended a theatre workshop.*

10.40 a.m. The Queen visited the Lyceum Theatre, London WC2, and met theatre staff and members of the cast of Oklahoma!

11.25 a.m. The Queen visited the Almeida Theatre and rehearsal rooms, London N1, and met members of the cast of Spear and Plenty.

12.15 p.m. The Queen and The Duke of Edinburgh visited Angel & Bermans, theatrical costumiers, London NW1.

1.00 p.m. The Queen and The Duke of Edinburgh attended a lunch hosted by The Society of London Theatre at The Ivy Restaurant, London WC1.

2.45 p.m. Her Majesty, Patron, visited the Royal Academy of Dramatic Art, London WC1.

3.30 p.m. Return to Buckingham Palace.

7.20 p.m. Left Buckingham Palace.

7.30 p.m. The Queen and The Duke of Edinburgh attended a performance of the Royal National Theatre's production of Oklahoma! at the Lyceum Theatre, London WC2.

THE QUEEN HAS BEEN CRITICISED, notably by thespians, for her lack of interest in the theatre. The Duke of Edinburgh has said that one reason they now go less often is the amount of swearing, for the audience turns to see what their reaction is. 'It did rather put us off,' he says. The Queen is making up for this with one of her new theme away days, when she and the Duke spend a whole day enjoying aspects of London's theatre. She begins at the Young Vic where she witnesses the death of a queen. 'O my dear Hamlet! The drink, the drink! I am poison'd.' Having watched Gertrude expire, the Queen talks to the actors and to the boys and girls who are working on sound and lighting, for this is a technical rehearsal for teenage schoolchildren.

The Almeida Theatre is strictly for professionals. This is one of the smallest, most highly regarded theatres in London, renowned for its dynamic and adventurous productions of both classical and modern works.

Angel & Bermans, theatrical costumiers, boasts five miles of rails hung with clothes. It is now in its sixth generation as a family business. Costumes, wigs and masks, jewellery, false noses and stubble paste – everything you want is here in authentic detail. And there, in the hall, is the costume worn for the role of her predecessor, Elizabeth I, in the film *Shakespeare in Love*, one of the firm's four 1999 Oscar nominations for Best Costumes.

The Queen talking to schoolchildren who are working as sound and lighting engineers at the Young Vic rehearsal for Hamlet.

The Ivy is the restaurant mecca of London theatre, and here the Queen is entertained to lunch. One performer later observes, 'Producers and theatre owners are gangsters. It was like the Pope dining with the Mafia – but then he wasn't invited. From there the Queen goes on to the Royal Academy of Dramatic Art. She watches with sympathy as a tightly bodiced young student rehearsing an Elizabethan tragedy is told to breathe more deeply as she lies dying. Remarking that she had been treated to rather a lot of death during her day, the Queen tells her, 'I started this morning at the Young Vic, and they were dropping like flies.'

It is time then for her to go back to the Palace before getting ready for the evening performance of *Oklahoma!*; she has called in at a dress rehearsal for this earlier in the day. It is said that a song from the original 1940s production, 'People Will Say We're in Love', has a special place in her heart. At about 11 o'clock she finishes her evening on the stage of the Lyceum, talking to the cast.

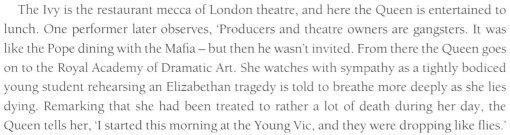

FRIDAY. *11.50 a.m. The Hon Mr Justice Bratza was received by The Queen upon his appointment as a Justice of the High Court when Her Majesty conferred upon him the honour of Knighthood and invested him with the Insignia of Knight Bachelor.*

12 noon. The Rt Hon Paul East was received by The Queen upon his appointment as High Commissioner for New Zealand in London.

12.20 p.m. Mr Assad Shomas was received by The Queen upon his appointment as High Commissioner for Belize in London.

12.30 p.m. The Queen received Fellows participating in the Commonwealth Foundation Fellowship Scheme to promote Commonwealth understanding. Afternoon. To Windsor.

LONDON
WESTMINSTER ABBEY

MONDAY 8TH MARCH. *Return to London.*
3.10 p.m. The Queen and The Duke of Edinburgh attended the Commonwealth Day Observance Service in Westminster Abbey.
6.10 p.m. The Chancellor of the Exchequer had an audience of The Queen.
6.45 p.m. The Queen and The Duke of Edinburgh attended a Reception to mark Commonwealth Day and the 50th Anniversary of the Commonwealth at Marlborough House, London.

TUESDAY. *11.00 a.m. The Queen held an Investiture.*
2.30 p.m. Portrait sitting with Mr Theo Ramos.

WEDNESDAY. *11.50 a.m. Her Excellency Madame Mariama Hima was received in audience by The Queen and presented the Letters of Recall of her predecessor and her own Letters of Credence as Ambassador of Niger to the Court of St James's.*
12.10 p.m. The Archbishop of Canterbury was received in audience by The Queen.
12.30 p.m. Meeting of the Privy Council. During the Council the Queen pricked the Sheriffs' Roll.
1.00 p.m. The King of Swaziland and Her Royal Highness Inkhosikati visited The Queen and The Duke of Edinburgh, and remained to Lunch.
6.30 p.m. Prime Minister's audience.

THURSDAY. *12.20 p.m. The Hon Timothy Lewin was received by The Queen and delivered up the Insignia of the Order of the Garter worn by his father, the late Lord Lewin.*

12.30 p.m. Mr John Macgregor (Warsaw), Mr William Erhman (Luxembourg)) and Dr Peter January (Tirana) were received by the Queen and kissed hands upon their appointment as Her Majesty's Ambassadors. Miss Linda Duffield was received in audience by The Queen upon her appointment as British High Commissioner to Colombo.

THE SECOND MONDAY IN MARCH is celebrated as Commonwealth Day. In 1958 this replaced Empire Day which was traditionally marked on Queen Victoria's birthday, May 24th. The Queen had recorded her message to the Commonwealth shortly after her return to London at the beginning of February. This is a personal message, one of only two speeches that she writes herself, with suggestions from her Private Secretary but without guidance from her ministers. The other is the Christmas Broadcast.

Since we were at the recce, it is interesting to be at the Observance for Commonwealth Day in Westminster Abbey. The Readings are taken from the scriptures or revered writings of the principal Commonwealth religions, and centre on five themes: Stewardship of the Earth, Human Worth, Justice and Peace, Love in Relationships, and Service and Sacrifice. Each is followed by an Affirmation of shared values spoken by the whole congregation. After the main part of the service there is a performance of classic Kathak dancing from north India, a form of storytelling that celebrates life in this universe. Then comes the final affirmation which endorses the theme of the day: 'We affirm our belief that through the joy of music, heard and performed, individuals and nations may progress towards greater harmony.' As the Queen comes out of the Abbey the music rings out, the photographers get their shots, the public see and speak to the Queen during her walkabout, and she finally steps into her car and is driven smoothly away.

MARLBOROUGH HOUSE

AT THE EVENING RECEPTION, Commonwealth guests, many wearing traditional dress, fill the elegant rooms of Marlborough House, the birthplace of George V. After his death it became the home first of Queen Alexandra, and then of the widowed Queen Mary. In 1959 the Queen loaned it to the government, and it now houses the Commonwealth Secretariat and the Commonwealth Foundation. The Commonwealth is something we have always taken for granted without really questioning its purpose, but we ask some of those we speak to what it means to them. 'Support', 'opportunity' – these are the two most repeated themes. In a world of political turmoil it is seen as something freely entered into, a positive and unifying force for good.

EACH COUNTY HAS A HIGH SHERIFF, an appointment which goes back to pre-Norman times, when he was the chief official, or reeve, for local administration in that shire. The Sheriff's role now is largely ceremonial, and the appointment is for one year.

Each March, during a meeting of the Privy Council, a long roll of paper, mounted on wooden rollers and bearing the names of the nominees, is presented to the Queen. She then pricks through the names of the new Sheriffs designate using a bodkin, a three inch-long steel spike mounted on a round brass knob. The tradition of pricking is said to date back to the day when Queen Elizabeth I was sitting in the garden sewing when the Sheriffs' Roll was brought to her. Until then the names had always been marked with a small black dot, but having no pen and only a bodkin – a real, sewing bodkin, not a ceremonial one as now – the Queen pricked the Roll with this.

The Queen with the Commonwealth Secretary - General, and the Prime Minister.

ESSEX
SOUTHEND AND BASILDON

The Bell Tower at Basildon is the first in the world to be made of glass and steel. It has eight bells, the oldest of which dates back to the mid-fifteenth century.

WHEN WE HEAR that the Queen's first engagement on her away day in Essex is to be the headquarters of Her Majesty's Customs and Excise – VAT – we decide to give that one a miss. It isn't just our dislike of those relentless quarterly VAT returns, or our apathy when we discover that each month half a million of these returns are processed, or even our lack of interest when we hear that the Queen is to start a new letter-sorting machine which will process 30,000 an hour – after all, from the beginning of the year we have seen that the buzz which surrounds a royal visit can give even the most mundane event an excitement. It is more that on these days it's often impossible to get to everything and we sometimes have to choose which event to go to. As the year progresses we hone the ordering of local taxis to a fine art, always leaving before the Queen so that we are away before the roads are temporarily closed for her car to go through, reaching the next venue in time to see her arrive. Of course, there are times when this system breaks down, generally when the driver doesn't know his own district, and then we see the blue lights of the outriders flashing away from us into the distance. On the whole, though, it works well.

But we haven't yet developed this skill, and so we go straight to the South East Essex College whose media centre of aspiring television technicians and interviewers is standing by to make a film of the Queen's arrival which they will show her during her visit. Meanwhile she goes to the studios to watch them at work.

From there we go to Southend's seafront, and the crowds who line the Golden Mile for what turns out to be an unusually long and happy walkabout. This is the first of two that

FRIDAY 12TH MARCH. *9.55 a.m. The Queen and The Duke of Edinburgh left Buckingham Palace by helicopter to travel to Essex.*
10.15 a.m. Her Majesty and His Royal Highness arrived in Southend.
10.25 a.m. The Queen visited Her Majesty's Customs and Excise Offices.
11.20 a.m. The Queen and The Duke of Edinburgh toured South East Essex College, where Her Majesty viewed the Learning and Media Centres.
12.15 p.m. Her Majesty and His Royal Highness did a walkabout on Marine Parade, Southend.
1.10 p.m. The Queen and The Duke of Edinburgh visited Basildon District Council Offices, to commemorate Basildon's 50th Anniversary as a New Town. Her Majesty and His Royal Highness were entertained to lunch.
2.30 p.m. The Queen and The Duke of Edinburgh visited the Towngate Theatre in the Basildon Centre to view a 50th Anniversary Exhibition, and met representatives of the business community. Her Majesty and His Royal Highness then opened the specially engraved doors of the Bell Tower, before attending a Service of Thanksgiving to mark the 50th anniversary of the foundation of Basildon New Town and the dedication of the Bell Tower at St Martin's Church.
4.00 p.m. The Queen left Basildon by helicopter. The Duke of Edinburgh left by car for a separate destination.
4.25 p.m. Arrival at Windsor.

day, for in the afternoon there is another in Basildon as the Queen makes her way from lunch in the Council Offices to the new Bell Tower.

The first royal walkabout was in New Zealand in 1970 when the Queen walked the last four hundred yards from her car to Wellington City Hall. It was an opportunity to meet ordinary people, those who had not been invited as guests to any of the ceremonies. Traditionally walkabouts are Aboriginal wanderings of escape from people and civilisation, but the Queen has given the word a new meaning as she moves in closer to people, talking to them, accepting presents of flowers and cards and chewed plastic toys, all of which she passes to her Lady-in-waiting so that her hands are free to receive yet more offerings. Small children are lifted over the crash barriers by their parents so that they can give the Queen their gifts; placards of welcome or protest are waved and always close beside the Queen is her Personal Protection Officer, who is trained to expect the unexpected and be ready to deal with it.

LONDON

ST JAMES'S PALACE

MONDAY 15TH MARCH. *Return to London.*

TUESDAY. *11.00 a.m. The Queen held an Investiture.*
6.30 p.m. Prime Minister's audience.

WEDNESDAY. *12.40 p.m. The Lord Somerleyton was received by The Queen when Her Majesty invested him with the Insignia of a Knight Grand Cross of the Royal Victorian Order.*
12.50 p.m. Major General the Lord Michael Fitzalan Howard was received by The Queen and delivered up the Stick of Office upon his relinquishing his appointment as Gold Stick.
6.30 p.m. The Queen attended a Reception for the College of Chaplains at St James's Palace.

THURSDAY. *12 noon. His Excellency Mr Khemaies Jhinaoui was received in audience by The Queen and presented the Letters of Recall of his predecessor and his own Letters of Credence as Ambassador of Tunisia to the Court of St James's.*
12.20 p.m. The Queen, Colonel-in-Chief, The Royal Green Jackets, received Lieutenant General Sir Christopher Wallace upon relinquishing his appointment as Colonel Commandant of The 2nd Battalion, and Major General Andrew Pringle upon assuming the appointment.
12.40 p.m. The Hon Mr Justice Burton was received by The Queen upon his appointment as Justice of the High Court when Her Majesty conferred upon him the honour of Knighthood and invested him with the Insignia of Knight Bachelor.
12.55 p.m. The Lady Hunt was received by The Queen and delivered up the Insignia of the Order of the Garter worn by her husband, the late Lord Hunt.

THE COLLEGE OF CHAPLAINS is part of the Queen's Ecclesiastical Household. It is composed of between forty and fifty clergy selected from all dioceses with the task of preaching at the two chapels in St James's Palace, and in Scotland.

We arrive at St James's Palace, by arrangement, in time for the service, but our names are not on the list. We ask to speak to whoever is in charge, but he knows nothing of us either and we are unceremoniously asked to leave. We can return later for the reception when the Queen arrives. As we leave at the end of the evening there are apologies from those who earlier conducted us out into the street. 'No one told us you were coming,' they say. It is a phrase that will become very familiar.

LONDON

BUCKINGHAM PALACE

FRIDAY 19TH MARCH. *11.45 a.m. The Queen presented a new Sovereign's Banner to the Royal Military Academy Sandhurst. Afternoon. To Windsor.*

MONDAY. *Return to London.*

TUESDAY. *12 noon. His Excellency Mr Choi Sung-hong was received in audience by The Queen and presented the Letters of Recall of his predecessor and his own his Letters of Credence as Ambassador of the Republic of Korea to the Court of St James's.*

THE ROYAL MILITARY ACADEMY SANDHURST trains Officer Cadets for the Army. In the forecourt of Buckingham Palace the Queen presents a new Sovereign's Banner to the Sovereign's Company, the company with the highest standards of achievement during the training year. It replaces the Standard presented by her in 1978, which is marched off parade during the ceremony and will be laid up in the Royal Memorial Chapel at the Academy.

LONDON HOUSE, MECKLENBURGH SQUARE

I T IS INTERESTING TO TALK to some of the Overseas Graduates when the Queen visits London House. Here students from the Commonwealth, the United States and Europe live together in a collegiate community, building up an international network of friends and avoiding the loneliness of city life in a strange country. Before the Queen arrives, there is an atmosphere of anticipation, with little sign of the bored cynicism combined with unwilling curiosity that we later see in some students' responses to her visits. Perhaps the cynics have kept away or maybe it's because these are older graduates, but we have found noticeably more interest in the monarchy among overseas students studying here than among our own.

After she has gone we speak to an orthopaedic surgeon who is here to do further training, and ask him how he has enjoyed the visit. 'We'd been told before she came, "Don't be worried – just imagine she's your Mum",' he says. 'When she was talking to me I felt this strange mixture of bewilderment and extreme respect. I thought she would be bored when I told her about my work, but she was really focussed, really interested in everything. She wanted to know how I'm going to use my training when I get home. In India we have this idea of the Creator, the Preserver and the Destroyer. She's the Creator and Preserver, really she is. I wish other people could see her, but sadly she doesn't pop into downtown Bombay too often.'

Some archaeologists who have been working on a dig in South America want a photographer to take a picture of them talking to the Queen in front of their display. They tell us that if they have a picture of themselves with her, it will give their work a stamp of approval which will help them to raise more money to go on with the dig.

WEST SUSSEX
WORTHING AND BURGESS HILL

FRIDAY 26TH MARCH. 10.05 a.m. The Queen and The Duke of Edinburgh left Buckingham Palace by helicopter to travel to West Sussex.

10.30 a.m Arrival at Broadwater Recreation Ground, Worthing.

THERE WERE SEVERAL REASONS for choosing Durrington High School for the Queen's visit, and one was the size of the school gymnasium and sports hall. So much space in one venue means that it can be a community event, with voluntary caring organisations and local industries setting up displays, giving their members a chance to meet and talk to the Queen. This kind of doubling up is arranged wherever possible, partly because more people can be involved and partly because it makes maximum use of the Queen's time. She and the Duke spend nearly four hours at the school – touring the classrooms, watching a theatrical performance, talking to community members and having lunch – far longer than they would normally be in one place. At lunch in the school cafeteria

the eighty guests, including pupils from the school, sit down at round tables of eight, an arrangement which the Queen prefers as it means she can talk easily to everyone at her table. The catering, the menu cards, the table flowers and the string orchestra all involve local colleges.

When we came down for the recce, the Triangle Leisure Centre was still a building site. What a transformation! The Queen is used to the smell of new paint – someone suggested we should call this book *Wet Paint and Handshakes* – but a lot of overtime must have been done to get this ready in time. It reminds me of a day in Oxford some years ago when the Queen was due to open a hall of residence. The important parts were finished but nothing else. On the day of her visit, the new building stood in a setting of trees and grass and flowers. The next day these had all gone, and it was a building site once more.

In the Triangle Centre the Queen visits the crèche on her way to the swimming pool. Royalty means nothing to small children, any more than it does to animals. To the despair of picture editors it's not her style to pick up and cuddle babies, but then, as far as the press is concerned, although the Queen is patient and accommodating she does things her way and not with an eye to an appealing picture.

10.40 a.m. Her Majesty and His Royal Highness visited Durrington High School where they toured the school and met pupils and staff. They also met representatives from caring organisations working in communities across West Sussex, representatives from local businesses, Queen's Award winning companies and winners of The Duke of Edinburgh Award. They were entertained to lunch at the school.

2.45 p.m. Her Majesty and His Royal Highness visited Church Walk Shopping Precinct, Burgess Hill, and walked to the West Sussex Local Authorities Help Point where they met staff and customers.

3.20 p.m. Her Majesty and His Royal Highness visited the Triangle Leisure Centre, Burgess Hill, where they toured the centre and attended a tea party.

4.30 p.m. Her Majesty and His Royal Highness left Burgess Hill by helicopter to travel to Windsor.

4.50 p.m. Arrival at Windsor Castle.

MONDAY. *Returned to London.*

TUESDAY. *12.55 p.m. The Queen received PC Thornborrow in Farewell Audience.*
2.30 p.m. The Princess Royal, Colonel, The Blues and Royals, was received by The Queen upon her appointment as Gold Stick and received from Her Majesty her Stick of Office.
3.00 p.m. Way Ahead Meeting.
6.30 p.m. Prime Minister's audience.

WEDNESDAY. *10.40 p.m. The Queen and The Duke of Edinburgh boarded the Royal Train to travel to Bristol.*

49

APRIL
STATE VISITS

WHEN THE QUEEN FIRST CAME TO THE THRONE, tours to Commonwealth countries could last up to six months with as many as fourteen destinations. Improved travel and increasing years mean the Queen now makes two, or occasionally three, much shorter overseas visits each year. One of these is a State Visit usually lasting four days. The other, of a week or more, is to part of the Commonwealth. She will also host two incoming State Visits from world leaders who will stay with her either at Buckingham Palace or at Windsor Castle. The purpose of all these visits is to foster good relations between the countries, sometimes endorsing and encouraging emerging democracies, and to build cultural, educational, business and trade links.

As Constitutional Monarch the Queen does not decide which Heads of State will be invited to Britain, nor which countries she might visit. Although the proposal will be put to her for approval, the choice of visiting leaders is made by the Foreign and Commonwealth Office representing the democratically elected government. She may dislike her visitor's regime, but the invitation is sent in her name as Head of State, and as hostess she must welcome her guest.

The Comptroller, Lord Chamberlain's Office is responsible for overseeing the programme of incoming State Visits, and for the ceremonial. Once the invitation has been accepted, his first task is to establish the Foreign Office objectives for the visit. He will then meet the Ambassador concerned to discover his country's wishes, and a programme will be drawn up followed by detailed recces. The Master of the Household, meanwhile, oversees all the domestic arrangements. These include accommodation for the Head of State and his party, the setting up of temporary offices with modern communications for them within the Palace or Castle, and the planning of meals including the State Banquet.

Although each is individually tailored for the particular guests, the visits follow an established pattern. They begin on Tuesday and finish on Friday. The Head of State, with his or her wife or husband, is met on arrival by a member of the Royal Family who accompanies them to the official welcome by the Queen and the Duke of Edinburgh. In London this now takes place on Horse Guards Parade, and at Windsor in the Home Park. There is then a State Drive down the Mall or through the streets of Windsor to the Palace or Castle, accompanied by a Sovereign's Escort of the Household Cavalry. The visitor is invited to inspect a Guard of Honour, then the Queen personally conducts her guests to their suite before an informal lunch for which she has chosen the menu. Afterwards presents, and possibly decorations, are exchanged. If the visit is in London, during the afternoon the Head of State generally goes to Westminster Abbey to lay a wreath on the Tomb of the Unknown Warrior; if they are staying at Windsor this will happen the following day. On the first evening there is a State Banquet to which leading public figures are invited, and others who might interest the visitors or who have particular links with their country. At the beginning of the Banquet both the Queen and her guest make speeches. The Queen welcomes her visitor, and they each set out the importance to them of the relationship between their two countries. The Queen's speech will have been written for her by the Foreign and Commonwealth Office.

The following day is occupied with political and diplomatic meetings in which the Queen plays no part, and on the third day the guests visit other parts of the country to see places that reflect their own particular interests. That evening there is a return banquet in their Embassy or a hotel. The following morning the guests bid their hostess goodbye.

The Queen's outgoing visits follow much the same pattern, with a mixture of ceremonial, formal entertainment and visits to places of interest. As soon as the visit is confirmed, a member of the British Embassy staff is appointed to coordinate it. Working with the hosts, the Palace, the Foreign and Commonwealth Office and the Department of Trade and Industry, the coordinator will draw up a suggested timetable. The official parts of the tour will be

pencilled in first, and then a schedule of visits will be built up, some to endorse trade or strengthen political links, others to see something of the country's culture and way of life. Plans will also be made for trade conferences and delegations which will use the goodwill engendered to create or develop bilateral links.

Once the broad timetable is agreed, two recce parties go out from the Palace, the first to look at the proposals and toss ideas around, the later one to work in detail over the agreed schedule and to make arrangements for security. When all the consultations are completed, the final programme is drawn up by the Palace. Embassy staff are often surprised by how much the Queen expects to do.

During the recces a representative of the Press Office will look for copy and photo opportunities. They will be hoping for one big story each day, although in practice this may not be the one they have planned. A hotel is booked for the press, and a fleet of small buses hired to take them round to the various rendezvous, and to return them speedily to their hotel so that they can file their copy in time for the morning papers, although increasingly both text and pictures are sent down the line by mobile phone.

The Queen meanwhile is briefed on the country's political and economic situation and will read about its history and culture, possibly visiting a museum to see something of this heritage. Her wardrobe will be chosen, bearing in mind not only the country's climate but also its particular cultural conventions. A British Airways plane will be chartered, and any necessary alterations made to its interior. Shortly before she leaves, the corridors of Buckingham Palace will fill with packing cases which look like old school trunks as the equipment necessary for the continuous running of her Private Office is crated. This will include anything from paperclips to filing cabinets and even desks. The Queen always travels with supplies of Malvern Still Mineral Water – a precaution which reduces the possibility of her being taken ill while abroad – oatcakes and marmalade for breakfast, and her own kettle, Twinings tea and Dundee cake, for she likes to pause during the afternoon and make herself some tea. She also brings her own feather pillows and pillowcases. The Queen will stay either in an official residence, or often more conveniently in a large hotel which has room to accommodate her staff. There are usually about thirty in her party, and, as with any large group, a corporate rate is negotiated.

The Queen always travels with her own doctor. Since early Royal Tours were by sea, he is by tradition a naval surgeon, and is there to give immediate medical help to any member of the Household. During the visit local hospitals will be on standby to offer more specialised treatment if necessary. Equipment and medical supplies, including the Queen's own blood, are taken.

When the visit is over, the FCO and the DTI, the businesses, investment bankers, educational establishments and cultural bodies begin to follow up leads and build on the goodwill that has been generated.

BRISTOL
BRISTOL CATHEDRAL

THURSDAY 1ST APRIL. *10.49 a.m. The Queen and The Duke of Edinburgh arrived at Bristol Temple Meads Station. Her Majesty and His Royal Highness drove to Bristol Cathedral where they attended the Maundy Service at which Her Majesty distributed the Royal Maundy. The Queen's Body Guard of the Yeomen of the Guard were on duty. Afterwards Her Majesty and His Royal Highness attended a Reception with members of the Cathedral and diocesan staff at the Chapter House.*

12.35 p.m. The Queen and The Duke of Edinburgh presented the 'Building a Better Bristol' Award to the Chairman of the Harbourside Project, Mr Nicholas Hood, before attending a Luncheon given by the Lord Mayor and the President of the Bristol Chamber of Commerce at the Mansion House.

SECURITY IS GOOD-NATURED but noticeably tighter than usual when we arrive at Bristol Cathedral for the Royal Maundy Service. We hear that anti-monarchy demonstrations are planned. Nearby Glastonbury is the home of travellers and known anti-monarchists.

The distribution of Royal Maundy is one of the oldest royal ceremonies. It derives from Christ's washing the disciples' feet at the Last Supper, and was first recorded in England in AD 600. The earliest known royal participation was in 1210 when King John washed the feet of the poor. In the early days the symbolism was less one of service than of Christ-like leadership. Since the reign of Henry IV the number of recipients of each sex has been the same as the sovereign's age.

By the early fourteenth century the monarch was providing a meal and gifts of clothing and food. Queen Mary I gave her gown to one of the women, but this led to squabbling and so Queen Elizabeth I substituted a red purse containing additional money. Charles I distributed the Maundy, but because of the plague he declined to wash the feet. At that time sweet-smelling herbal nosegays were first carried to keep away the plague. Half a century later James II wiped and kissed the feet 'with wonderful humility', but he was the last monarch to do so, for William III instructed his Almoner to carry out the task for him. By the mid-eighteenth century the sovereign had ceased to attend the ceremony, although the

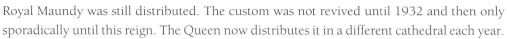

Royal Maundy was still distributed. The custom was not revived until 1932 and then only sporadically until this reign. The Queen now distributes it in a different cathedral each year.

Maundy money is legal tender. Like all British coinage it became decimal in 1971, and there is talk of special legislation to preserve it in sterling if Britain adopts the euro. It is given now to pensioners who have made a particular contribution to local Christian charities. Each receives a red purse and a white purse containing seven sets of specially minted silver Maundy coins – one for each decade of the Queen's life – plus a single three-pence coin for the extra years. The purses are carried on huge heavy platters by Yeomen of the Guard who process in front of the Queen as she leaves her seat in the sanctuary and goes down to distribute them, one of the rare ceremonial occasions when the Monarch goes to the people. She and the attendant clergy carry their nosegays, and those with her wear white linen towels recalling the washing of feet.

During the distribution the cathedral choir sings anthems, including Handel's magnificent 'Zadok the priest', one of the many occasions when we wish that music could be put within the pages of a book. They are joined, in their scarlet and gold Tudor State coats, by the ten Children of the Chapels Royal whose choir dates back to the thirteenth century.

After the service the Queen comes outside to pose for photographs and then walks straight across to the crowd of people waiting to see her, including the protestors now shouting slogans. Her Personal Protection Officer is close beside her but, although the police later make two arrests, the crowd is welcoming and there is no real trouble.

BRISTOL

ROYAL WEST OF ENGLAND ACADEMY

THE QUEEN IS PATRON OF THE ROYAL WEST OF ENGLAND ACADEMY, and she is visiting it as part of a £5 million appeal for redevelopment. The building, which was opened in 1858, houses an art school as well as galleries and a conservation department. As part of its educational programme the Academy encourages visits from schoolchildren, and she watches a group act their interpretation of a painting of trees. Some move in the wind, but one child who attracts her attention is as unmoving as the picture itself. 'You're a very still tree,' she observes with a grin.

The hosts decide whether they wish to fly a Royal Standard during the Queen's visit. If they do, they can borrow a flag in one of two sizes from the Palace. It is flown only while the Queen is actually in the building. The Royal Standard is never flown at half-mast, for one monarch is succeeded by the next at the moment of death.

Colin Edwards from Macclesfield is a familiar face on royal walkabouts. In seventeen years he has made nearly a hundred trips to see the Royal Family, and the Queen often stops to talk to him or to his grandchildren who sometimes come with him.

The Royal Standard waiting to be raised outside the Royal West of England Academy.

THURSDAY 1ST APRIL. *2.40 p.m. The Queen visited the Royal West of England Academy, where she met artists and members of the Academy as well as children from a local primary school. The Queen afterwards joined The Duke of Edinburgh at Cameron Balloons where they met Mr Brian Jones and M Bertrand Piccard, who circumnavigated the world in the balloon Breitling Orbiter 3.*
3.45 p.m. The Queen and The Duke of Edinburgh left Bristol by helicopter from Ashton Court Park.
4.20 p.m. Arrival at Windsor.

CAMERON BALLOONS

IN A LAST-MINUTE ALTERATION to her timetable, the Queen visits Cameron Balloons in Bristol. Two weeks earlier Brian Jones and Bertrand Piccard were the first people to circumnavigate the world in a balloon. The Queen had been monitoring their progress, and on one of their blackest days over the Gulf of Mexico they received a satellite fax from the Palace saying that if they completed the journey the Queen would like to meet them on their return. Their balloon was made in a Bristol factory already on the Duke's itinerary, and the Queen joins him there.

The maker of the balloon, Don Cameron, looks on as the Queen meets the balloonists, Brian Jones and Bertrand Piccard.

WINDSOR

WINDSOR CASTLE

IN AN EXCHANGE PROGRAMME with the Coldstream Guards, C Company 2nd Battalion of the Jamaican Defence Regiment mounts guard at Buckingham Palace and Windsor Castle during the week of 12th April, the first time that the Jamaican defence force has stood guard outside the Queen's residence.

THE RECEPTION for VCs and GCs is being held in St George's Hall. In the Windsor fire of November 1992 its ancient timber roof and painted heraldic ceiling were completely destroyed. It took six years to rebuild, and the first event after the restoration was the State Banquet in December 1998 during the visit of the President of Germany. We were there that evening in a dummy-run for our royal year, and from the balcony we had a chance to see at close quarters the splendid modern craftsmanship involved in the restoration, in particular in the woodcarving and repainting of the ceiling.

We are here again now for the gathering of holders of the Victoria Cross and George Cross. Britain's highest award for gallantry, the VC is awarded for acts of bravery on active service regardless of rank. Instituted by Queen Victoria in 1856, it has precedence over all other British Orders and decorations. The medals, each a bronze cross with a crimson ribbon, are coined by the Royal Mint from guns captured from the Russians during the Crimean War, and are inscribed with the words 'For Valour'. The George Cross, awarded to civilians, was instituted by George VI during the Second World War 'for acts of the greatest heroism or of the most conspicuous courage in circumstances of extreme danger'. The cross is silver with a dark blue ribbon, and has the inscription 'For Gallantry'.

Subedar Major Umrao Singh, Indian Army (below), received his VC fighting against the Japanese in Burma in December 1944.

Surviving VCs and GCs used to meet every year, with the expenses of those travelling from Commonwealth countries being paid for out of the public purse. As their numbers dwindle these gatherings are now held every other year, and the Queen has invited them to Windsor during this year's meeting.

Our friend Richard Annand of The Durham Light Infantry (seated on the left in the illustration opposite), received his VC during the retreat from Dunkirk; his father, whom he never knew, was killed in 1915 at Cape Helles on the southern tip of the Gallipoli peninsula. On the night of 15th –16th May 1940 Second Lieutenant Annand led his platoon against a German party which was attacking a blown bridge over a river. When the ammunition ran out he twice went forward over open ground by himself and drove out the attacking party with hand grenades. He was wounded, but he had his wound dressed and carried on in command. When the order was received to withdraw he led his platoon back, but as they went he heard his batman had been wounded and left behind. He returned at once and brought him away in a wheelbarrow, before losing consciousness because of his wounds. Profoundly deaf as a result of his war experiences, Mr Annand has subsequently worked for the welfare of the deafened.

WHILE THEY ARE AT WINDSOR IN APRIL, the Queen and the Duke of Edinburgh give two 'Dine and Sleep' parties. About twenty guests are invited, arriving at the Castle in the evening at 6.30. Pre-dinner drinks are served in the Green Drawing Room, followed by dinner in the State Dining Room. Afterwards the Queen takes her guests to the Royal Library to show them some of its treasures, which have been laid out for them by the Librarian. They leave after breakfast the following morning, a meal for which the Queen does not join them.

LONDON

BUCKINGHAM PALACE

THE PRESS CONFERENCE for the Korean State visit is held in the Chinese Dining Room at the Palace, with its oriental furnishings which came originally from George IV's Pavilion in Brighton. Mary Francis, the Queen's Deputy Private Secretary, and Penny Russell-Smith, her Deputy Press Secretary, brief royal correspondents and a number of Korean journalists representing their newspapers in London.

This is the first State Visit to Korea by a British Head of State. It was initially proposed in 1986 but for political reasons could not then go ahead. When President Kim Dae-jung came to the United Kingdom in April 1998, he issued a formal invitation to the Queen which has led to this visit. Its timing is particularly appropriate, for as well as underlining support for the government of President Kim Dae-jung it also marks the fiftieth anniversary of the renewing of British–Korean diplomatic ties following the Japanese colonisation of the country between 1910 and 1949. Britain was the first European country to have diplomatic links with Korea, in 1883.

The President's reforms have led to unprecedented UK investment in Korea as it rebuilds its infrastructure, and to Korean investment in the UK, a two-way association which will be reflected during the visit. The country's economy is showing strong signs of recovery after the slump of 1997, and Britain is now its largest European trading partner.

There are also strong cultural and educational links. The Queen has particularly asked to see something of the traditional culture of the country, and the itinerary has been planned with this request in mind. In preparation for the visit, she has been to see the 'Arts of Korea' exhibition at the British Museum, with artefacts from neolithic times to the Choson dynasty (1392–1910).

WITH THE WINDING DOWN OF THE QUEEN'S FLIGHT for financial reasons, the Royal Family now travels abroad on a specially chartered British Airways plane, generally a 767. About five days before they are due to leave, the plane is taken out of service so that a number of adaptations can be made.

The seats are removed from the First Class area, which is made into a private cabin with two beds, a hexagonal table and four chairs. Screwed-down bedside lamps are added. The silver St Christopher medallion with which the Queen always travels will later be fixed by Velcro to the cabin wall. Shower and lavatory accommodation forward of the cabin has to be shared with those on the flight deck. Any accompanying Minister and senior members of the Royal Household travel in the Cabin Class area, the rest further back.

For tours with multiple destinations – like that to Africa later in the year – there are two complete crews, as they will be flying for longer periods than one crew is allowed to by law. Each crew has a chief pilot and two others. The food is supplied by British Airways. A miniature Royal Standard is carried, and once the plane has landed and before it taxis forward, the pilot places this in position outside the aircraft. It is not possible to estimate flying time exactly, but, since the timing of the reception ceremony is precise, the plane will arrive early and circle until it is due to land. In 1997 British Airways had replaced the Union Flag colours with ethnic designs on all tailfins, except those of Concorde. This policy is now being changed, and the Queen's 767 is the first to sport the new stylised red, white and blue motif.

KOREA

SEOUL

SUNDAY 18TH APRIL. *6.50 p.m. The Queen and Duke of Edinburgh left Heathrow Airport, London, by British Airways 767 for the State Visit to the Republic of Korea.*

WE LEAVE FOR KOREA ahead of the Queen on the 10 p.m. Air Singapore flight, arriving in Seoul at 7 o'clock on Saturday morning. This gives us a day to acclimatise before the first briefing session at the Hilton on Sunday evening. The Queen is due to arrive on Monday afternoon.

It's a far more vibrant country than we had expected. I suppose our idea of it was formed from images of the Korean War, when Seoul was almost totally destroyed, and from what we have heard about continuing North–South confrontation. Certainly that is a menacing presence here, especially in a city so close to the border with North Korea, but the people are delightful, and everywhere we look there is new building – huge new bridges across the Han-gang River, and quantities of very fine skyscrapers. From our hotel window we look

out over endless construction sites in among the other buildings, and the never-ending sound of cement mixers mingles with the insistent traffic noise. Even after a few hours it's apparent that this visit is going to be very interesting.

At the briefing the Queen's Deputy Press Secretary, and the Second Secretary at the British Embassy who has organised the day-to-day timetable of events, go through the itinerary. There was an attempt on the President's life a few months ago, so security will be very tight. The press are issued with brightly coloured armbands, and we are given lapel-badges which will give us access to all the places the Queen will visit. Because of the Kosovo crisis, there are fewer press than had been expected. The Foreign Secretary has had to remain in Britain and will be sending the Foreign Office Minister, Derek Fatchett.

A shop-front in Seoul (above).

The press briefing (left) where the Queen's timetable is discussed, item by item, press opportunities and arrangements for transport explained, and information packs and press passes distributed. (Left to right) Simon Walker of The Times, *Tim Rooke of Rex Features, Colin Brazier of Sky News, Ian Jones of the* Daily Telegraph, *Robert Hardman of the* Daily Telegraph, *Michael Cassell of the* Financial Times, *Ros Sparrow, Second Secretary at the British Embassy, Alan Hamilton of* The Times, *Fiona Hanson of the Press Association.*

KOREA

SEOUL

MONDAY 19TH APRIL. *2.30 p.m. The Queen and The Duke of Edinburgh arrived in the Republic of Korea and were welcomed at the Military Airbase, Seoul, by the Foreign Minister, Mr Hong Soon-young.*

3.00 p.m. Her Majesty and His Royal Highness drove to the National Cemetery and laid a wreath.

3.20 p.m. The Queen and The Duke of Edinburgh were welcomed at the Blue House by HE President Kim Dae-jung and the First Lady, Mrs Lee Hee-ho.

4.15 p.m. Her Majesty and His Royal Highness visited Midong Elementary School and watched a display of Taekwondo.

6.00 p.m. The Queen and the Duke of Edinburgh received Commonwealth Ambassadors at the Hyatt Hotel.

6.30 p.m. The Queen and the Duke of Edinburgh gave a Reception to members of the media at the Hyatt Hotel.

THERE'S A LOT OF INTEREST HERE IN THE VISIT. In London during the past few weeks we have met a Korean camera crew on all the Queen's public engagements, and theirs is just one of a number of television programmes about her to have gone out in the past few days. We hear that last week's dress rehearsal took number one spot on the evening news above a State Visit to Korea by President Mubarak of Egypt. Today's papers are full of it. An editorial in *The Korean Times* talks of a special day for Korean democracy as the country welcomes the head of the world's most stable and mature democracy, and speaks of the affinity between a centuries-old monarchy and Korea's traditional Confucian values. It even suggests that if Korea comes together as a unified democratic country, serious thought should be given to the possibility of reinstating a monarchy. In a society that respects age, it is seen as a great compliment that the Queen has chosen to spend her seventy-third birthday here.

The Queen and the Duke arrive at the Military Airbase at 2.30 p.m. after an eleven and a half hour flight. They go straight from there to the National Cemetery where, like all senior visitors to the country, they lay a wreath and place incense on the eternal flame. This was first built as a military cemetery during the Korean War and is a memorial to the 102,000 soldiers from that war who have no known grave. From the cemetery they go on to the official reception at the President's residence, where they are welcomed by

Kim Dae-jung and the First Lady. Both the Queen and the Duke look very tired. Even though their flight is made comfortable, they are both now in their seventies and must find the journey a strain. Their Korean hosts suggest they might like to rest after the welcoming formalities, but the Queen likes to keep going through the first day and has asked to visit Midong Elementary School to meet the children and watch their display of Taekwondo, a Korean martial art.

In the evening they receive Commonwealth Ambassadors to Korea at the Hyatt Hotel where they are staying, and then host a reception for members of the British and Korean press. It is now nearly sixteen hours since they left Heathrow.

Police motorbikes outside the Hyatt Hotel, Seoul. The Queen and her staff have taken over the top floor of the hotel, the rest of which continues to operate normally but with increased security during her stay.

KOREA

SEOUL

I N HIS FIGHT FOR A FREE AND DEMOCRATIC COUNTRY, President Kim Dae-jung spent many years in prison. Sentenced to death, twice exiled, and the first opposition leader to become President, his election brought Korea a new political era.

His official home is the Chong Wa Dae, or 'House with a Blue Tile Roof', which is built along an energy-giving axis. Here a Guard of Honour greets the Queen and the Duke on their arrival. It is formed of Korean troops, with a ceremonial Presidential Guard, some of whom are actors in traditional uniforms.

SEOUL

THE FLIGHT TAKES US BACK to Seoul, where the long line of cars is speeded through traffic lights to the Hyatt Hotel. Here, after only a slight pause to recover, the Queen hosts a tea party for Parliamentarians before getting ready for the evening's concert of British and Korean music and dance, her turn to entertain the President and the First Lady. At the end, the British soprano Lesley Garrett leads a choir of schoolchildren in singing 'Happy birthday'. For all the banality of the song, it is curiously moving and the Queen seems genuinely touched. Indeed those closest to her later say that there were tears in her eyes.

KOREA
ANDONG PROVINCE

WEDNESDAY 21ST APRIL. *The 73rd anniversary of the Birthday of The Queen. 7.00 a.m. The Queen left the Hilton Hotel for Seoul Airbase, travelling by British Airways 767 to Andong Province. 11.15 p.m. Her Majesty arrived at Hahoe Village where she viewed a family house and watched a masked dance. 12.25 p.m. Her Majesty visited Andong wholesale fruit market. 1.00 p.m. The Queen visited Pongjong Buddhist Temple. After this visit she returned by British Airways 767 to Seoul. 4.20 p.m. The Queen had Tea with Korean and British Parliamentarians at the Hyatt Hotel. 7.25 p.m. The Queen and The Duke of Edinburgh attended a Concert of Korean and British music and dance with the President and First Lady at the Korean Broadcasting Service Hall, Seoul. After the concert Her Majesty and His Royal Highness hosted a Reception for Korean and British guests.*

LIKE ANY COUNTRY WITH ANCIENT TRADITIONS, Korea has had to decide how to preserve customs that have come down from earlier times. Part of their solution has been to designate some of these as Important Intangible Cultural Properties, guaranteeing their survival. In the province of Andong, whose main city is considered the spiritual home of Korea's Confucianism, traditional culture is still passed down as a way of life, and it is here that the Queen has chosen to go. She is the first foreign Head of State to visit Andong, and since the announcement of her visit tourist numbers have increased threefold.

We leave early in the morning for the Seoul Military Airbase, where we board the Queen's plane for the fifty-minute flight to Yechon. From there the procession of cars drives past rice fields and flag-waving, music-playing Koreans to the Folk Village of Hahoe, which is designated Important Folklore Object No. 122. Each village in Andong is comprised of a different clan, and each has its principal family. The Queen goes first to the home of one of these, called Ch'unghyodang or the 'house of loyalty and filial piety'. Having first taken off her shoes, she goes inside to see women preparing *kimch'i*, Korea's powerful national dish of cabbage pickled in chilli and garlic. She then watches ox-ploughing before going to the Talking House, or village hall, to be greeted by elders and to see the colourful, ebullient Hahoe Mask Dance. Dating back eight hundred years, this was devised to placate the local goddess and to exorcise evil spirits. It is accompanied by *nong-ak*, traditional Korean farmers' percussion music, and combines ancient shaman ritual with bawdy satire. Allegorical figures represent types – the arrogant aristocrat, the depraved Buddhist monk, the coarse butcher – whose absurd and abandoned performance was designed to defuse social tensions within the village. Villagers crowd onto the straw roofs of nearby houses to watch.

The Queen then meets the dancers, and a birthday table is placed in front of her laden with almond cakes, rice, savouries and sweetmeats, a tradition dating from the fourteenth century. Since it is the forty-sixth birthday of one of the performers, he and the Queen toast one another in rice wine.

Stopping next at the Andong modern and utilitarian fruit market, which each day handles over five hundred tons of locally grown fruit, the procession of cars drives up into the hills to the Pongjong Buddhist Temple. According to legend, a revered monk in the seventh century made a phoenix out of paper, flew on it from a nearby mountain and built the temple where it landed. The Queen's journey is not so simple. Her car brings her as close as possible to the temple compound, but she has a final steep climb up rocky steps. The large temple bell is rung twenty-eight times each morning – signifying the twenty-eighth heaven – to wake all the creatures of creation, and thirty-three times each evening – the thirty-third heaven – to summon them to sleep. Following a Buddhist tradition bringing good fortune, the Queen adds one more stone to the pile in the temple courtyard.

Traditional court dress (left) is now only used
by performers, but the Korean national dress,
hanbok, is still worn.

The Queen was served a seven-course menu
including pine-nut porridge; broiled silver codfish
with pan-fried squash, shiitake and shrimp with
eggs; casserole 'Shin-Sul-Lo'; and steamed rice with
black beans and beef soup.

河回別神굿탈놀이

KOREA
SEOUL

I T IS THE CUSTOM NOW FOR SPEECHES to be made at the start of State Banquets, which is unfortunate for the Duke of Edinburgh, who might have benefited from the first course of ginseng, served with cucumber and mustard sauce. Ginseng is famous for its restorative powers and its ability to increase stamina. 'Duke of 'ed in soup,' blazes the London headline next morning, for we watch the Duke's head slipping slowly forward during the Queen's speech as he almost loses his battle against tiredness. But the newspaper comments are more questioning than critical. Do we ask too much of him – or more accurately, does he, at seventy-eight, demand too much of himself?

The seven-course State Banquet comes at the end of a long and busy first full day. The Duke has visited seven different locations, from an electronics factory to a bridge construction site, and has given a pre-lunch speech at the UK–Korean Conference, where he spoke on the importance of environmental issues and the need for considerations of ethics and morality in a knowledge-driven economy. It is a purposeful, crippling schedule which he himself has chosen.

Korean music and dance have their origins in ancient seasonal religious festivals, and developed over the centuries through cultural contact with China and the introduction of Confucianism and Buddhism. Court music and dance are designed to create a calm asceticism of the inner spirit.

During the banquet the red-carpeted corridor, along which the procession of dignitaries has just sedately passed, is transformed into a kitchen as trestle tables and mobile ovens are put speedily in place, and waiters with trays and white napkins suddenly appear. The meal, prepared by one of Seoul's leading hotels, is served and cleared away, and when the doors open once more at the end of the meal no one would know a thing.

After the banquet the Queen and the Duke exchange presents with their hosts, including a wooden box for the President, 'made by my nephew' [Viscount Linley], as the Queen explains; an engraving of Clare Hall, Cambridge, where the President had been a student; and a Shetland wool scarf for the President's wife. 'I hope it keeps you nice and warm,' says the Queen.

Then there is a performance of traditional court music and dance. One of the dances, 'Taepongmu', is a prayer for long, healthy life for the King and Queen. It is delicate, gracious and serene, very different from the performance the Queen will watch in Andong.

KOREA

SEOUL

TUESDAY 20TH APRIL. *10.20 a.m. The Queen and The Duke of Edinburgh visited the Daewoo Design Forum and met engineers from the Daewoo technical centre in Worthing, UK.*
11.10 a.m. Her Majesty visited Ani Dream Animation Studio.
12.20 p.m. The Queen, with The Duke of Edinburgh, met Korean and British business leaders at the Hyatt Hotel.
2.45 p.m. The Queen visited Ehwa Women's University.
3.35 p.m. The Queen visited Insadong, and called at calligraphy, pottery and hanbok shops.
7.30 p.m. The Queen and The Duke of Edinburgh attended a State Dinner given by the President and First Lady at the Blue House.

THE KOREAN RESPONSE to this visit is astonishing. 'Queen-mania rocks Seoul: Monarch is given pop star welcome during state visit' is the headline that Peter Archer, the Press Association correspondent, has filed for the British papers after the Queen's first full day here.

It begins relatively sedately with the morning visit to the Daewoo factory to see the latest designs in cars manufactured for the Korean firm at Worthing. As she crosses the city the Queen is surrounded by American-style security, something she is not used to. Nor is she used to decoy cars and official tasters, both of which we have seen here. This security edginess is a constant reminder of the continuing division between North and South Korea. It is still quiet at the Ani Dream Animation Studio, which has recently purchased £1 million of computer software from a Cambridge company. But at the Ewha Women's University things change. Here her reception is rapturous. 'The students seem quite cool about this rare celebrity, concerned more about their midterm exam schedule,' says one of the senior academics hopefully, but the undergraduates are having none of it. Instead they surge, cheering and shouting, against the security cordons to greet the Queen. The University was established by an American Methodist missionary in 1886 at a time when the education of women outside the home was considered improper and grossly against Confucian traditions. It is now the largest women's university in the world, with over 18,000 students, and the Queen's endorsement of their campus thrills them. During the Korean War the university was used as a field hospital for British and American troops.

In the Pharmacology Department of the university, the Queen visits two laboratories. In one (above) she watches undergraduates conducting experiments, and in the other she meets graduate students who are carrying out research on the chemical composition of Korean Red ginseng roots.

KOREA

SEOUL

At INSA-DONG, WHERE THE QUEEN GOES NEXT, her reception is no less ecstatic. Insa-dong is a narrow street in central Seoul which once linked the northern aristocratic village of Pukch'on with the commercial district of Chongo. In the 1930s it became a gathering place for shops trading in Korean crafts and antiques, and now it is an exciting cultural centre with hundreds of small shops, galleries and restaurants. With its exotic shop-fronts it is already colourful and festive, but it is made even more so by the crowds hanging from windows, by Korean flags, Union Jacks and paper lanterns, and by music that booms from loudspeakers. The streets and pathways and pavements are packed with thousands of excited, cheering people. There is nothing stage-managed about this, and one realises how a country that is only now emerging into hard-won democracy envies the continuity and stability the Queen represents.

The Queen's visit begins in the tiny shop owned by Mr Lee Si-Kyu, where the shelves are stacked with long rolls of paper and soft, sweeping-headed brushes of every size. He is used to VIPs; last year Bill Clinton came to watch him creating his Korean calligraphy. Leaving there, the Queen crosss the road to see the work of Mrs Park Young Sook, who has revived traditional Korean potting techniques for the modern table. As the Queen saw at the 'Arts of Korea' exhibition at the British Museum, this country has a long history of fine porcelain, pottery and ceramics. For her last stop, the excited crowds are pushed back once more to allow her to get to a hanbok shop where she is shown modern examples of the elegant traditional dress still worn by Korean women. She is presented with a shawl, which they slip over her shoulders. 'Would you like to see in a mirror?' they ask. The Queen smiles as she declines the offer. 'I'm sure it looks very nice,' she says.

Statue of Confucius (551–479 BC). Nothing has had more influence on Korean thought than Confucianism. Its values permeate the national approach to life.

Children from the British Council school line the route as the Queen walks to the Anglican Cathedral. Educational links between the two countries are strong. Each year about 22,000 Koreans enquire about studying in Britain, and about half of these come to the UK.

77

THURSDAY 22ND APRIL. *10.20 a.m. Mr
Stephen Brown, British Ambassador to
the Republic of Korea, was received by
The Queen when Her Majesty conferred
upon him the honour of Knighthood and
invested him with the Insignia of Knight
Commander of the Royal Victorian
Order. The Queen then held an
Investiture.
11.10 a.m. The Queen and The Duke of
Edinburgh visited the British Council,
and the Anglican Cathedral in Seoul.
11.50 a.m. Her Majesty and His Royal
Highness attended a Reception at the
British Residence for British and
Commonwealth veterans of the Korean
War and met Embassy staff and their
families.
1.30 p.m. The Queen and The Duke of
Edinburgh departed Seoul for the UK.
6.30 p.m. The Queen and The Duke
of Edinburgh arrived at Heathrow
Airport, London.*

KOREA

SEOUL

THE CENTRAL EVENT OF THE QUEEN'S LAST DAY is a party for Korean War veterans in the garden of the British Embassy. She goes first to the British Council, whose role is to strengthen Britain's educational, scientific and cultural relations with Korea. From there she walks past flag-waving children wearing traditional Korean dress to the Anglican Cathedral, where General Sir Anthony Farrar-Hockley, who fought in the Korean War, shows her the Roll of Honour listing the war dead.

South Korea has not forgotten those who fought alongside them in the war; returning veterans pay their own air fares, but once they arrive in the country they are distinguished guests of the government. The Queen herself is almost certainly unaware of the problems the garden party has created for some of the Australian, Canadian and New Zealand veterans who, with eighty-four of their British comrades, are in Seoul for their annual reunion. It was to have been one of the highlights of a visit that for many has included their first return to the battlefields and cemeteries of nearly fifty years before. They and their wives had all been invited but, on the evening before, a message came through to their hotel saying that the Embassy garden is not large enough for them all and their number is to be restricted, with no wives allowed. Whoever is to blame, this muddle causes a great deal of distress and anger and does nothing to enhance what is for many of them an already equivocal view of the Crown.

PANMUNJON AND GLOSTER VALLEY

WE STAY ON AFTER THE QUEEN HAS LEFT KOREA so that we can go with the veterans to Panmunjon on the border with North Korea, where Prince Philip was a few days ago. In the demilitarized zone there is a sense of eerie menace. At a service of commemoration in Gloster Valley, site of one of the bloodiest and bravest battles of the war, the newly knighted Ambassador reads a message from the Queen.

We hear from someone in the Press Office that we cannot observe any part of the Service for the Royal Victorian Order, inside or outside the chapel. This spectacular event happens only once every four years and we wonder whose decision this is.

TUESDAY 27TH APRIL. *1.00 p.m. The Queen and The Duke of Edinburgh entertained the Governor-General of Australia and Lady Deane to Lunch.*

WEDNESDAY *Mrs Mary Francis was received by The Queen upon relinquishing her appointment as Deputy Private Secretary when Her Majesty invested her with the Insignia of Lieutenant of the Royal Victorian Order.*

THURSDAY. *10.30 a.m. The Queen, Sovereign of the Order, accompanied by The Duke of Edinburgh, was present at a Service of the Royal Victorian Order held in George's Chapel, Windsor Castle. Detachments of Her Majesty's Body Guard of the Honourable Corps of Gentlemen at Arms, the Queen's Body Guard of the Yeomen of the Guard and the Military Knights of Windsor were on duty in St George's Chapel. After the Service The Queen and The Duke of Edinburgh gave a Reception at Windsor Castle for those who had attended.*

FRIDAY *To Wood Farm, Sandringham.*

MAY

THE QUEEN AS
CONSTITUTIONAL MONARCH

THE UNITED KINGDOM has no written constitution, and the Queen's constitutional role is determined by convention as well as by statute. Growing from the thirteenth-century reforms embodied in the Magna Carta, the Bill of Rights at the end of the seventeenth century was designed to protect Parliament and the people from interference by the Sovereign. Four centuries after the Magna Carta, Charles I sought to rule without Parliament, arguing that the Monarch answered only to God and not to man. His actions led to the Civil War, his execution and the Commonwealth. The monarchy was restored, but his second son, James II, attempted to reintroduce arbitrary monarchical rule, and was deposed and forced into exile. When in 1688 the throne was offered to his daughter Mary and her husband, William of Orange, the Bill of Rights was drawn up restoring the traditional rights of Parliament against the Sovereign. This Bill, reinforced in 1701 by the Act of Settlement, forms the basis of the relationship the Monarch now has with government, the Church, the judiciary and the armed forces.

With the principles established, modifications slowly developed. George I understood very little English, and since he could take no real part in Privy Council discussions the ministers began to meet without him in what was to become the Cabinet. This shift in the centre of government towards the elected House of Commons was strengthened by the passage of the Reform Bill in 1832. There were dips in this process as individual monarchs took independent stands over often quite small constitutional matters, but throughout the eighteenth and nineteenth centuries the progress was steady. Members of the House of Commons were elected by the people to decide matters of policy, and the Monarch became a Head of State who, in the words of Walter Bagehot in his hugely influential book *The English Constitution* published in 1867, had 'the right to be consulted, the right to encourage, and the right to warn'. By the end of the nineteenth century the Sovereign had become a person of influence rather than power.

But this influence constitutes a vital part of the Monarch's role. It is the Queen's actual responsibility to express her opinion on government policy to her ministers, in particular in her weekly audiences with the Prime Minister. In 1986 her then Private Secretary, Sir William Heseltine, laid down the three rules that govern this aspect of the Queen's work, saying that she has the right and duty to express her views on government policy, that she must abide by the advice of her ministers, and that communications between her and her ministers must remain confidential. As a source of advice, the present Queen can draw on fifty years of experience and reading of government and international documents, as well as on discussions with ministers and world leaders of every kind. This gives her a perspective that few of her ministers can have. 'Occasionally you are able to put your point of view,' she says. 'Perhaps they hadn't thought of it from that angle.' But it is they who have the final say, and she must abide by this. The substance of these meetings remains confidential. No minutes are kept, and the Prime Minister does not even report back to the Cabinet on what has been said. This guarantees the Queen's political impartiality, but also means that the extent of her influence cannot be assessed, although from the memoirs of earlier Prime Ministers it would seem that it is real.

Although without direct political power, as Head of State the Queen still fulfils public duties relating to Parliament. The most visible of these is her annual Speech from the Throne, in which she opens the new parliamentary session by setting out her government's policy. This is prepared for her by the government, and expresses no thoughts of her own. She must also give the Royal Assent to the passing of all new laws, for no Act of Parliament becomes law until she has signed it, and she enacts certain measures with her ministers in the Privy Council.

The Privy Council dates back to Norman times and is the oldest form of legislative assembly to have survived. Originally a group of close advisers to the Monarch, its main business is now conducted in Cabinet. The Privy Council, however, still functions as part of the machinery of government, through which the Queen in person approves Orders and Proclamations, acting on the advice of the Council and deriving her power from the royal prerogative and from various acts of Parliament. Through Orders in Council, the Queen orally signifies her approval of subordinate legislation which does not then need to be re-presented to Parliament, grants royal charters of incorporation and makes certain appointments. The Privy Council also issues Proclamations such as the dissolution of Parliament. When a Proclamation has been approved in Council, it is signed by the Queen, and the Great Seal of the Realm is then affixed. The Privy Council has about four hundred members. The number of Counsellors summoned to any meeting is usually only four, and so that its business should not be unduly protracted the meetings are conducted standing up.

There are still some areas of the personal prerogative where the Queen might have to act without ministerial advice. The appointment of the Prime Minister and the dissolution of Parliament are still, in theory at least, her decisions. In normal circumstances it would be unthinkable for her to appoint as Prime Minister anyone who was not also leader of the party with the largest number of seats in Parliament, but as recently as 1963 the Queen was called upon to choose between four contenders for the role. This she did after consultation with senior party figures. Since then, all the leading political parties elect their own leaders and the issue has not arisen again. However, although the choice of Prime Minister rests with the party, the actual appointment is the responsibility of the Queen as Head of State. A defeated party leader remains Prime Minister tendering his or her resignation to the Queen, and after a general election or change in leadership she summons the incoming Prime Minister to the Palace where she invites the new Premier to form a government.

The decision to dissolve Parliament usually rests with the Prime Minister and the Cabinet. They decide when it is time to go to the country, and the Prime Minister then asks the Sovereign to grant a dissolution. It is a request rather than a demand, for there are theoretical circumstances in which the Queen could believe it unwise to grant the request, for example if she judged the existing Parliament to be still viable and capable of carrying out its work even though the Prime Minister may have lost the party's support.

The idea of the Monarch as the country's 'Fount of Justice' goes back to Anglo-Saxon times. The King oversaw a single judicial system which prevailed over competing local, civil or ecclesiastical jurisdictions. The Bill of Rights secured the position of the judges by making their appointments dependent upon good behaviour

rather than on the pleasure of the King. The country's jurisprudence now derives from the Crown and is carried out by those acting in the Queen's name. Her Majesty's judges sit in the Queen's Courts administering the Sovereign's laws, and those found guilty may be sent to Her Majesty's Prisons.

Although the Monarch no longer has control over the Church, the judiciary or the armed forces, the Act of Homage or Oath of Allegiance is sworn to the Crown embodied in the Monarch and not to the government of the day, and with high-ranking appointments this is confirmed in a private audience with the Queen. This means that these bodies operate independently of the government. Indeed, these slowly evolving constitutional changes have led to a paradoxical reversal. There is no longer any need to protect the people against the arbitrary power of the monarchy. Instead, the monarchy now stands against the threat of arbitrary political power.

LONDON
WESTMINSTER ABBEY

TUESDAY 4TH MAY. *Returned to London.*

WEDNESDAY. *11.30 a.m. The Queen attended a Service for the Centenary of King Edward VII Hospital for Officers in Westminster Abbey. Her Majesty later attended a Reception at College Gardens. 6.30 p.m. The Queen attended a Reception at St James's Palace to mark the 50th Anniversary of the Council of Europe.*

THURSDAY. *11.50 a.m. Her Excellency Mrs Monica Nashandi was received in audience by The Queen and presented the Letters of Recall of her predecessor and her own Letters of Commission as High Commissioner for Namibia. 12.10 p.m. The Queen, Colonel-in-Chief, Corps of Royal Engineers, received General Sir John Stibbon upon relinquishing his appointment as Chief Royal Engineer. Her Majesty received Lieutenant General Sir Scott Grant upon his appointment as Chief Royal Engineer and upon relinquishing his appointment as Colonel, The Queen's Lancashire Regiment. The Queen, Colonel-in-Chief, received Brigadier Alex Birtwistle upon his appointment as Colonel, The Queen's Lancashire Regiment. 12.40 p.m. His Excellency Monsieur Mahmoud Hammoud was received in farewell audience by The Queen upon His Excellency relinquishing his appointment as Ambassador from Lebanon to the Court of St James's. 2.30 p.m. Portrait sitting.*

FRIDAY. *To Badminton Horse Trials.*

D URING THE BOER WAR, two sisters, Agnes and Fanny Keyser, opened their London house in Grosvenor Crescent as a nursing home for sick and wounded officers. Such private enterprise was not uncommon at the time, and was to burgeon a few years later when countless private houses became nursing and convalescent homes during the First World War. What was different about this was that Agnes Keyser was a bridge-playing friend of Edward VII, himself a vigorous supporter of charitable enterprises. In offering a passport into royal circles, with shoots at Sandringham and envied social endorsement, Edward VII extended an unspoken condition – that those he benefited should in turn benefit others. When the war ended, he was anxious that Miss Keyser's hospital should continue, and he prevailed upon twenty-four of his friends to give money to make it a permanent foundation.

A hundred years later, the Queen as Patron is at Westminster Abbey to celebrate the centenary of the King Edward VII Hospital for Officers. It has continued to enjoy royal patronage and in the most practical way, for the Queen Mother, Princess Margaret and the Princess Royal have all been patients there, as has the Queen herself. In 1982 she went there for the removal of a wisdom tooth, the first time that she had ever been in hospital.

ST JAMES'S PALACE

T HE RECEPTION TO MARK the fiftieth anniversary of the Council of Europe is hosted by the Foreign Secretary. It is held at St James's Palace, where the original agreement had been signed; it has been brought from the Public Record Office for the evening. The multinational list of guests represents the wide range of work of the Council of Europe. There is emphasis on youth, including young people from both sides of the Irish divide – a girl in traditional Irish dress presents the Queen's posy.

As Constitutional Monarch, the Queen expresses no opinion on the European Community. It is left to others to wonder what long-term effect the organisation she is celebrating will have on the constitution of this country, and with it the monarchy.

B ADMINTON HORSE TRIALS is a three-day event in which horses and riders compete in dressage, cross-country and show jumping. It is a tough competition of all-round skill; the Princess Royal was an Olympic three-day eventer. The weather this year is appalling, making conditions difficult and the arduous course even more of a test. No one is seriously injured, although this later turns out to be a black year for eventing.

Peta Beckett receives a silver rose bowl from the Queen. She was to suffer a fatal fall a few weeks later at the Savernake Forest Horse Trials.

LONDON
NATIONAL MARITIME MUSEUM, GREENWICH

BOTH HENRY VIII and his daughter Queen Elizabeth I were born at Greenwich, and the palace there remained a centre of court life until the time of the Civil War. For centuries British life was dominated by the sea, and Greenwich has a long naval tradition. Much of the defence of Britain against the Spanish Armada at the end of the sixteenth century was planned here, and both the Duke of Edinburgh and the Prince of Wales spent some of their naval training at the Royal Naval College.

The National Maritime Museum was opened by George VI in 1937, when his daughter Princess Elizabeth was with him. She is here again to open Neptune Court, a central courtyard covered now by a soaring, dramatic free-span glass roof, the largest of its kind in Europe. She and the Duke, who has been a trustee of the Museum for fifty years, see Prince Frederick's barge, built in 1732 for the eldest son of George II as Prince of Wales. It was

The Lord Lieutenant of Greater London, Lord Imbert, is at Greenwich to greet the Queen. As Sir Peter Imbert, he was Commissioner of the Metropolitan Police from 1987 to 1993.

84

then pulled by twenty-one oarsmen in full livery, and on its first day afloat took Queen Caroline and the Prince from Chelsea to Somerset House to inspect the cleaning of the royal paintings. It was last used in 1849 by Prince Albert. It was later sawn into three pieces, and for a hundred years was stored in the Royal Barge House at Windsor.

The six Doggettmen are Royal Watermen who have won the Doggett's Coat and Badge in a sculling race on the Thames between London Bridge and Chelsea. The race has been rowed on or near 1st August each year since 1715, and celebrates the accession a year earlier of George I. Thomas Doggett, a staunch Hanoverian, was a comedian and actor associated with the Theatre Royal Drury Lane and the Haymarket Theatre. He gave funds in perpetuity to provide the winner with an orange-coloured (now red) livery with a large silver badge to be worn on the left arm bearing the White Horse of Hanover and representing Liberty.

Prince Frederick's barge

WEDNESDAY 12TH MAY. *11.30 a.m. Portrait sitting with Mr Chen Yan Ning.*
1.00 p.m. The King and Queen of the Hashemite Kingdom of Jordan visited The Queen and remained to Lunch. The Queen invested the King with the Insignia of an Honorary Knight Grand Cross of the Most Distinguished Order of St Michael and St George.
Afternoon. To Royal Windsor Horse Show.

THURSDAY – SUNDAY. *Royal Windsor Horse Show.*

MONDAY *9.35 a.m. Left Windsor Castle.*
10.00 a.m. Arrived at RAF Northolt.
11.15 a.m. Arrived at Edinburgh Airport and drove to the Palace of Holyroodhouse. The Rt Hon Donald Dewar, MP, MSP, was received by The Queen upon his appointment as First Minister of the Scottish Executive.
1.15 p.m. Arrived at Edinburgh Airport.
2.30 p.m. Arrived at RAF Northolt.
3.00 p.m. Arrived at Buckingham Palace.

TUESDAY. *11.40 a.m. Colonel Sir Piers Bengough was received by The Queen and delivered up his Stick of Office upon relinquishing his appointment as Standard Bearer of Her Majesty's Body Guard of the Honourable Corps of Gentlemen at Arms. Major Anthony Arkwright was received by The Queen upon his appointment as Standard Bearer of Her Majesty's Body Guard of the Honourable Corps of Gentlemen at Arms, and received from The Queen his Stick of Office.*

LONDON
BUCKINGHAM PALACE

THE CONVENTION OF COURT PAINTER, possibly with a studio producing replicas, has now gone. Although at the beginning of the Queen's reign there was still a handful of favourites who painted her many times, there is now a more adventurous wish to give younger or less well-known artists a chance; indeed the Queen has sat to more individual painters than any monarch in history.

When a portrait is proposed – perhaps for a regiment or an organisation of which the Queen is Patron – the commissioning organisation writes to the Palace to ask if the Queen would be prepared to sit. If she agrees, they will then either propose their own artist or ask the Palace for advice. It is usually the Private Secretary who puts forward a possible name.

Sittings are held in the Yellow Drawing Room, at the front left-hand corner of the first floor of the Palace. The light is not ideal, and early in her reign the Queen would go to the artist's studio, but that is no longer regarded as practicable. The clothes she is to wear are discussed by the Private Secretary and the painter before the first sitting. The choice is dictated partly by where the picture is to hang; for a regimental picture she may wear a day dress with the regimental badge, but for a large, formal picture she may be painted in the robes of one of the Orders of Chivalry. Sittings last for about an hour, and the painter is generally left alone to get on, although a Private Secretary may use the opportunity to talk through non-sensitive things with the Queen. Conversation flows freely and informally,

often with the Queen giving a running commentary about what is going on outside the window. It is alleged that the tip-chinned, imperious look of the famous 1955 Annigoni picture came about because he spoke little English and she spoke little Italian, and after talking in French for a while they lapsed into silence. To fill the time she lifted her chin so that she could look out of the window and see what was going on outside.

It is a very cold, very wet day when the new King Abdullah II of Jordan and Queen Rania arrive at Buckingham Palace to have lunch with the Queen. I thought that the ceremony was to be indoors, and have worn a woollen frock and no coat. As we wait in the rain for the King to arrive before inspecting the Guard of Honour in the Quadrangle, I ask someone from the Press Office if I might borrow the rolled umbrella that I see propped against the wall close by. This is not possible, and as I get wetter and colder I swear that for the next out-of-doors event I shall wear something warm and practical.

HOLYROODHOUSE, SCOTLAND

T O SIGNIFY THE IMPORTANCE of the new appointment, the Queen makes a special visit to Scotland for her first, twenty-minute audience with Donald Dewar, Scotland's new First Minister, a break with the usual convention that political leaders go to the Queen for audiences. The British Prime Minister has a weekly audience with the Queen, but distance means that she will have only irregular audiences with the First Minister.

12 noon. His Excellency Dr Lal Jayawardena was received in audience by The Queen and presented the Letters of Recall of his predecessor and his own Letters of Commission as High Commissioner for Sri Lanka in London.
12.20 p.m. Lieutenant General Sir Michael Jackson was received by The Queen upon his appointment as Colonel Commandant Adjutant General's Corps.
12.30 p.m. Sir Robertson Young (New Delhi) and Mr Anthony Smith (Kingston) were received in audience by The Queen upon their appointment as British High Commissioners. Mr John Grant (Stockholm) and Miss Kay Coombs (Ulaanbaatar) were received in audience by The Queen and kissed hands upon their appointment as Her Majesty's Ambassadors.
2.30 p.m. Portrait sitting with Mr Chen Yan Ning.
6.30 p.m. Prime Minister's audience.

WINDSOR
WINDSOR CASTLE

I T WAS SOMEHOW INEVITABLE that the event for which I wear my warm, practical clothes is one where the guests are wearing morning dress and hats. I should of course have known that the presentation of New Colours to the 1st Battalion Coldstream Guards at Windsor would be a formal affair. It is the wrong event for trousers and a thick jersey, but the Officer who greets us at the St George's Gate courteously ignores my discourtesy as he conducts us to an embarrassingly prominent position.

It is a spectacular setting for a beautiful occasion, the kind of ceremonial that the British Army does supremely well. In Quadrangle of the Upper Ward and against the backdrop of the Round Tower – built originally of wood by William the Conqueror in the 1070s and rebuilt in stone by Henry II a hundred years later – the officers and men perform the traditional ceremony of marching the Old Colours off Parade. The Queen, who is Colonel-in-Chief of the Regiment – as she is of thirty-six other regiments – is received on Parade and inspects the Regiment in their brilliant scarlet Dress Uniforms and black Bearskins, the officers carrying swords. The New Colours are consecrated, and then presented by the Queen. As she takes the salute, the music of the Band of the Coldstream Guards echoes round the medieval walls.

St George's School, for which the Queen attends a reception at the Castle, was established as part of the Order of the Garter in 1348, with the task of educating choristers for the Castle chapels including St George's Chapel, the spiritual home of the Order.

Bella, Ollie and Sam in their St George's School uniform. Although established as a choir school, St George's now takes other children between the ages of three and thirteen.

OXFORD
UNIVERSITY COLLEGE

OXFORD IS THE OLDEST English-speaking university in the world, and University College, endowed in 1249, was the first college to be founded – although two other colleges, Merton, and Balliol contest this claim. As Visitor, the Queen is consulted on matters relating to the statutes and higher appointments in the college. Oxford's links with the monarchy, which go back to its earliest days, were strengthened in the seventeenth century when the Royalists set up their headquarters here during the Civil War. There is a story that during his stay Charles I asked if he might borrow a book from the Bodleian, the University Library, but he, like every member of the university before and since, was told that no book could be taken away.

Although it is late May the day is wet, cold and blustery as the clerics and academics wait outside St Mary's for the Queen to arrive for the service of celebration for University College. When she steps out of her car, the Queen is greeted first by the Lord Lieutenant.

The Queen and the Duke of Edinburgh are greeted by the Chancellor of Oxford University, Lord Jenkins of Hillhead, and the Master of University College, Lord Butler of Brockwell.

FRIDAY 21ST MAY. *10.00 a.m. Left Windsor Castle by car.*
10.55 a.m. The Queen, Visitor, and The Duke of Edinburgh, Honorary Fellow, attended a Service of Thanksgiving for the 750th Anniversary of University College, Oxford, at the University Church of St Mary the Virgin.
11.40 a.m. Her Majesty and His Royal Highness visited the Bodleian Library to view an exhibition celebrating 'University College – the First 750 years'.
11.55 a.m. Her Majesty and His Royal Highness arrived at University College, where they attended a Reception of Fellows, members and staff of the College, and representatives of the University and the City. They then visited the Junior Common Room before being entertained to Lunch in College Hall.

2.35 p.m. The Queen visited the Union
Street Education Complex, Oxford,
where Her Majesty watched South Asian
Song and Dance, talked to youngsters in
discussion groups, watched the Asian
Youth Project Football Team practising
with Oxford United professionals, and
met representatives of Adult Education
and English for Speakers of Other
Languages. The Queen and The Duke of
Edinburgh then attended a Reception
with members of community groups.
3.30 p.m. The Queen and the Duke of
Edinburgh left Oxford by car.
4.25 p.m. Arrival at Windsor Castle.

of Oxfordshire, Hugo Brunner. He will be her overall host throughout the day. Since the reign of Henry VIII each county has had its own Lord Lieutenant. Their original responsibility was to control the King's military forces in their county, but in 1871 this was transferred to the Crown. Since then they have acted as the Monarch's personal representative locally. They play an important part in the organisation of any royal visit, for they know the district and can advise the Palace on the most suitable venues for the day.

After the Service in St Mary's, the Queen walks across Radcliffe Square to the Bodleian. A small crowd has gathered outside All Souls to greet her and give her flowers. Inside the Library she is shown a letter from Charles I written in 1643 asking University College for financial support for his army. It's not known for certain if the request was granted.

The Queen then goes by car to the College, where members line the paths as she makes her way to a marquee for a reception, before going into Hall for a lunch of smoked salmon mousse with fresh asparagus, chicken supreme, and lemon Cotswold with mango coulis. We ask some of the undergraduates what they think about the visit. Some have no interest in it at all, others have blossomed into uncharacteristic grey suits, and one tells us that he is reserving judgment until the Queen returns his bicycle which she has stolen.

UNION STREET EDUCATION COMPLEX

I N THE AFTERNOON THE QUEEN visits the Union Street Education Complex where pupils from three to eighty take part in Lifelong Learning. Oxford is a busy commercial city with a multi-ethnic population, and she watches children perform a dance from Rajasthan, and a team of Asian boys practising football with Oxford United players. She then talks to a group of adults who are learning English as a foreign language. Each one has been asked to bring along some object about which they can talk to her, and she sits and listens intently, asking questions and laughing with them. The Duke, who has been visiting Oxford Brookes University, joins her to meet members of local community groups, and, as they leave, staff and children from the 'After School Club' line the route.

LONDON
CHELSEA

THE QUEEN IS PATRON OF THE ROYAL HORTICULTURAL SOCIETY, and each summer she and members of her family visit the Flower Show which is held in the grounds of the Royal Hospital, Chelsea. The Royal Hospital was founded in 1682 by Charles II as a home for old soldiers. The building was designed by Sir Christopher Wren, and is the home of four hundred army veterans known affectionately as Chelsea Pensioners. In their scarlet coats and tricorn hats they are a familiar sight in London.

The Royal Horticultural Society was founded in 1804, and although its early aims were scientific its purpose now is to help and encourage amateur gardeners to make the most of their gardens. It is the most important showpiece of the year for seedsmen and growers, not only for flowers but also for fruit and vegetables. Britain's top garden designers create show gardens, and there are factual displays. One explains the breeding capacity of pests; we discover that a single aphid can have 250 million tons of descendants at the end of one year.

The Chelsea Flower Show is now so popular that on the public days it is impossibly crowded, but today we can move easily and comfortably around. The Queen stays for about an hour and a half, looking at the gardens in the rain and going round the exhibits in the Great Marquee. After she has left and before guests begin to arrive for the evening Gala Preview, we delight in wandering through an almost empty marquee with its brilliant displays. We are unaware of problems which explode in the following day's newspapers.

One of the exhibits that the Queen is shown is a new lily called 'The Crusader' which will be part of the floral decoration at the wedding of Prince Edward and Sophie Rhys-Jones in June.

To bring minibuses with minor members of the Royal Family and their friends to Chelsea through the evening rush hour, the police used outriders to hold back the traffic. Most drivers would accept this special treatment for the Queen, if only for security reasons, but they very much resent the congestion it has caused already harried motorists. The Queen, who insists on a mimimum disruption of traffic as she moves around, is reported to be very angry.

MONDAY 24TH MAY. *Returned to London. 5.30 p.m. The Queen, Patron, and The Duke of Edinburgh visited the Royal Horticultural Society's annual Chelsea Flower Show in the gardens of the Royal Hospital, Chelsea, London SW3.*

TUESDAY. *11.10 a.m. The Queen and the Duke of Edinburgh attended the Service of Commemoration and Thanksgiving for the work of the Colonial and Overseas Civil Services, the Centenary of the Corona Club and the Golden Jubilee of Corona Worldwide, at Westminster Abbey.*
6.30 p.m. Prime Minister's audience. 10.40 p.m. The Queen, The Duke of Edinburgh and The Prince of Wales left Euston Station on the Royal Train to travel to Wales.

WESTMINSTER ABBEY

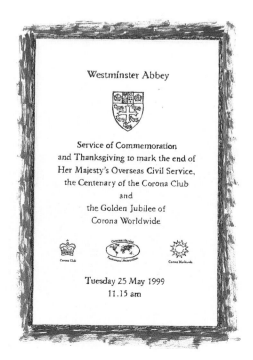

WITH THE HANDING BACK of Hong Kong to the Chinese in 1997, the work of the British Colonial Service came to an end. The service in the Abbey is a final act of thanksgiving which acknowledges the failures of Empire, but celebrates its many achievements and the dedication of those who worked in the Colonial Service. In her message, the Queen speaks of the friendships which were developed during those years, and which act as a powerful force for good in today's Commonwealth.

We have been trying to sort out arrangements for the forthcoming trip to Wales for the opening of the new Welsh Assembly. We have just been told – too late – that these are to be made through the Welsh Office and not through the Palace. All the passes to all the events have already been handed out. Why weren't we told earlier?

CARDIFF

THE WELSH NATIONAL ASSEMBLY

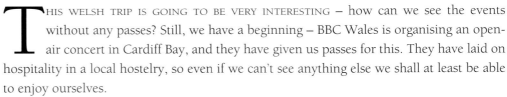

T HIS WELSH TRIP IS GOING TO BE VERY INTERESTING – how can we see the events without any passes? Still, we have a beginning – BBC Wales is organising an open-air concert in Cardiff Bay, and they have given us passes for this. They have laid on hospitality in a local hostelry, so even if we can't see anything else we shall at least be able to enjoy ourselves.

With the opening of the new Welsh Assembly it will be the first time that Wales has had a say in its own government for nearly six hundred years. The country was conquered by the English at the end of the thirteenth century, and Edward I installed his son as the first Prince of Wales. Just over a hundred years later the rebel warrior Owain Glyndwr rose up against England's oppressive rule, and the struggle for Welsh independence began. He established a Welsh Parliament and held out against the English for ten years. His rule was eventually brutally suppressed and anti-Welsh laws were passed. Henry VIII restored civil

WEDNESDAY 26TH **MAY.** *10.28 a.m. The Queen, The Duke of Edinburgh and The Prince of Wales arrived at Cardiff Central Station, and then drove to Llandaff Cathedral, Cardiff, where they attended a Multi-faith Service.*

12.35 p.m. Her Majesty and Their Royal Highnesses attended a Luncheon at the National Museum of Wales, at which Ambassadors, overseas representatives and representatives of companies located in Wales were present.

3.00 p.m. Her Majesty and Their Royal Highnesses attended the Opening Ceremony of the National Assembly at Crickhowell House, Cardiff.

4.00 p.m. The Queen, The Duke of Edinburgh and The Prince of Wales, Patron, attended The Prince's Trust Event at Cardiff Castle.

8.05 p.m. The Queen and The Duke of Edinburgh attended a Dinner given by the First Secretary and Secretary of State for Wales, the Rt Hon Alun Michael, MP, AM, before watching the finale and fireworks of the open-air 'Voices of the Nation' Concert, attended by The Prince of Wales, at Cardiff Bay open-air Stadium.

10.40 p.m. The Queen and The Duke of Edinburgh left Cardiff Station on the Royal Train to travel to Swansea.

rights to the Welsh in exchange for union with England, but the cause of Welsh nationalism has never gone away.

We begin the day outside Llandaff Cathedral where crowds, including small children in traditional Welsh dress, have gathered to welcome the Queen. Then we go on to the National Museum, but there's nothing we can do there except admire the red carpet and the statue of Lloyd George in the park opposite. The Royal Regiment of Wales is here with its mascot goat, Shenkin II; we saw him on Monday at the Chelsea Flower Show. Thinking of animals, today's paper reports that the two last Welsh pit ponies retired yesterday; there have been ponies in the Welsh coal mines since about 1750. These two have gone to live in Milton Keynes.

As there is no point in staying, we decide to go down to Cardiff Bay and the temporary home of the Assembly. Here our BBC passes work wonders, and we're given a conducted tour of the building. We clamber up ladders to the press point on scaffolding immediately opposite the Assembly. The Welsh Office representative arrives. 'I wish I had known earlier you were coming. Nobody told me,' he says, and as he is happy for us to stay, we are able to watch the royal procession arrive.

Sadly we have no passes for The Prince's Trust celebrations inside the Castle. What colourful drawings we could have got there – dancers, musicians, stilt-walkers... Still, the day is not yet over.

CARDIFF BAY

WE ENJOY MORE HOSPITALITY courtesy of BBC Wales, then make our way to the 'Voices of the Nation' Concert. This turns out to be spectacular, with a cast of Welsh talent from Robert Tear and Shirley Bassey to Max Boyce and Tom Jones. The rain holds off, the sun goes down and the crowd enjoys itself, revelling in music, sentiment and iconoclasm and in an especially Welsh way. The Prince of Wales is here throughout the concert, the Queen arrives later from her dinner with politicians, and the black sky is lit by thunderous explosions of fireworks.

SWANSEA

THURSDAY 27TH MAY. *10.15 a.m. The Queen
and The Duke of Edinburgh arrived at
Swansea High Street Station.
10.30 a.m. Her Majesty and His Royal
Highness visited Cefn Hengoed School,
Bonymaen. Her Majesty joined an
Information Technology lesson, sat in on
a Welsh Language class, visited the
Family Centre and met pupils, staff and
adult students.
11.30 a.m. The Queen and the Duke of
Edinburgh visited 3M United Kingdom
Plc. Her Majesty and His Royal Highness
met company personnel and were present
for the opening of a new production line.
12.15 p.m. The Queen and The Duke of
Edinburgh visited The Maritime and
Industrial Museum, Swansea. Her
Majesty and His Royal Highness toured
exhibits and met Museum personnel.
1.00 p.m. The Queen and The Duke of
Edinburgh were entertained to Luncheon
at the Guildhall by The Lord Mayor of
the City and County of Swansea and The
Lady Mayoress.
2.55 p.m. Her Majesty and His Royal
Highness visited Crofty, where Her
Majesty met members of the local tourist
industry and His Royal Highness toured
the Cockle Factory and met local cottage
industry workers.
3.35 p.m. Her Majesty and His Royal
Highness left Swansea Fairwood Airport.
5.30 p.m. Arrival at Aberdeen Dyce
Airport.
6.30 p.m. Arrival at Craigowan on the
Balmoral estate.*

WE SPEND THE NIGHT AT MUMBLES, and then set out to see what we can do today. The Queen has moved from Cardiff to Swansea overnight on the Royal Train, and this will be an ordinary away day – yesterday's celebrations are over. We can't go to the school, which has reinvented itself with huge improvements over the last two years, but there's less demand for passes to the 3M factory where the Queen is to open a new state-of-the-art computer-controlled production line, so we go there. Factories like this, which is part of a multinational American foundation, are playing an important role in rebuilding the Welsh economy after the decline of the traditional mining and iron industries. This particular factory is regarded as a European Centre of Excellence.

We arrive and wait, and our friend from the Welsh Office turns up. Unfortunately he hasn't brought a pass for himself – after all, as he explains to the security guard on the gate, he made all the arrangements for the visit and doesn't need one. But he's obviously not to be trusted, and they won't let him in. A television crew arrives with cameras and Royal Rota

passes, but by now the security man is deeply suspicious and won't let them in either. As he says, 'How do I know they're not forged?' It's beginning to resolve into a rather enjoyable farce, but some urgent telephone calls are made and just before the Queen's car arrives we are at last allowed inside.

The Royal Standard, borrowed from Buckingham Palace for the day, is raised outside the 3M factory in Cardiff as the Queen arrives.

The Queen speaking to Mrs Mary Bennett, who has spent her life picking cockles on the Gower Peninsula.

CROFTY

THERE ARE NO PASSES LEFT for the Maritime and Industrial Museum, where large crowds have gathered as the Queen goes inside to tour the museum's woollen mill and to see plans for a new extension, nor for the walkabout in the Maritime Quarter – what a great shame to miss that one. Instead we make our way to the small village of Crofty where the Duke is to visit the cockle factory and the Queen will meet some of those who work in the local cockle and cottage industries. We are given a warm welcome by the people here, including ninety-seven year–old Mary Bennett, who is now wheelchair-bound but has been picking cockles since she was twelve. She is introduced to the Queen, who tells her, 'I'm so glad to have had the chance to meet you.' Cockle-picking on this part of the Gower peninsula has been going on since Roman times. It is now licensed so that the cockles can't be over-harvested, and they've installed a new EU-approved plant. Their business, they tell us, may be small but their tradition is great.

JUNE
THE QUEEN AND FINANCES

No area of the queen's life has caused more adverse comment than money. It is here, rather than in any constitutional element, that the greatest threat to public support for the monarchy lies. It is here also that there is the most ignorance.

The Queen is perceived by some as one of the world's richest women (conjectural estimates have put her wealth as high as £13 billion) who, despite her wealth, each year asks Parliament – you and me, the taxpayer – for yet more money. Many ordinary citizens, their lives dominated by unemployment and poor housing or by high levels of taxation and the burden of mortgages, see a Head of State who is living off the fat of our land. And it's not even as though she earns it, for what does she actually *do* apart from riding around in a big car and going to Ascot?

But such an estimate, even if it were accurate, ignores the fact that the largest part of the Queen's apparent wealth belongs not to the Monarch but to the monarchy, and through the monarchy to the country. Certainly she can enjoy the use of Windsor Castle and Buckingham Palace, the paintings, drawings, sculpture and furniture in the Royal Collection, and the Crown Jewels (although not everyone would want to wear the Imperial Crown, at least not for long) but they do not belong to her.

There is no doubt though that the Queen is a very rich woman. She personally owns Balmoral and Sandringham and, as the result of an arrangement made in 1399 by Henry IV, she, rather than the monarchy, receives the income from the Duchy of Lancaster. In the year to 31 March 1999 this brought in a pre-tax figure of £5.968 million. The larger part of this is used to meet the official expenses of those members of the Royal Family who fulfil public functions but do not receive anything from the Civil List. The value of the Queen's portfolio of shares is not known but it is substantial, partly because until she volunteered to pay tax its value increased exponentially.

Since 1993 the Queen has paid income tax, capital gains tax, and inheritance tax except on bequests made to her successor as Monarch. The long-outdated notion that it is unbecoming for a Monarch to pay tax had meant that until then she had paid no direct taxes. When this was brought to widespread public attention for the first time during a deepening recession – complicated by the issue of whether the taxpayer was to pay for rebuilding after the Windsor fire – it caused a deep and damaging resentment. She had, in fact, already offered to pay tax, but this had not happened. When she eventually did so it was perceived as grudgingly reactive. Perhaps if she had been putting an equivalent sum into a Queen's Trust for young no-hopers, the homeless and the unemployed, the public would not have responded as it did.

The Civil List, paid to the Queen by the government, dates back to the Restoration in 1660 but was set up in its present form in 1760 on the accession of George III. It was agreed then that all the costs of civil government, which had previously been paid by the Sovereign, would henceforth be met by Parliament. In exchange, the King would surrender to the Treasury, after due expenses, his hereditary income as Monarch. This income came principally from the Crown Estate, land spread around the country and under the sea and including property in prime London sites and almost all the United Kingdom seabed to a limit of twelve miles from the shore. In the year 1998–9 the Crown Estate was worth £3.3 billion, producing an income for the government of £125.8 million.

The Civil List payment for each year is £7.9 million, plus parliamentary annuities of £1.002 million paid to the Queen Mother and the Duke of Edinburgh. (As a point of comparison it is worth noting that the cost to the taxpayer of the Royal Shakespeare Company for the year 1998–9 was £9.18 million.) Contrary to popular belief, the Civil List is not a personal salary but is a payment made to the Queen, the Duke of Edinburgh and Queen Elizabeth the Queen Mother to cover the expenses that they incur in the course of their work. About seventy per cent of it goes in salaries for the members of the Royal Household. It also covers the cost of entertaining British and foreign visitors.

When the Queen came to the throne the amount payable from the Civil List was fixed for the length of her reign, but by the early 1970s the level of inflation meant that the original sum was no longer adequate. After a Report by a Select Committee and a lively debate in the House of Commons, in 1972 the Civil List Act was passed agreeing an increase which would be reassessed each year. In 1990 this arrangement was changed, allowing Parliament to set the amount for ten-year periods. At the end of each period it would be looked at again, and any surplus would be carried forward. If, during that period, inflation fell so low as to make that surplus substantial, as has happened recently, payments would be suspended until this had been absorbed.

Apart from the three principals no other member of the Royal Family now receives any money from Parliament, for since 1993 the annual parliamentary allowances totalling just over £1.5 million paid to them through the Civil List have been repaid by the Queen in full to the Treasury out of her income from the Duchy of Lancaster. This has helped to defuse the widespread criticism of royal hangers-on. The criticism still lingers, but apart from the cost of security it is no longer justified for financial reasons.

Royal security figures are not published by the Home Office but are estimated at about £30 million a year. The Chilcot report on royal security recommends substantial cuts in the annual protection bill, particularly for minor members of the family, and the Queen has asked the Home Secretary to examine ways of implementing this.

There have been substantial reforms in all financial areas in recent years, notably in the 1991 creation of the Grants-in-aid

which has meant the transfer of responsibility for the administration of funds away from government departments to the Palace. It now oversees its own expenses within the given budget, subject still to supervision by those departments. There are two parts to these Grants-in-aid. The first is the Property Maintenance Grant-in-aid, an annual sum for maintaining and servicing the Occupied Royal Palaces – those buildings used as offices and living accommodation by senior members of the Royal Family – apart from the Palace of Holyroodhouse, which is the responsibility of the Scottish Office. It does not pay for all the expenses, and increasingly ways are sought to make departments within the Palaces more cost-efficient or even independent. The department responsible for the Royal Collection draws its income entirely from Royal Collection Enterprises Limited, and over seventy per cent of the cost of rebuilding Windsor Castle after the fire was met by entry charges to Buckingham Palace and Windsor Castle. The money needed for rebuilding The Queen's Gallery will come from the same source. A 450-foot-deep borehole has been dug in the Palace garden to supply the water needed for air conditioning for the new Gallery, and water 'hippos' have been placed in cisterns to reduce the amount of water required for what is called by insiders 'the royal flush'.

Since 1997 a second Grant-in-aid relates to travel, and covers the travel costs of the nearly 3,000 official engagements carried out by the Royal Family each year. Since the decommissioning of HMY Britannia, which cost £12 million a year, it pays for the maintenance and function of the Royal Train, the helicopter and the chartering of commercial aircraft for official visits abroad. The cost of car travel for the Queen is covered by the Civil List.

All public spending on the monarchy is audited and the results published, and it has been described as the most accountable and most efficient use of public funds there is. In recent years it has fallen within, and sometimes substantially below, budget. For example, in 1991–2 the cost of maintaining the Occupied Royal Palaces was £23.9 million; in 1999–2000 this had gone down to £15 million. For the year to 31 March 2000, the Grant-in-aid for royal travel was £8.6 million, compared with £17.3 million in 1997–8, a reduction in real terms of 58 per cent since the Royal Household took responsibility.

The Prince of Wales has spoken of the importance of the Monarch retaining a degree of independence from the state; financial dependence would put the monarchy into the pocket of the government and take away its ability to act as a constitutional safeguard. Certainly if the cost of maintaining the monarchy is a central argument for its abolition, putting aside all other issues it is worth noting that presidents do not come free, and that automatic inheritance costs rather less than presidential election.

LONDON
BUCKINGHAM PALACE

CARDINAL BASIL HUME, OSB, ARCHBISHOP OF WESTMINSTER, was appointed to the Order of Merit on 27th May. It is an inspired award. This is one of the most highly esteemed of all honours and is in the Queen's personal gift. It is given to those who have made an outstanding independent contribution to national life, and its previous holders have included Florence Nightingale, Thomas Hardy, Edward Elgar and Henry Moore. At any time there are no more than twenty-four members; the Cardinal brought the current number up to twenty-one.

He is the first Catholic prelate to have received this honour, and with characteristic humility he shares it among his fellows. 'I would like to think that it is a recognition of the part played by Her Majesty's loyal Catholic subjects – laity, clergy and bishops – in the life of the nation,' he says. But why so late? He is ill with cancer, and within three weeks he will be dead. Ted Hughes, the late Poet Laureate and the last person before Hume to be awarded the OM, was also mortally ill and died less than two weeks after his investiture. It is sad that they have had so little time to enjoy it.

TUESDAY 1ST JUNE. *p.m. Return to London.*
6.30 p.m. Prime Minister's audience

WEDNESDAY. *10.15 a.m. Cardinal Basil Hume, Cardinal Archbishop of Westminster, was received by The Queen when Her Majesty invested him with the Insignia of a Member of the Order of Merit.*
10.30 a.m. The Queen visited the Royal Kitchens.
11.30 a.m. The Queen and The Duke of Edinburgh held a Reception for the World Cricket Cup teams and management.
2.30 p.m. Portrait sitting with Mr John Wonnacott.
5.00 p.m. Meeting of the Privy Council.
6.30 p.m. The Queen and The Duke of Edinburgh gave a Reception for recently retired Senior Ambassadors.

The Queen and the Duke of Edinburgh greet the cricketers in the White Drawing Room (left). With his invitation, each player has been sent a card printed with his name. This is handed to the Master of the Household who then announces him.

THE QUEEN VISITS THE ROYAL KITCHENS before they close for redevelopment. As well as complete refurbishment and modernisation, the ceiling is to be lowered, a new floor put in, and the space above incorporated into The Queen's Gallery. While this work is going on, State Visits will take place at Windsor.

The Royal Chef heads a staff of sous-chefs, senior cooks, cooks, apprentices and porters – twenty-six in all. He prepares the Queen's private menus which are recorded in the Royal Menu Book which she sees each morning and from which she chooses the day's menus, and also those for all the official functions and for staff meals. The kitchen staff move with the Queen to other royal residences, and a chef travels with her when she goes abroad on State Visits to oversee the preparation of food for any receptions that the Queen may give, including return hospitality for her host, and receptions for local and visiting parliamentarians, award scheme winners, or the British and local press for whom the Queen always gives a reception on the first evening of any overseas State Visit.

FOR SOME BRITISH PEOPLE cricket is a philosophy. For most Americans it is a mystery. It's not a mystery to us, but it did seem an awful waste that we should be at the reception held by the Queen and the Duke of Edinburgh for the World Cup cricketers when we know so little about it and can recognise so few of the players. I'm not sure that the Queen knows many of them either, although Prince Philip obviously does. Cricket began in this country and is one of our incomparable cultural exports. All twelve teams in the competition were part of the UK or were once British colonies.

THURSDAY 3ʳᵈ JUNE. *12 noon. His Excellency Senhor Rubens Antonio Barbosa was received in farewell audience by The Queen and took leave upon His Excellency relinquishing his appointment as Ambassador from the Federative Republic of Brazil to the Court of St James's.*

12.10 p.m. Professor Andrew Motion was received by The Queen upon his appointment as Poet Laureate in Ordinary to Her Majesty.

12.20 p.m. Mr Les Murray was received by The Queen when Her Majesty presented him with the Queen's Gold Medal for Poetry. The Poet Laureate was present.

12.30 p.m. Air Chief Marshal Sir Peter Squire was received by The Queen upon his appointment as Air Officer Commanding-in-Chief Strike Command.

12.40 p.m. The Queen, Colonel-in-Chief, received Lieutenant-Colonel Colin Martin upon relinquishing his appointment as Commanding Officer 1ˢᵗ Battalion The Royal Welch Fusiliers, and Lieutenant-Colonel Roderick Porter upon assuming the appointment.

LONDON

BUCKINGHAM PALACE

ANDREW MOTION has replaced Ted Hughes as Poet Laureate. This post, which is given for life, goes back unofficially to 1616 when James I gave Ben Jonson a pension of £72 a year and a 'butt of sack' – 126 gallons of wine – to oil the wheels of creativity. The first official Poet Laureate was John Dryden, with a salary of £200 a year, and the wine. In exchange he had to write poems marking national events.

Some later Laureates have rued the decision of Henry Pye, who in 1790 asked for money instead of wine. It was then valued at £27, and when John Betjeman suggested that he might return to the earlier tradition he duly received the wine – just £27 worth.

REGENT'S PARK

THERE ARE QUIPS about one endangered species meeting another as the Queen arrives at London Zoo to open the new Millennium Conservation Centre. Outside the new building there is a large bronze sculpture of a dung beetle, once revered as the Ancient Egyptian scarab and now respected as one of nature's most efficient recyclers.

The exhibition 'Web of Life' features biodiversity in a new building inspired by termites. Tall ventilators echo the chimneys of termite nests sunk deep into cool boreholes in hot

Education is one of the main purposes of any well-run modern zoo. Nearly a third of the visitors to London Zoo are children. There are seventeen members of the Children's Committee, coming from all over the country.

3.00 p.m. The Queen, Patron, and The Duke of Edinburgh, Honorary Fellow of the Zoological Society of London, visited London Zoo, Regent's Park, where Her Majesty opened the new Millennium Conservation Centre and toured the 'Web of Life' exhibition. The Queen and The Duke of Edinburgh met children engaged in craft activities and subsequently met Zoological Society of London Council and Board Members, staff and volunteers at a Reception on the Main Lawn.

10.50 p.m. The Queen and The Duke of Edinburgh left King's Cross Station on the Royal Train to travel to Hull.

habitats. Nearby, there are new underground lavatories built into the anteater paddock. Somehow they don't sound entirely inviting.

The role of zoos has changed fundamentally in recent years, and the developments in London reflect the importance of conservation and education. The Queen is greeted by members of the Children's Committee carrying huge stick insects, and giant African land snails who regard her with horns aquiver. They may be a long way from home, but they can look forward to a more secure future than their cousin escargots which we will see for sale in Accra market later in the year.

The Duke of Edinburgh is President of the Worldwide Fund for Nature, but is he aware of facts which the Centre teaches, that one acre of English meadow may contain two million spiders with each web catching up to 500 insects a day, or that there are between 15 and 20 million plant and animal species in the world of which only 1.4 million have been described by scientists?

FRIDAY 4TH JUNE. *9.50 a.m. The Queen and The Duke of Edinburgh arrived at Paragon Station, Hull. The Lord Mayor surrendered to Her Majesty the Sword of the City, which The Queen returned to him. Her Majesty and His Royal Highness drove to King George Dock, where The Queen, with The Duke of Edinburgh, met groups associated with the fishing industry and the flood defence scheme and opened the new lock-gates. Her Majesty and His Royal Highness embarked in the launch Humber Ranger and proceeded upstream to view riverside regeneration projects before disembarking at Horse Wash.*

11.10 a.m. The Queen and The Duke of Edinburgh attended a Service at Holy Trinity Church, Hull, to celebrate the 700th anniversary of the City of Hull.

11.45 a.m. Her Majesty and His Royal Highness walked through the market square to the covered Victorian Market and met stall holders and other members of the public.

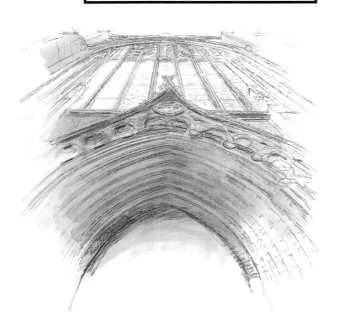

HULL

KING GEORGE DOCK AND CITY CENTRE

IT IS SEVEN HUNDRED YEARS since Edward I granted Kingston upon Hull a Royal Charter, and the Queen's visit, with its crowded schedule, is the highlight of Hull700, 'Celebrating the past – Pioneering the future'. It is a city which has had to face huge problems. As a major port it suffered heavy bombing during the Second World War, and more recently the decline of the fishing industry, and of the port in the 1970s, brought high unemployment and a sense of hopelessness to many parts of the city. Now it is moving forward once more, recapturing its pride and its prosperity. As the Royal Train draws into Paragon Station, a choir of a hundred schoolchildren and young people sing 'Hull in our Hands', a song specially written for the day.

Hull is one of the UK's principal trading ports, with easy access to Europe and the Baltic states and to worldwide shipping routes. The Queen and the Duke of Edinburgh drive first to the King George Dock where, in a cold, gusting wind, she opens new lock gates. Most of the city lies ten feet below the highest tide, and computer predictions of global warming, rising tides and strong winds anticipate major flooding along this coastline in 2045. The gates are part of an overall flood defence programme which will protect not only the half million or so people who live and work around the Humber estuary, but also some of the most important wildlife and conservation sites in the country.

We are very glad not to be on the Queen's launch as it sails out through the newly opened gates into uncomfortably choppy seas on its way down the estuary. It has started to rain hard, but by the time the Queen comes out of Holy Trinity Church after the service celebrating Hull's 700th anniversary it has stopped, and she watches members of the Hull Press Gang in period costume re-enact the infamous eighteenth-century naval recruiting methods. She talks to some of the crowd who have waited in the rain, and then walks to the nearby covered fruit and vegetable market.

HULL
GUILDHALL

KINGSTON UPON HULL was the birthplace of the anti-slavery campaigner William Wilberforce; he was baptised in Holy Trinity Church, and married the vicar's daughter. After a Civic Lunch in the Guildhall the Queen presents the annual Wilberforce Medal to Archbishop Desmond Tutu for his contribution to the battle for human rights in his fight against apartheid and poverty in South Africa. The medal bears the words of the anti-slavery movement: 'Am I not a man and a brother.'

FRIDAY 4TH JUNE. *12.30 p.m. The Queen and The Duke of Edinburgh attended a Luncheon at the Guildhall, Hull. Afterwards Her Majesty presented the Wilberforce Medal to the Most Reverend Archbishop Desmond Tutu.*

2.30 p.m. The Queen visited Noddlehill Youth Centre, Noddlehill Way, Hull, and met young people and representatives from local community and activities groups, and sports clubs.

3.10 p.m. Her Majesty visited The Garths housing estate, Hucknell Garth, Hull, and met the residents.

4.00 p.m. The Queen and the Duke of Edinburgh left Hull by helicopter.

5.00 p.m. Arrival at Windsor Castle.

BRANSHOLME ESTATE

The Queen is given a model made from nuts and bolts by two twelve-year-olds working with the Bransholme Urban Motor Project.

RANSHOLME ESTATE is one of the most needy housing estates in the country. It has been a place of low educational attainment and low aspiration, with unemployment more than fifty per cent above that in the rest of the city and high levels of truancy and crime. Part of the estate, The Garths, is composed of about two thousand 1960s system-built houses which had been allowed to deteriorate. In 1990 an organisation called CityVision set up a working party to look at how the estate could be revived and the way of life there improved, and in 1994 a seven-year, £41.5 million programme of regeneration was begun. This included improving the houses and the surrounding environment, and setting up support groups for people of all ages. From the beginning, local people have been involved in the changes as plans were set in motion for creating jobs through training and employment opportunity schemes, improving health, raising educational standards and reducing crime. A scheme has been launched to take young offenders off the streets. At Noddle Hill Youth Centre, BUMP – Bransholme Urban Motor Project – is tackling the problem of car crime by teaching youngsters engineering skills so that they can rebuild cars and motorbikes, with younger boys learning to make go-carts. The Queen watches as they race them at high speed round a newly constructed track.

The Queen's visit has been planned so that she can see as much as possible of what has been achieved and can meet people, young and old, representing different aspects of the work. The atmosphere here is terrific, and when I speak to the Regeneration Manager some weeks later he tells me that local morale is still high. The Queen's visit has given the people there a sense of self-worth, and a realisation that she is not only concerned about the problems of their lives, but is also endorsing and encouraging the work they are doing to improve their own community. Talking to those who have been at the heart of the achievement, the Queen says that she realises it has been a long haul but it is good to see what has been achieved. The disgust expressed to me later by a Hampstead acquaintance and well-known novelist who thinks the visit patronising and condescending is a point of view not shared by any of the Garth Estate residents to whom we have talked.

Members of Karen's Country Kickers give the Queen a demonstration of line dancing. Classes in line dancing are one of the activities offered at the Bransholme Women's Centre.

EPSOM

EPSOM DOWNS

SATURDAY 5TH JUNE. *Derby Day.*
12.50 p.m. Royal Procession down the
Epsom racecourse.

SUNDAY. *At Windsor.*

MONDAY. *Afternoon. Returned to London.*

THE DERBY, FIRST RUN IN 1780, is one of the most important classic races in the world and is the only one that a Queen's horse has not yet won, although Edward VII had three Derby winners. Traditionally Derby Day is a day out, with roundabouts and swings and gypsy fortune-tellers. At the height of its popularity about half a million people would be on the downs where, it is said, the people's funfair and the royal fanfair unite the crowds and the Crown.

The threatening rain holds off for the race itself, but then the heavens open. In the Royal Box the Queen is shielded from the downpour, but there is no protection for those on the downs, and the funfair takings fall dramatically as thousands head for home.

LONDON
BUCKINGHAM PALACE

TUESDAY 8TH JUNE. *11.45 a.m. Farewell audience.*

11.50 a.m. General Sir Roger Wheeler, Chief of the General Staff, was received by The Queen .

12.10 p.m. Sir William Gladstone, Bt, was received by The Queen when Her Majesty conferred upon him the honour of Knighthood and invested him with the Insignia of a Knight Companion of the Most Noble Order of the Garter.

12.15 p.m. The Duke of Abercorn was received by The Queen when Her Majesty conferred upon him the honour of Knighthood and invested him with the Insignia of a Knight Companion of the Most Noble Order of the Garter.

12.20 p.m. The Queen received the Bishop of Leicester, the Right Reverend Timothy Stevens, who did homage upon his appointment. The Rt Hon Jack Straw, Secretary of State for the Home Office, administered the Oath.

12.30 p.m. Mr Richard Ralph (Romania), Mr Ronald Nash (the Kingdom of Nepal) and Mr Charles Mochan (the Republic of Madagascar) were received in audience by The Queen and kissed hands upon their appointment as Her Majesty's Ambassadors. Mr Peter Harborne was received in audience by The Queen upon his appointment as British High Commissioner to the Republic of Trinidad and Tobago.

6.30 p.m. Prime Minister's audience.

AUDIENCES FORM A REGULAR PART of the Queen's working life. The Prime Minister's weekly audience is in the evening, as is the twice-yearly pre-Budget audience with the Chancellor of the Exchequer. Almost all other audiences take place towards the end of the morning. Each lasts ten or twenty minutes and is private; no official record is kept of what is said. They are held in either the White Drawing room or in the 1844 Room at the back of the Palace overlooking the garden. Although these adjoin the formal State Rooms, they are domestic in scale. Many of those who come are anxious and on edge, but they are not stuffy occasions, for the Queen makes a point of putting her visitors at ease. After the initial introductions and any formalities – handing over Letters of Credence, the presentation or return of insignia, being dubbed as a knight – other visitors such as an ambassador's retinue may be presented, or she may invite her guests to sit in the comfortable chairs by the fireplace.

During our year we are with the Queen at the beginning of several audiences. In early June she sees first the Chief of the General Staff, followed twenty minutes later by Sir William Gladstone, who is invested as a Knight of the Garter.

When a newly appointed Bishop comes to do homage, he kneels in front of the Queen, who places her hands around his, and the Oath of Allegiance is sworn on a Bible which is a duplicate of the one on which she swore her Coronation Oath, and which is brought from the Royal Library at Windsor.

The investiture sword and insignia outside the 1844 Room. The sword used by the Queen is George VI's Scots Guards sword, which she prefers because it is light.

The Queen presents Sir William Gladstone with his insignia as a member of the Order of the Garter. Sir William Gladstone's insignia is on loan to him during his lifetime. After his death it will be returned to the Queen by his family, and will then be given to whoever fills his place in the Order. As with members of the Order of Merit, the Order of the Thistle and the Royal Victorian Order, Knights of the Garter are chosen personally by the Queen without consultation with the Prime Minister.

PREPARATIONS FOR THE GARDEN PARTIES

DURING THE SUMMER altogether about 24,000 guests come to the three Garden Parties at Buckingham Palace. Work in the garden goes on all year round, not only in preparation for these public events but also in preserving wildlife habitats.

The forty acres have gradually evolved since they were first laid out nearly three hundred years ago as a mulberry orchard. In the early eighteenth century the Duke of Buckingham commissioned a formal garden, and this was replaced a century later when George IV oversaw its complete remodelling, including the creation of a three-acre lake.

Mark Lane is the Head Gardener, with nine full-time assistant gardeners. It takes a week to mow the lawns, the part most familiar to visitors. But Garden Party guests are free to explore, and many are drawn to the magnificent 175-foot herbaceous border. It is here that we watch Mr Lane and some of his assistant gardeners at work.

As important as the appearance of the gardens is its ecology. The Palace garden is said to be one of the finest wildlife areas in Britain. A recent three-year survey recorded 1,500 varieties of trees and shrubs, fifty-eight species of birds, and many rare moths and butterflies. Large stretches of long grass are mown only twice a year – in August and late October – and provide a habitat for insects and small mammals. There is minimum use of chemicals, and the lawnmowers are run with biodegradable oils. This care echoes the approach to the environment in all the Royal Estates.

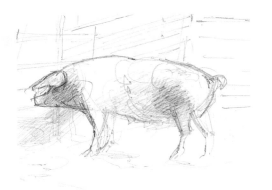

LONDON

DOCKLANDS

WEDNESDAY 9TH JUNE. *Noon. Private audience.*

12.05 p.m. The Rt Hon John Major, MP, was received by The Queen when Her Majesty invested him with the Insignia of a Member of the Order of Companions of Honour.

12.25 p.m. His Excellency Mr Arthur Foulkes was received in farewell audience by The Queen and took leave upon His Excellency relinquishing his appointment as High Commissioner for the Commonwealth of the Bahamas.

12.35 p.m. Mr Stephen Gomersall was received in audience by The Queen and kissed hands upon his appointment as Her Majesty's Ambassador to Japan.

12.45 p.m. His Excellency Khalil Haddaoui was received in farewell audience by Her Majesty and took leave upon His Excellency relinquishing his appointment as Ambassador from the Kingdom of Morocco to the Court of St James's.

2.45 p.m. The Queen visited Mudchute Community Park and Farm, Pier Street, London E14.

3.10 p.m. Her Majesty embarked in the Port of London Authority barge Royal Nore and travelled downstream, viewing Sea Scouts, Sea Cadets and young disabled people from Millwall Sailing Club on the water. The Queen's Bargemaster and Watermen were on duty. Her Majesty disembarked at Poplar Dock Marina where she met community groups.

4.10 p.m. The Queen visited Workhouse Leisure Centre, and met local athletes.

THE QUEEN'S VISIT to the Isle of Dogs began with an invitation by the Docklands Development Corporation for her to open the new Poplar Dock Marina, part of the revitalised Docklands. Once the busiest port in Europe, from the late 1960s London Docks declined and much of the area fell silent and derelict.

The Queen goes first to Mudchute Farm. It is a place with an extraordinary story. In the mid-nineteenth century, silt from the new Millwall Dock was washed down by the tide, building up an earth wall which created a reservoir. Using smelt and clinker from local iron ore works, a permanent high wall was built and the dredged slurry from Millwall was pumped into the reservoir – the mud shute – which gradually became a land site. Then in the early 1900s there was an outbreak of diphtheria. The 52-acre site was thought to be a health hazard and was closed. Left undisturbed, the silt settled and solidified. Grass and saplings grew and flowers self-seeded, including exotic imported seeds blown from nearby ships. Years passed, the Second World War came and with it the Blitz, in which the docks suffered severely. The land was used for allotments – 'Digging for Victory' – and for anti-aircraft gun emplacements.

After the war, though littered with concrete and debris, it became an open space where people walked their dogs and children played. Meanwhile, on the Isle of Dogs protests were afoot. There was no secondary school, and nothing was being done about it. For the locals that wasn't good enough, and in 1970 they sealed off the island, which can be reached only

by one bridge and one road, and demanded independent borough status with the right to control their own lives. They didn't get it, but the point was made and a school was opened.

Then, in 1974, the Greater London Council decided to built a huge housing estate on the Mudchute. The local people didn't want it, and again they took matters into their own hands. Once more they sealed off the island, this time to show that if developers tried to move in they could stop them. The developers withdrew, the GLC sold the land to Tower Hamlets Borough Council and they in turn passed it over to the local community. 'You want it, you run it,' they said, and local volunteers began to turn it into a microcosm of the countryside. The rubble was cleared, more than ten thousand trees and hedges were planted and someone suggested bringing in farm animals. There were doubters who thought that the children would be frightened of them, or chase them, or feed them with buns until they burst. So they introduced them gradually. First there were six Jacob's Sheep, then another six, and then cows and horses and pigs and goats and chickens and geese. The Mudchute is run as an active small farm, not as a zoo of farm animals. It receives no public funding, but money has been raised locally and it has somehow survived. It is the largest city farm in Europe, and on the day of the Queen's visit children pick bunches of wild ox-eye daisies and give them to her.

LONDON

HORSE GUARDS PARADE AND KNIGHTSBRIDGE BARRACKS

THE QUEEN HAS COME AS A SPECTATOR to the ceremony of Beating Retreat by the Massed Bands of Her Majesty's Royal Marines. The Duke of Edinburgh is Captain General Royal Marines, and the Queen watches from the window of Horse Guards Building as he takes the salute to mark his seventy-eighth birthday in a ceremony that is performed each year by the Army, Royal Navy or Royal Marines in rotation.

It goes back to the days when night brought an end to fighting in battle. As light faded, Beat Retreat was sounded as a signal to disengage, and to call outlying troops back to the safety of the encampment before night fell and picquets were set.

Originally the call of Retreat was sounded by drums alone, but over the years fifes were added, and then the bugle, and long after it had ceased to have any military purpose the marching ceremony was added to create spectacle. In the 1930s it was much enjoyed by Admiral Sir William Fisher, Commander-in-Chief Mediterranean Fleet, who used it to impress when his Fleet was in foreign ports.

We go early to watch the Household Cavalry preparations in Hyde Park Barracks in Knightsbridge for tomorrow's Trooping the Colour. While we are there the new guard is getting ready for today's Changing of the Guard.

Since the Restoration of the Monarchy in 1660, the privilege of guarding sovereigns and their palaces has belonged to the Household Troops. At the beginning of her reign Queen Victoria moved to Buckingham Palace, but the Court officially remained at St James's. The archway into Horse Guards on Whitehall is still the official entrance to both, and each morning at 10.30 the new guard leaves Hyde Park Barracks to ride to Horse Guards for the ceremony of the Changing of the Guard in Whitehall. Foot Guards, rather than these mounted guards, protect the two palaces themselves. At 10 o'clock we watch as they go through a detailed inspection. The best turned-out men and horses are rewarded with the shortest guard duty.

As well as the preparations, we see young soldiers training in Hyde Park. Before qualifying for ceremonial duty, they do ten weeks' basic training, followed by five weeks' unmounted training in London. They then go to Windsor for sixteen weeks' horsemanship, before returning to London for four weeks' Kit Ride – learning to ride in ceremonial uniform. With the high, stiff leather boots, getting on and off the horse is a skill in itself. Some then go straight into a two-year ceremonial secondment. Others on ceremonial duty have undergone additional military training and are fully trained operational soldiers in an armoured reconnaissance regiment which is part of the Army's rapid deployment force; a detachment of the Household Cavalry leaves for Kosovo the day after we are with them. Some choose to stay with the horses, specialising as saddlers, farriers or blacksmiths, as riding staff breaking and training the animals, or as vets.

THURSDAY 10TH JUNE. *10.45 a.m. The Lord Chamberlain had an audience of The Queen.*
6.30 p.m. The Queen and The Duke of Edinburgh attended Beat Retreat by the Massed Bands Royal Marines on Horse Guards Parade, Whitehall, to mark the Birthday of The Duke of Edinburgh, Captain General, who took the Salute.

FRIDAY. *11.40 a.m. The Rt Hon George Robertson, MP, Secretary of State for Defence, had an audience of the Queen.*
12 noon. His Excellency the Marqués de Tamarón was received in audience by Her Majesty and presented the Letters of Recall of his predecessor and his own Letters of Credence as Ambassador from Spain to the Court of St James's.
12.20 p.m. Mr Stephen Brady, Ambassador of the Commonwealth of Australia to the Kingdom of Sweden, was received by Her Majesty.
12.30 p.m. The Queen, Colonel-in-Chief, received Lieutenant Colonel David James upon relinquishing his appointment as Commanding Officer, 1st Battalion, The Queen's Lancashire Regiment, and Lieutenant Colonel Stephen Davies upon assuming the appointment. Her Majesty, Colonel-in-Chief, also received Lieutenant Colonel Michael Shearman upon relinquishing his appointment as Commanding Officer, 4th (Volunteer) Battalion, The Queen's Lancashire Regiment, upon the Battalion's amalgamation with the 4th Battalion, The King's Own Royal Border Regiment.
12.50 and 12.55 p.m. Private audiences.

LONDON

HORSE GUARDS PARADE

I N THE EARLY YEARS of the Queen's reign, one of the most familiar images of her was mounted on horseback wearing a scarlet tunic and tricorn hat as she took the Salute at the annual Trooping the Colour. This is one of the most spectacular events in the royal calendar and is still regularly televised.

It is the first time we have watched the ceremony, which has marked the Sovereign's Birthday since the reign of George III. George III was born in June, but some later Monarchs have had winter birthdays, and Edward VII, born in November, decided to celebrate an Official Birthday in the summer. The Queen's actual birthday is in April, but she has kept the tradition and observes her Official Birthday on a Saturday in June.

The originally purpose of trooping the colour, or flag, was to march it slowly past the ranks of soldiers so that they could be familiar with it and recognise it in battle. Over the centuries this has evolved into a precise and elaborate ceremony. Each year it is a different Colour, but always it belongs to a regiment of the Household Division traditionally in attendance on the Monarch. The Colour we see being trooped is the one that the Queen presented to the 1st Battalion Coldstream Guards at Windsor in May.

Accompanied by a Sovereign's Escort of the Household Cavalry, the Queen leaves Buckingham Palace shortly before 11 o'clock. Since the retirement in 1986 of her black mare Burmese, she no longer travels on horseback but instead rides in the Ivory Mounted Phaeton, a small open carriage drawn by two Greys. She is greeted at Horse Guards by a Royal Salute and is then driven slowly down the lines to inspect the Guards and Mounted Troops. She takes her place on the saluting base, and the Massed Bands and Drums first

slow march and then quick march across the parade ground before the Ensign receives the Colour. This is trooped down the lines of Guards. Then comes the March Past, with the Colour lowered in salute as it passes the Queen. The Guards re-form in their original positions, and it is the turn of the Mounted Troops to walk past and then trot past. Throughout, the Massed Bands are playing. As the ceremony ends, a final Royal Salute is given, and then the Queen drives at the head of her Guards back down the Mall to the Palace. Here she again takes the Salute, this time in the Centre Gateway.

There are huge crowds, and as the procession makes its colourful, musical way back to the Palace it is difficult to get through them to the position we have been given on the steps of the Victoria Memorial, but we are there in time to watch the royal party come out onto the balcony. A Royal Air Force fly past had been planned but, although the threatening rain has held off all morning, the low cloud has not shifted and this has had to be cancelled.

121

SATURDAY 12TH JUNE. *11.00 a.m. Her Majesty was present at The Queen's Birthday Parade on Horse Guards Parade at which The Queen's Colour of the 1st Battalion Coldstream Guards was trooped. The Queen was accompanied by The Duke of Edinburgh, Colonel, Grenadier Guards, The Duke of Kent, Colonel, Scots Guards, The Prince of Wales, Colonel, Welsh Guards, and The Princess Royal, Colonel, The Blues and Royals and 1st Dragoons. On the conclusion of the Parade, Her Majesty drove in a carriage back to Buckingham Palace at the head of The Queen's Guard, preceded by the King's Troop Royal Horse Artillery, the Massed Mounted Bands of the Household Cavalry, the Sovereign's Escort of the Household Cavalry, The Life Guards and the Massed Bands of the Guards Division. On arrival at Buckingham Palace, The Queen's Guard entered the Forecourt and formed up opposite the Old Guard, the remaining Guards marching past Her Majesty.*
12.52 p.m. Royal Salutes were fired by the King's Troop Royal Horse Artillery in Green Park, and from the Tower of London Saluting Battery by the Honourable Artillery Company.
1.00 p.m. The Royal Air Force fly past was cancelled due to bad weather.
Afternoon. To Windsor.

SUNDAY *3.30 p.m. The Queen attended the Final of the Alfred Dunhill Queen's Cup for Polo at Smith's Lawn, Windsor Great Park, and presented the awards.*

WINDSOR

THE ROYAL MEWS

O N THE MORNING of the Hungarian State Visit we go to the Royal Mews at Windsor to watch them prepare. They have done it all so many times that they know exactly what they must do, and there is a sense of purpose without panic. The last few weeks have been an unusually busy time for the Mews. The Opening of the Welsh Assembly in May was followed in June by the Trooping the Colour, the Garter ceremony, Ascot and the royal wedding. The Opening of the Scottish Parliament and the Thistle ceremony are still to come at the beginning of July.

Work began in the Mews at 3.30 this morning. The Greys were lightly exercised to work off their surplus energy and take away stiffness. They were then washed off to remove stable-stains, and dried and groomed. Breakfast was at seven. The harness – The Queen's Harness dating from 1899, Round Buckle and Ascot – was prepared the day before, apart from the brass which needed final polishing. A last burnish is being given to the carriages that will be used – the 1902 State Landau drawn by six Windsor Greys in which the Queen will ride with the President, the semi-State Landau drawn by four Greys carrying the Duke of Edinburgh and Mrs Göncz, an Ascot Landau drawn by four Greys to take Prince and Princess Michael of Kent, who will be meeting the President and his wife at Heathrow, and

When the preparation of horses and carriages is complete, the animals are backed into the carriage shafts, or put to, ready to leave for Windsor Home Park.

Guardsmen line the route for the State Drive from Windsor Home Park up the steep hill to the Castle.

THE MONTH OF JUNE sees one colourful spectacle after another for the Royal Family, and of these the Garter ceremony at Windsor is perhaps the most splendid of all.

The Most Noble Order of the Garter is the senior British Order of Chivalry. It was founded by Edward III in 1348, with the motto 'Honi soit qui mal y pense' ('Shame on him who thinks this evil'). As well as his son the Black Prince, Edward installed twenty-four knights, some as young as twenty, who were skilled in tournament and in the arts of battle. Each year these Knights came together for three days of celebration. They feasted in St George's Hall and gathered for worship, for this was a religious as well as a military fellowship. From the beginning its spiritual home was the Chapel at Windsor Castle, where each Knight had his own stall in which hung the banner bearing his coat of arms. After two centuries these gatherings became less frequent and by the early nineteenth century they had all but ceased, although appointments to the Order still continued. On the 600th anniversary of the Order in 1948 the Knights gathered once more, and the event as we see it today was re-created.

The first part of the ceremony takes place in the Throne Room of the Castle. Here, at a Chapter of the Order, the Queen formally invests new Knights with the Garter, the Riband, the Star, the Mantle and the Collar. Then comes lunch in the Waterloo Chamber. After this it is the task of the Heralds to gather and organise the various parts of the procession in St George's Hall. Meanwhile, dismounted squadrons of the Household Cavalry take up positions along the ceremonial route, followed, as we watch, by the Bands of The Irish Guards and of The Blues and Royals.

From our positions on the Guard Room roof and inside the Chapel we see with fascination the unfolding pageant as it makes its slow way down from the Castle to St George's Chapel in the beautiful setting of the Lower Ward. First comes the Governor of the Castle, then the Military Knights of Windsor, retired officers who attend matins in the Chapel each Sunday on behalf of the Knights of the Garter. The Officers of Arms come next, Pursuivants and Heralds wearing medieval tabards and black knee-breeches. They are followed by the Knights and Ladies of the Garter (for there are now women in the Order) in their dark blue velvet robes and black velvet bonnets with swirling ostrich feathers.

The Order is no longer composed of lusty twenty-year-olds but instead is made up of distinguished elder statesmen and public figures; the oldest, apart from Queen Elizabeth, who has been driven to the Chapel, is Lord Longford, aged 93. There are the old sparring partners Sir Edward Heath and Lady Thatcher, and their erstwhile political adversary Lord Callaghan. They are followed by the Officers of the Order, including Black Rod and Garter King of Arms. Then come the Queen and the Duke of Edinburgh, and behind them Field Officer in Brigade Waiting and Silver Stick. Finally there are the Officers of the Yeomen of the Guard, and sixteen Yeomen in their scarlet Tudor uniforms.

Inside the Chapel, as a fanfare of trumpets sounds, the Knights go to their separate stalls, except for those yet to be installed. The Duke of Abercorn, and Sir William Gladstone whom we saw invested in the Palace a few days ago, remain in the Quire until the Queen gives her permission for their Installation. They are then conducted to their stalls and the service begins, including the joyous 'Te Deum Laudamus', a thanksgiving to God for his creation and renewal of the world. Afterwards, the Queen and the Duke drive back to the Castle in an open carriage.

WINDSOR

WINDSOR CASTLE

MONDAY 14ᵀᴴ JUNE. *12.15 p.m. The Queen, accompanied by The Duke of Edinburgh, Queen Elizabeth The Queen Mother, The Prince of Wales, The Princess Royal, The Duke of Gloucester and The Duke of Kent held a Chapter of the Most Noble Order of the Garter in the Throne Room, Windsor Castle. Her Majesty invested the Duke of Abercorn and Sir William Gladstone, Bt, with the Insignia of Knights Companion of the Most Noble Order of the Garter.*
1.00 p.m. The Queen and the Duke of Edinburgh gave a Luncheon Party.
3.00 p.m. The Installation Service for the Most Noble Order of the Garter was held in St George's Chapel.

The Garter Procession makes its way down from the Upper Ward in Windsor Castle. The Castle has been in continuous use since the site was chosen by William the Conqueror. In the background is the twelfth-century Round Tower, and on the left are St George's Chapel and the Tudor buildings of the Lower Ward.

four further Ascot Landaus drawn by Bays for the senior members of the President's party, each with someone from the Royal Household.

The horses are dressed, some standing quietly but others tossing their heads and eyeing us histrionically, their white socks chalked and their hooves oiled to make them shine, then the coachmen and postilions put on their full State Livery. These liveries are handed down from one generation to the next, some of them going back to Queen Victoria's reign. Her Majesty's Bargemaster and eight Royal Watermen will also be in the Procession, recalling a time when the visitors arrived by boat and were brought up the Thames to Westminster in the Royal Barge. The carriages are hauled out into the yard and at 10.30 the horses are put to, or backed into the shafts. Within minutes they are on the road towards Home Park where the procession will begin.

The Queen's Bargemaster and Royal Watermen (right) hold two of the oldest appointments in the Royal Household, dating back to a time when the Sovereign regularly travelled by barge on the River Thames.

Horses are brought to Windsor from London for the busy round of royal events in June. Younger, friskier horses are paired with older, steadier ones.

WINDSOR
ASCOT

Ascot racecourse was built on part of the Windsor estate by Queen Anne in 1711, and the Royal Family went regularly to racing meetings. However, after Prince Albert's death in 1861 Queen Victoria gave up racing, and it was not until Edward VII came to the throne that the four-day meeting of Royal Ascot once more became fashionable. At the beginning of each afternoon, in a convention begun by George IV, the Queen and her guests drive down the course in open carriages.

For many people Ascot is a champagne day out and the racing is almost incidental. Others take it more seriously. On the afternoon we are there the Queen's horse, Blueprint, the favourite at 4–1, wins the final mile-and-a-half race, her first Ascot win since 1995. Beaming happily, she goes down to the Winners' Enclosure to congratulate the horse and jockey. The win brings in £35,520 towards the cost of running the Royal Studs.

On the Wednesday of Ascot week, after the racing the Queen invites a number of boys from nearby Eton – godchildren, sons of friends, and in recent years her grandsons William and Harry – to watch polo at Smith's Lawn, to tread in the divots and to have strawberries and cream with her.

WINDSOR CASTLE

Fleet street is not happy with Prince Edward's wish that his wedding to Sophie Rhys-Jones should be a low-key, family affair with little media coverage. They feel that, whether he likes it or not, this is a royal wedding and there is going to be enormous interest around the world. But television passes are handed out only to the BBC, and most camera crews have to use their ingenuity in finding locations.

In keeping with this low-key approach the wedding is in Windsor rather than in London, the first time for more than a century that the child of a sovereign has been married here, and the guests are predominantly friends of the couple, not State guests.

About six thousand members of the public have been invited into the Castle precincts to watch, but unlike most royal weddings there are no processions and there is no military ceremony. The only people in uniform are the police. The six hundred guests have left their cars in Windsor Home Park and are brought up to St George's Chapel in a fleet of minibuses. Prince Edward and his two brothers meanwhile walk down from the Castle. The bride arrives in a Rolls-Royce from the Royal Mews, but after the service she and the Prince drive through Windsor and then up to the Castle in an Ascot Landau drawn by four Windsor Greys, the same carriage that the Queen used earlier in the week for her drive down the racecourse at Ascot.

Prince Edward and his bride, now the Earl and Countess of Wessex, pose for photographs at the west door of St George's Chapel before being driven away in an open Ascot Landau.

WINDSOR
WINDSOR HOME PARK AND CASTLE

FOR TODAY'S STATE VISIT THE QUEEN will be welcoming President Göncz of Hungary with his wife. Now aged seventy-eight, President Göncz fought against Nazi oppression as a young man and against Communist oppression later on. He was involved in the Hungarian rising of 1956, and was expelled from university, tried, and sent to prison for life. Six years later he was released under an amnesty. While in jail he taught himself written English. Barred as a dissident from other employment, he began translating American and English books, and – like Václav Havel of Czechoslovakia – he became a playwright. He continues to speak out on human rights, the dignity of the individual and reconciliation. This is a welcome State Visit.

The President and his wife are driven by car from Heathrow to Windsor Home Park where the Queen and the Duke of Edinburgh are waiting to welcome them in a specially erected medieval-style Royal Pavilion. Against the backdrop of the Castle the President inspects a Guard of Honour, and The King's Troop fires a 21-gun salute. Then comes the State Drive in open carriages through the streets of Windsor. At the Castle there are further welcoming ceremonies in the Upper Ward before the Queen and the Duke and members of the Royal Household settle down with their guests and the Hungarian Suite to an informal lunch in the State Dining Room. After lunch the Queen and the President exchange presents.

It is customary, on the first afternoon, for visiting Heads of State to call on Queen Elizabeth the Queen Mother and to have tea with her. In London they go to Clarence House, but when she is in Windsor Queen Elizabeth lives at Royal Lodge in Windsor Park. Earlier in the afternoon the President went to Runnymede to see the site where Magna Carta was signed, while Mrs Göncz went to the Savill Garden, close to Royal Lodge, now in the full splendour of summer colour. After tea, they have time to catch their breath and relax for a couple of hours at the Castle before getting ready for the State Banquet.

Led by the Mounted Band of The Blues and Royals, the King's Troop Royal Horse Artillery prepare to march past the Queen and President Göncz of Hungary in the Quadrangle of Windsor Castle.

TUESDAY 22ND JUNE. *12 noon. The Queen and The Duke of Edinburgh welcomed The President of the Republic of Hungary and Mrs Göncz in Windsor Home Park at the start of their State Visit. They then drove in a Carriage Procession with a Sovereign's Escort of the Household Cavalry to Windsor Castle. Gun salutes were fired in the Home Park by The King's Troop Royal Horse Artillery and from the Tower of London by the Honourable Artillery Company. Guards of Honour were provided at Windsor Great Park by Nijmegen Company Grenadier Guards and at Windsor Castle by the 1st Battalion Welsh Guards, who later marched past. The King's Troop Royal Horse Artillery marched past and the Sovereign's Escort of the Household Cavalry ranked past.*

1.15 p.m. The Queen and the Duke of Edinburgh entertained The President and Mrs Göncz to Luncheon in the State Dining Room, Windsor Castle. After Luncheon, decorations and presents were exchanged in the White Drawing Room, when The Queen invested the President of the Republic of Hungary with the Insignia of an Honorary Knight Grand Cross of the Most Honourable Order of the Bath.

WINDSOR
WINDSOR CASTLE

TUESDAY 22ND JUNE. *8.30 p.m. The Queen and The Duke of Edinburgh gave a Banquet in honour of The President and Mrs Göncz in St George's Hall, Windsor Castle.*

I T TAKES MOST OF THE DAY to prepare the table for the State Banquet. The individual places are carefully measured, not just for perfection but to prevent arriving at the far end with several unlaid places still to go. Late in the afternoon the Queen comes down to inspect the table. We are there at 6 o'clock for our own viewing, arriving at the same time as the Pipers, who are just getting out of their minibus.

The 160 guests start arriving at the State entrance of the Castle at about ten to eight, and they assemble with an *aperitif* in the Waterloo Chamber. Meanwhile, in the Grand Reception Room official photographs are being taken. The guests then come through to be presented by the Lord Steward to Queen Elizabeth the Queen Mother, the Queen, the President, Mrs Göncz and the Duke of Edinburgh, then go on into St George's Hall to take their places. Among the guests are the President of the National Federation of Hungarians in England, the wine writer Hugh Johnson who has a particular interest in Hungarian wines, the Artistic Director of Shakespeare's Globe, Bernard Matthews of turkey fame, and Sir John Harvey-Jones.

The Royal Family and principal guests process in, and the Queen and the President take their places in the middle of the long table. An interpreter sits in a chair immediately behind and between them. The Duke and Mrs Göncz face them on the other side. The speeches, first by the Queen and then by the President, are at the beginning of the evening, which means that they can then relax and enjoy the dinner. The speeches, but not the dinner itself, are televised.

A four-course meal is being served. The first course is a vichyssoise, followed by suprême of turbot. Then comes chicken poêle jeanette with cauliflower, broad beans, roast potatoes, and salad. The pudding is a raspberry ice-cream soufflé. Plates are cleared as individual diners finish. Champagne for the toasts is poured out shortly before the guests come in. With the soup there is an amontillado sherry, with the fish a Chassagne-Montrachet 1990, with the chicken a Château Talbot 1982, and with the pudding the famous Hungarian dessert wine from Tokaji served in its rarest and most exquisite form of 6 Puttonyos. There is also vintage port. Coffee, *petits fours* and liqueurs are served in the Waterloo Chamber.

The Orchestra of The Scots Guards, up in the musicians' gallery, plays a programme of largely Scottish music. Later, music by Pipers of the Royal Scots Dragoon Guards echoes round the rafters of the Hall and brings the banquet to a close.

Fresh English summer flowers, gold plate and English cut glass decorate the single long table in St George's Hall (opposite).

PLYMOUTH

DEVONPORT

WEDNESDAY 23RD JUNE. *10.00 a.m. The Queen and The Duke of Edinburgh left Windsor Castle by helicopter to travel to Plymouth.*
11.10 a.m. Her Majesty and His Royal Highness arrived in Plymouth, where they visited HMS Drake on the occasion of the Centenary of the Field Gun Competition and watched a slow and fast run. They then visited the Drill Shed where they met staff and members of HMS Somerset and HMS Turbulent ship's company and toured an exhibition before being entertained to Lunch in the Wardroom Dining Room.
2.20 p.m. The Queen visited North Prospect Primary School where she toured classrooms and met parents before visiting the Toddler Centre.
3.15 p.m. The Queen visited Gleason Factory where she toured the factory and met apprentices and those involved in the Gleason Foundation.
4.00 p.m. Her Majesty and His Royal Highness departed by helicopter to travel to Windsor Castle.

BECAUSE OF DRIVING RAIN and low cloud there is some question about whether the Queen's helicopter will be able to land at HMS Naval Base Devonport at Plymouth. The band is playing 'Raindrops keep falling on my head', but they tell us they're not playing it specially – it was always part of their musical programme. The rain certainly keeps falling, but the clouds break up enough for the helicopter to come in. The Queen is coming to watch training for the Field Gun Run which grew out of events in the Boer War a hundred years ago. Then Naval Brigade Gunners, on their way to relieve Ladysmith which was being besieged by the Boers, manhandled heavy field guns across large areas of the South African veldt with almost impossible physical obstacles. These dramatic events were first re-enacted as a competitive spectacle in 1912, with teams from Portsmouth, Chatham and Devonport, and since then the Run has become one of the highlights of the annual Royal Tournament.

We are standing beside the cinder training ground only a few feet from the competing teams as they use ropes, pulleys and blocks to manhandle 2,088 pound cannon and limber over the obstacle course of walls, ramps, a 28-foot wide chasm and narrow passes, dismantling and reassembling them as they go – gun carriages, gun barrels, limbers, wheels. In 1948 they recorded the first 4-minute run, and this is now down to 2 minutes 40.6 seconds. The daily results of the competition at the Royal Tournament are signalled to Ships and Establishments all round the world.

After watching the Run, the Queen goes to the Drill Shed where she cuts a centenary cake, and she then plants a tree, the first time this year she has done so.

PLYMOUTH

BOTH THE QUEEN'S AFTERNOON VISITS acknowledge success in the local community. North Prospect Primary School has applied for Early Excellence Status, and has submitted a proposal within the Sure Start initiative supporting individuals and families within the community. She goes from there to Gleasons, an American manufacturing firm, where she tours the factory and hears about the work of the Gleason Foundation, which makes grants to a wide variety of voluntary and other organisations in the local community.

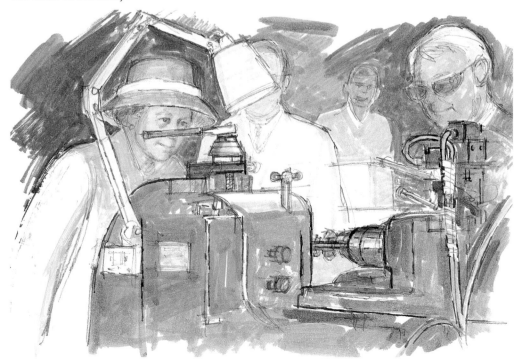

WINDSOR AND LONDON
MARLOW AND WINDSOR

FOLLOWING THE NORMAL PATTERN in State Visits, the President of Hungary and his wife host a return dinner on their last night. Since they are staying in Windsor rather than in London it is more convenient to entertain the Queen and the Duke of Edinburgh at a nearby hotel rather than in their Embassy, and the riverside Compleat Angler at Marlow is chosen.

The Queen is celebrating a centenary when she goes to visit the Sea Cadets in Windsor. On a glorious summer day she inspects the Thames barge *Wyvenhoe* moored by Windsor Bridge, then goes below decks to see an exhibition recording a hundred years of Sea Cadet history.

MOORFIELDS EYE HOSPITAL

IT IS ANOTHER VERY WET DAY on the morning of the Queen's visit to Moorfields Eye Hospital, and as we walk with our heads down from the Underground station we follow the large yellow arrows painted on the pavement to help those with impaired sight find their way to the hospital.

The Queen is Patron of the hospital and is here to mark the centenary of its move to City Road. Moorfields, originally called The London Dispensary for Curing Diseases of the Eye and Ear, was founded nearly two hundred years ago for soldiers returning from the Napoleonic wars in Egypt. Many of them came back with potentially blinding tropical conjunctivitis. It was run then as a charity, and patients were given an admission card that

read: 'This letter is granted to the applicant in being poor. Its acceptance therefore by anyone not really poor constitutes an abuse of charity.'

The hospital moved to its present site in 1899. In 1935 the Queen's father, then Duke of York, opened the new George V extension, but in 1944 it was almost completely destroyed by a direct hit from a doodlebug. It reopened in 1946.

In one of the operating theatres the Queen is told the history of cataract operations in some detail, and she then watches a televised consultation with patients from another hospital who key in to Moorfields.

In the afternoon the Queen has a final fitting for the outfit she will be wearing in three days' time at the opening of the new Scottish Parliament. It is being made by the Scottish designer Sandra Murray and is still a closely guarded secret. Meanwhile, in the yard at the side of the Palace the Queen's luggage, and luggage for the Royal Household, is being loaded into the lorry for its journey north to Scotland.

JULY

THE QUEEN AND THE
WELFARE MONARCHY

THE MONARCHY HAS COME A LONG WAY from the earlier idea of kingship for the King. Henry VIII showed scant sense of responsibility towards his subjects when, in the sixteenth century, he dissolved the monasteries, destroying the welfare network of the country and using the money to wage war. It was more than a hundred years before the political upheavals of the Commonwealth and the Restoration forced the monarchy, not altogether willingly, to adjust to the idea that the King was the servant of the people, in spite of the deference with which he was surrounded. Slowly the Monarch's role shifted towards a benefi-cent paternalism, a growing awareness and practical response to the needs of the people.

George III concerned himself with the welfare of his subjects in a way no previous Monarch had done, and in doing so he earned their affection and respect. Of course this philanthropic awareness was not entirely disinterested, for social ills brought threats of civil disorder; at a time when the monarchy was lampooned for its excesses, and crowned heads were tumbling just across the Channel, to be seen to be doing good was a sensible move. But expediency went hand in hand with genuine concern, and by the time Queen Victoria was on the throne the notion of the monarch's responsibility for the well-being of the people was established beyond question.

This was made easier by the shift in the monarch's power from authority to influence. As the opportunity for political leadership declined, so the possibility for moral leadership grew. Prince Albert worked conscientiously to extend this role by assuming patronage of organisations and charities, by encouraging improvement and initiative and, with the coming of the railways, by visiting more of the country so that he could see conditions for himself.

However, this concern coincided with worsening deprivation and social inequality. The incongruity of ladies-bountiful appearing from that very layer of society which bled working people dry still evokes a spectre of imperious do-goodism. In fact many of these people were honest and good, but it seemed that only the state could dispense welfare without condescension. Certainly none but the richest and most efficient voluntary organisations had the resources to maintain and dispense welfare on the scale that was obviously needed, and with the creation of the National Health Service in 1948 the state assumed this responsibility.

From the time of George III, members of the Royal Family had supported the development and welfare of voluntary hospitals. Now many of these, and other voluntary organisations with which they had been involved, were absorbed into the National Health Service. Once nationalised, they were run by the government. But the monarchy could not involve itself in government. Where did interest in welfare end and political involvement begin? Was there any role for the Royal Family within the welfare state, or would it have to give up its traditional function of endorsing and encouraging the many voluntary organisations that had been absorbed into the Health Service? In the late 1940s these issues had to be addressed.

After much discussion it was agreed that the Royal Family could continue its involvement, but as figureheads – patrons rather than presidents. And so they found themselves inside yet set apart from this new creation of the state, with no power of decision-making but in a new position of being able to endorse independence of spirit and action. For, essential though state intervention was, the personal involvement of individuals still offered something special to both giver and receiver. Good works were not just an opportunity for the ruling classes to feel virtuous. For one thing they did not have a monopoly of these good works; a desire to contribute voluntarily to the welfare of the less fortunate and to press for the good of local communities, particularly where these were threatened by a faceless and uncaring bureaucracy, was found in all social groups. The determination and independence it represented was something vitally important to society as a whole.

The voluntary system may not have had the resources to bring about the radical changes which were needed, but it was an expression of the British character which should not be dismissed. 'As a people we want to maintain our democracy not only in a parliamentary way, but in our social service,' wrote one commentator at the time.

To an extent not then foreseen, the Royal Family would come to represent a personal face in a public monolith. Nowhere is this more plainly seen than in the encouragement which the Queen – and other members of the Royal Family – can give to those struggling to cope with often overwhelming odds in their daily lives. On most away days her visits endorse the work of voluntary organisations, from local housing associations to care for the elderly and lonely immigrants, from comfort for the bereaved and those in pain to efforts to get young people off the streets, encouraging those who are struggling to overcome the forces which keep them down – and not only voluntary organisations, but hospitals, fire stations, ambulance depots. This contradicts the belief of three-quarters of the population, expressed in an opinion poll, that the Queen is out of touch. She speaks to more people from more walks of life about the difficulties and problems of their lives, than most people do. Of course, she cannot go everywhere and only a few can benefit directly from this involvement, but for those who can it is of incalculable value, and its ripples spread.

During our year we saw this pattern of endorsement over and over again. We saw it in Hull. We saw it in Glasgow. We saw it in London's Docklands. One of those responsible for the long battle to save Mudchute Farm, Ted Johns, who was born on the Isle of Dogs and has lived there all his life, told us: 'I think Mudchute has been and is a tremendous expression of how communities can take something like this and believe in it because it's theirs. These are people who own practically nothing, but here in the centre of the island is a huge piece of land which is *theirs*, somewhere where the kids can run free. When the Queen came

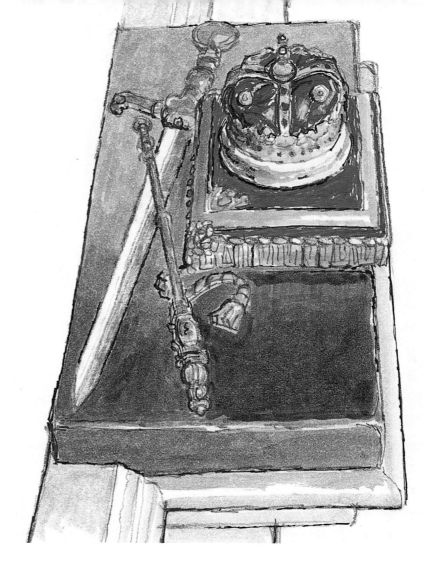

The Queen's pew in Canongate Kirk, Edinburgh, is decorated with painted wooden carvings of the Honours of Scotland – Scottish Crown, Sceptre and Sword of State.

she was acknowledging that it is ours. You've only got to look at the photos, at the look on the people's faces. They're not just meeting the Queen, but the Queen is coming to *them*, to their home. It makes them so proud. This is *our* Mudchute, and this is the Queen coming here, to us.'

As with so much of what we have seen this year, it was not what we had expected. We imagined her away days to be a round of opening factories and exchanging pleasantries with local mayors. Instead, although these happened, we found a persistent and enriching theme of encouragement and endorsement which gave people a sense of their own worth because of what they have themselves achieved or overcome. Of course, the monarchy has no monopoly in this, but we have observed that it can do it particularly well.

EDINBURGH
HOLYROODHOUSE

REMEMBERING WHAT HAPPENED IN WALES we have taken no chances with the Scottish trip and are in touch with the Scottish organisers in good time. Our support and guide is Sandy Sutherland from the Scottish Office. Throughout our stay in Scotland his quiet and unassuming professionalism allows us maximum access with minimum fuss.

At the Palace of Holyroodhouse we wait in the forecourt for the Queen, who has flown up from London. First to alight from the car is a bevy of corgis, who trot purposefully into the Palace. Behind them the Queen's Private Secretary hurries in carrying one of the red boxes.

Holyroodhouse is one of the oldest of the Royal Palaces. It was here that Mary Queen of Scots married Lord Darnley, witnessed the murder of her secretary Rizzio and later married the Earl of Bothwell. After James VI moved south to London it was rarely used until Queen Victoria established the custom of an annual visit by the Sovereign.

The Ceremony of the Keys takes place in the forecourt of Holyroodhouse each time the Queen visits Edinburgh. The Keys of the City, carried on a red velvet cushion, are presented

The Queen and the Duke of Edinburgh are greeted outside St Giles' Cathedral by Sir David Steel, the Presiding Officer of the Parliament, and Donald Dewar, First Minister.

to her by the Lord Provost. The Queen thanks him and returns them, saying that she is perfectly convinced that they cannot be in better hands than those of the Lord Provost and Councillors of her good City of Edinburgh.

We go from Holyroodhouse up the Royal Mile to St Giles' Cathedral for the Kirking of the Parliament, where the congregation of politicians asks for God's blessing on their work. On the principle that taxi drivers are a source of endless wisdom, we use whatever chance we have to find out what they think about the new Parliament. Without exception they are proud of Scotland and of being Scots, but they see this as just another layer of bureaucracy. It's jobs for the boys, they say, with well-paid holidays, and seats and salaries for some in two parliaments here and at Westminster. And then there's the scandal of the cost to the taxpayer of the new Parliament building which is going up opposite Holyroodhouse, and which is escalating out of control. Still, taxi drivers always were pessimists, and as it grows dark there is an atmosphere of celebration about the city. We go up onto Calton Hill to see the bonfires being lit. From here we have a wonderful view across the city to Edinburgh Castle, and, as we watch, the beacons light up the night sky.

Leaders of all religious denominations in Scotland are invited to the Kirking (right). There is no chaplain to the Scottish Parliament; each week a minister from a different faith says opening prayers.

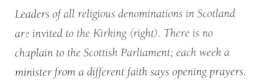

EDINBURGH

ASSEMBLY HALL

WEDNESDAY 30TH JUNE. *2.15 p.m. The Queen and The Duke of Edinburgh left Buckingham Palace by car.*
2.45 p.m. Arrival at RAF Northolt.
4.40 p.m. Arrival at Edinburgh Airport.
5.00 p.m. Arrival at the Palace of Holyroodhouse.
5.30 p.m. The Rt Hon The Lord Provost of Edinburgh surrendered to The Queen the Keys of the City, which Her Majesty returned to him. A Guard of Honour found by the 1st Battalion The Black Watch (Royal Highland Regiment) was mounted in the Forecourt.
6.30 p.m. The Queen and The Duke of Edinburgh attended a Service in St Giles' Cathedral for the Kirking of the Parliament.

THURSDAY. *11.15 a.m. The Queen and The Duke of Edinburgh drove in a Carriage Procession to the Assembly Hall, Edinburgh, to open the First Session of the Scottish Parliament. A Guard of Honour was found at the Palace of Holyroodhouse by The Queen's Body Guard for Scotland.*
12.15 p.m. Her Majesty and His Royal Highness viewed a parade of young people, and witnessed a fly past of Red Arrows and Concorde.
6.00 p.m. The Queen and The Duke of Edinburgh met members of the Scottish Executive in the Palace of Holyroodhouse.
6.10 p.m. The Queen and the Duke of Edinburgh gave a Reception for members of the Scottish Parliament.

EDINBURGH CASTLE has perched high on a rocky hill overlooking the city since the ninth century. It has served as fortress and Royal Palace, as treasury, barracks and military prison. It was besieged by Cromwell, but he failed then to plunder The Honours of Scotland – the Scottish Crown, Sceptre and Sword of State. Part of this regalia is the centrepiece of the first ceremony on the day of the opening of the new Scottish Parliament, when the Scottish Crown is delivered into the hands of the Duke of Hamilton. He will take it to the Assembly Hall – as in Wales, the new building is not yet ready – where the Scottish Parliament voted itself out of existence in the Act of Union of 1707, and where today's new Parliament will be declared.

Arguments about the form of today's events have raged in Scotland over the last months. Some feel that pageantry would emphasise the historic nature of the events, but others believe that this is a day for the people. No robes, no flummery, no pomp or ceremony. The Queen herself has expressed no views, believing that it is a matter for the Scottish people to decide.

In the end there are compromises. The Scottish Crown, symbol of sovereignty, goes back to at least the thirteenth century, and was used three hundred years later for the coronation

EDINBURGH
HOLYROODHOUSE

T HE PALACE OF HOLYROODHOUSE was founded by King David I of Scotland as the Augustinian Abbey of the Holy Rood. While hunting below Arthur's Seat, the great rise of hill beside the Palace, a fierce stag bore down upon him, but he was saved when the sign of the cross appeared between its antlers. He built the Abbey in thanksgiving, naming it after the relic of the True Cross which had been given to his mother, the devout Margaret, wife of King Malcolm III.

It is a beautiful setting for today's Garden Party, to which about 8,000 people will be coming. At the start of the afternoon we are in the garden as the Queen stops to talk to some of her guests. A guide dog nuzzles against her as she listens to its blind owner, and we see the same empathy she has with dogs that we saw at Sandringham in January.

Later, we go up onto the roof of the Palace, and look down over the lawns and beyond to Salisbury Crags and Arthur's Seat. These are part of Queen's Park, 640 acres of ancient landscape with fields, moorland and glens, marshes, lochs and hills. It contains archaeological sites and a wealth of animal and plant life, and, in keeping with so many of the ecologically conserved Royal Estates, is a site of Special Scientific Interest.

The Scottish Crown, a symbolic link with the past, is carried out of Edinburgh Castle by the Duke of Hamilton (above) on its way to the new Scottish Parliament.

The Queen arriving at the Assembly Hall (opposite page) for the opening of the Scottish Parliament with Donald Dewar, the First Minister (on the left) and Sir David Steel, the Presiding Officer.

of the infant Mary Queen of Scots. In the Great Hall of the Castle we watch as the Duke accepts it into his safe keeping, and it is then slowly driven, preceded by the Pipes and Drums of the Argyll and Sutherland Highlanders, in a Royal Mews Phantom Rolls-Royce which has been specially adapted so that the Crown on its dark blue cushion can be seen by those lining the streets.

The Scottish State Coach is not used, but there is a carriage procession, with the Queen, the Duke of Edinburgh, and Prince Charles as Duke of Rothesay, in a semi-State Landau on the door of which the Scottish Coat of Arms has been painted. It is led by a small escort of troopers from the Household Cavalry. As it drives from Holyroodhouse up the Royal Mile, an Irish Nationalist protestor runs out into the road and is dragged back by the police. It stops close to the Assembly Hall, and the royal party walks the last few hundred yards. The Queen is wearing an ankle-length woollen dress covered with silver metallic lace, and a mauve silk coat with a bolt of Isle of Skye tartan plaid, an interpretation of the Scottish national emblem, the thistle.

The ceremony inside the Assembly Hall is low-key. The Scottish Crown is carried before the Queen as she processes in. In her speech she wishes the new Parliament success, and presents a mace made of Scottish silver with an inlaid band of gold panned from Scottish rivers. It is the symbol of the new Parliament's lawful authority. The Burns song 'A Man's a Man for a' that' is sung. It is an anthem of republicans worldwide, hailing working men above posturing lords and princes.

Outside, the Queen walks down to a viewing dais to watch the procession of children. They are carrying brilliantly coloured Tibetan banners, Buddhist prayer flags each with a symbol of Scottish life – a computer screen for technology, a bird for wildlife. Overhead, Concorde and the Red Arrows sweep by.

EDINBURGH

DYNAMIC EARTH AND HOLYROODHOUSE

THE AREA ROUND THE PALACE OF HOLYROODHOUSE is being redeveloped. When Edinburgh New Town was built at the end of the eighteenth century all the rich people moved there, and the Canongate district of aristocratic, fashionable Old Edinburgh – what is now the Royal Mile – descended into slums. Gasworks and breweries nestled against the Palace, and so that Queen Victoria would not have to come through this unsalubrious district the Palace entrance was moved. Now the gasworks and breweries have gone, and in their place are rising the new Scottish Parliament and Dynamic Earth, a modern white butterfly of a building housing a fascinating interactive display which traces the development of the planet.

It is pouring with rain when the Queen arrives for the official opening. There is some windswept cover for the press who are gathered outside, but they are in no mood to be messed around and they don't take kindly to the senior official from Dynamic Earth who comes out and tells someone to 'get these people away from here'. We have been talking to a German television cameraman who had been planning to do a piece about it for German television. 'In Germany they want you to talk about their projects, and they really help you,' he tells us as he packs up his camera to go. As he says, he doesn't need the story, but it's sad, after all the work their Press Office must have put in over recent weeks, that when the press do turn up they are treated so discourteously. We've seen it so often this year, and it's not something we realised when we began. Yet these same people enjoy it if their picture is in the newspaper, or if they appear on television with the Queen.

FRIDAY 2ND JULY. *11.00 a.m. The Queen opened the Dynamic Earth Galleries, Edinburgh, and toured the galleries.*

12.30 p.m. Mr Thomas Drysdale, former Deputy Keeper of the Signet, had an audience of The Queen.

12.40 p.m. Lord Hogg of Cumbernauld, Lord High Commissioner to the General Assembly of the Church of Scotland, was received by The Queen and reported on the recent proceedings of the General Assembly.

12.55 p.m. Lieutenant Colonel Malcolm Ross was received by The Queen when Her Majesty conferred upon him the honour of Knighthood and invested him with the Insignia of a Knight Commander of the Royal Victorian Order.

6.30 p.m. First Minister's audience.

SUNDAY. *11.15 a.m. The Queen attended Divine Service at Canongate Kirk.*

MONDAY. *11.00 a.m. The Queen held an Investiture at Holyroodhouse.*
7.45 p.m. The Queen, Colonel-in-Chief, was entertained to Dinner by the Officers of The Argyll and Sutherland Highlanders (Princess Louise's) at the Assembly Rooms, Edinburgh.

Canongate Kirk is the Kirk of Holyroodhouse. Wherever she is, the Queen always attends Divine Service on Sunday.

Investitures in Holyroodhouse take place in the Great Gallery, hung with portraits of the Scottish kings. Although they follow exactly the same pattern, they are altogether more intimate affairs than those at Buckingham Palace. Instead of the Yeomen of the Guard there are members of the Royal Company of Archers.

The selection of light music is played by the Orchestra of The Scots Guards. Military musicians are trained at the Royal Military School of Music at Kneller Hall. In times of war, and during military operations, they act as medical orderlies and stretcher bearers; the musicians of the Scots Guards served in the Gulf War. The Drummers, and the Pipers of the Scots and Irish Guards, are trained infantrymen.

In an adjacent room each recipient has the insignia, which the Queen has just given to them, unhooked and placed in a presentation box. They then go back into the Great Gallery, where the empty seats are gradually filled as they return.

EDINBURGH
CITY CENTRE

THIS IS THE CENTENARY OF CHEST, HEART AND STROKE SCOTLAND, and as the first stop on her morning out and about in Edinburgh the Queen, as Patron, visits their centre at Meadowbank. Here she talks to some of the patients, and watches others relearning lost skills.

The building now known as The Hub – the new administrative centre of Edinburgh's International Festival which the Queen is to open – once housed the Assembly Hall and offices of the Church of Scotland. Situated at the top of the Royal Mile, it lay empty for many years and became increasingly derelict. It is an 1840s Pugin building which presented a

The Queen watches stroke patients as they relearn their skills through occupational therapy (above).

TUESDAY 6TH JULY. *10.30 a.m. The Queen,
Patron, visited Meadowbank Centre,
Edinburgh, to commemorate the
Centenary of Chest, Heart and Stroke
Scotland.*

*11.20 a.m. The Queen, accompanied by
the Duke of Edinburgh, opened the new
Edinburgh Festival Offices at the Hub.
They then toured the building and met
those involved with the Festival.*

*12.50 p.m. The Queen was entertained to
Lunch by Scottish Financial Enterprise at
Scottish Widows Headquarters,
Edinburgh.*

*Afternoon. Mr Anthony Cox, winner of
the annual shooting event of the Queen's
Body Guard for Scotland, Royal
Company of Archers, was presented to
Her Majesty and received The Queen's
Prize.*

*4.00 p.m. The Queen and The Duke
of Edinburgh gave an Afternoon Party
in the Garden of the Palace of
Holyroodhouse.*

challenge to the renovators. They decided to take up his architectural themes but to add powerful creations from contemporary artists – a glowing glass track, decorated windows, light sculpture, terrazzo panelling and a brilliant cacophony of colour in the Main Hall. Most exciting of all are the two hundred terracotta-red plaster figures grouped against the walls of the main stairway representing past Festival performances of theatre, dance, music and opera. The Queen seems fascinated to hear from the sculptor, Jill Watson, how she went about making the models.

It is the first time that the Festival, which draws artists and artistic daring from all over the world, has been able to offer round-the-year facilities in one buzzing location. It is, as they tell us, a glorious celebration of the creativity and fun of Edinburgh's festivals.

155

GLASGOW

GLASGOW IS AN HOUR'S DRIVE FROM EDINBURGH, and the Queen arrives by car to begin her away day. In 1997 the city was elected Cultural Capital of Europe, and two years later it is the UK City of Architecture and Design. It has a strong artistic heritage, centred partly round the Glasgow School of Art, and the Queen begins her day by visiting the first public building commission from one of the city's most famous sons – Charles Rennie Mackintosh. He designed it in the early 1890s as the headquarters of the *Glasgow Herald,* but the newspaper moved out in 1984 and, like Edinburgh's Hub, the building has lain empty for many years. The Queen is here to open it as The Lighthouse: Scotland's Centre for Architecture, Design and the City. It is in a part of Glasgow city centre which has become run down and abandoned, and its re-creation is a step towards the regeneration of the whole district.

From the city centre, the Queen and the Duke of Edinburgh go to the Castlemilk Estate. Her first call here is to the bungalow of a young widow who has had a series of strokes. They sit together at Mrs McCarron's table and drink tea – and next day the newspapers have a

WEDNESDAY 7ᵀᴴ JULY. *11.00 a.m. The Queen and The Duke of Edinburgh opened the New Scottish Centre for Architecture at the Lighthouse Project, Mitchell Street, Glasgow.*
11.55 p.m. Her Majesty and His Royal Highness visited Craighale Housing Association, Castlemilk Estate, and met residents. They then visited Castlemilk Sports Centre.
12.35 p.m. The Queen and The Duke of Edinburgh visited Hampden Park National Sports Stadium and attended a Lunch for sportsmen and women and sports administrators.

156

At the Castlemilk Sports Centre (below) the Queen sees stroke patients using walking machines to rebuild coordination and strengthen their muscles.

field day, a miserable example of selective picture editing. Sitting in her upright chair, a cup of tea in front of her, the Queen is portrayed as stuffy, toffee-nosed and unyielding, an image that rings no bells with those who know her. Only one paper carries a picture of a smiling, outgoing Queen leaning forward to talk to her hostess. With headlines like 'Let Them Drink Tea', the rest of the newspapers create the image and the story they want.

At the Sports Centre, a few hundred yards down the road, she talks to stroke victims who are exercising on machines, and to young Down's Syndrome people, who interrupt their game of football to crowd round her, giving her an excited greeting.

Her final morning stop is again football – this time to see the redesigned National Sports Stadium at Hampden Park, the home of international football in Scotland for nearly a century. Here she watches as a hundred boys and girls between the ages of ten and fourteen take part in a football festival.

GLASGOW

WEDNESDAY 7TH JULY. *2.35 p.m. The Queen visited the Buchanan Bus Station, Killermont Street, Glasgow.*
2.55 p.m. Her Majesty visited Buchanan Galleries Shopping Centre.
3.30 p.m. The Queen and The Duke of Edinburgh visited the Royal College of Physicians and Surgeons of Glasgow.
8.00 p.m. The Queen and the Duke of Edinburgh gave a Dinner Party at the Palace of Holyroodhouse.

AFTER LUNCH AT HAMPDEN PARK, the Queen goes back into Glasgow to see more of the regeneration of the city centre. Her first stop is Buchanan Bus Station, and as this is a busy place she has asked that there should be as little fuss as possible so that it can carry on with its business as usual. Only the presence of extra police and a handful of press photographers and reporters gives any indication that something out of the ordinary is happening. When she arrives the people look disbelieving, uncertain if they are really seeing what they think they are seeing. One woman, busy buying her ticket, turns round to find the Queen standing just behind her.

Ann Gloag, the daughter of a bus conductor, is Britain's wealthiest businesswoman – she is more than twice as rich as the Queen. She grew up in a council house in Perth and left school with no qualifications. In 1980 she and her brother together bought two second-hand buses with £25,000 from their father's redundancy money and a loan from an uncle.

With the deregulation of bus services a year later they moved into a new gear, taking over state franchises and creating the huge transport network Stagecoach. Mrs Gloag is standing beside one of her Stagecoach buses when the Queen comes out to meet her.

From the bus station the Queen is driven round to the new Buchanan Galleries, a shopping centre built on land that had lain derelict for twenty years. This huge development with its eighty shops has brought a new vitality to what has been until now a sadly depressed area of inner-city Glasgow.

The Queen's last stop of the day is at the Royal College of Physicians and Surgeons of Glasgow. Here she is shown new surgical techniques, before going into a reception to meet Fellows of the College.

Computers play an important part in modern medicine. Some of the latest advances are explained to the Queen at the Royal College of Physicians and Surgeons.

EDINBURGH
ST GILES' CATHEDRAL

THURSDAY 8TH JULY. *11.30 a.m. The Queen and The Duke of Edinburgh attended a Service in St Giles' Cathedral for the Installation of the Lord Mackay of Clashfern as a Knight of the Most Ancient and Most Noble Order of the Thistle. A Guard of Honour was mounted in Parliament Square West by The Queen's Body Guard for Scotland, Royal Company of Archers.*

1 p.m. The Queen and The Duke of Edinburgh gave a Luncheon at the Palace of Holyroodhouse for the Knights of the Most Ancient and Most Noble Order of the Thistle.

3.30 p.m. The Queen left Edinburgh Airport for London.

5.15 p.m. Arrival at Buckingham Palace.

FRIDAY. *11.00 a.m. The Queen attended the Wedding of HRH Princess Alexia with Don Carlos Morales Quintana. Afternoon. To Windsor.*

THE MOST ANCIENT AND MOST NOBLE ORDER OF THE THISTLE is Scotland's highest honour, the Scottish equivalent of the Order of the Garter. Its origins are uncertain. Legend traces it back to the reign of King Achaius in 809, but it was probably founded in the fifteenth century. Originally it consisted of the Sovereign and twelve Knights Brethren, 'in allusion to the Blessed Saviour and his Twelve Apostles', and it was given in reward to Scottish peers who supported the King's religious and political aims. Since 1827 there have been sixteen members of the Order, and it now includes women.

This year there is one new Knight to be installed. Members of the Royal Company of Archers, the Sovereign's Body Guard in Scotland, stand guard in the forecourt of the Cathedral in their dark green uniforms. The design of these is thought to owe much to the romantic vision of Sir Walter Scott, who was himself a member of the Company. Earlier they marched down from Castle Esplanade with colours flying. As well as fulfilling ceremonial duties, they encourage archery, and members compete for the Queen's Prize, which she presents during her stay in Scotland.

We wait outside during the service and talk to some of the men whom we met earlier in the year at the Windsor Mews. This is the last of a busy round of summer engagements – they will now have a pause until the second State Visit of the year in October, and then the State Opening of Parliament in November. Twelve horses – six Bays and four Greys and a

The Queen, accompanied by her page and by members of the Royal Company of Archers, processes into St Giles' Cathedral for the Service of Installation.

spare of each – were brought up to Scotland in two horseboxes; in processions an older horse is teamed with a younger one to give it confidence. The horses travelled with a groom in each box. They had hay-nets, but there were stops for water and to check that the horses were not getting too hot. A Royal Mews horsebox carried the harness and a 40-foot hired transporter took the carriages. Because of the stops, the journey took about ten hours.

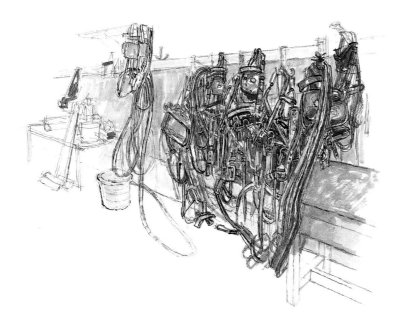

Members of the Royal Company of Archers, the Sovereign's Body Guard in Scotland, seen beyond the 1850 semi-State Scottish Landau as they wait outside St Giles' Cathedral.

MONDAY 12TH JULY. *12.15 p.m. The Queen visited the Royal Military Academy Sandhurst.*

6.30 p.m. The Queen and The Duke of Edinburgh held a Reception for MPs.

TUESDAY. *11.50 a.m. Mr Graham Allen, MP, Vice-Chamberlain of the Household, was received in audience by The Queen, and presented an Address from the House of Commons to which Her Majesty was graciously pleased to make reply.*

12 noon. HE Dr Kyaw Win was received in audience by The Queen and presented the Letters of Recall of his predecessor and his own Letters of Credence as Ambassador from the Union of Myanmar (Burma) to the Court of St James's.

12.20 p.m. HE Signor Paolo Galli was received in farewell audience by Her Majesty and took leave upon His Excellency relinquishing his appointment as Ambassador from the Italian Republic to the Court of St James's.

12.30 p.m. Mr Richard Lewington (Republic of Kazakhstan), Mr Stephen Nash (Republic of Latvia), Mr Douglas Scrafton (Democratic Republic of Congo) and Mr William Sinton (Democratic and Popular Republic of Algeria) were received in audience by The Queen and kissed hands upon their appointment as Her Majesty's Ambassadors.

4.00 p.m. The Queen and the Duke of Edinburgh gave a Party in the Garden of Buckingham Palace.

WEDNESDAY. *11.00 a.m. The Queen held an Investiture.*

SANDHURST
ROYAL MILITARY ACADEMY

THE QUEEN IS ENTERTAINED TO LUNCH at Sandhurst by members of Intake 3, who are celebrating their Sovereign's Parade fifty years ago. As Princess Elizabeth, she was Sovereign's Representative on that day. She is the first female member of the Royal Family to have served as a full-time active member of the armed forces. In February 1945 she was commissioned into the Auxiliary Territorial Service (ATS).

LONDON
BUCKINGHAM PALACE

THIS IS THE FIRST RECEPTION that the Queen has given for Members of Parliament. About three hundred guests from all parties have been invited. As a result of the last General Election a large number of new MPs arrived in the House. Although the Queen sees a number of these as she travels round the country, there are many whom she has not yet met. This, and a second party planned for next year, will give her a chance to do so.

Looking out of the window during the reception, we can see last-minute preparations for tomorrow's Garden Party, one of two to be held this week.

12.30 p.m. Capt Michael Fulford-Dobson
RN was received by The Queen upon his
retirement as a Gentleman Usher when
Her Majesty invested him with the Insignia
of a Commander of the RVO.
2.30 p.m. Portrait sitting.
6.30 p.m. Prime Minister's audience.

THURSDAY. 12 noon. HE Mr Gholamreza
Ansari was received in audience by The
Queen and presented the Letters of Recall of
his predecessor and his own Letters of
Credence as Ambassador from the Islamic
Republic of Iran to the Court of St James's.
12.20 p.m. Gen John de Chasterlain was
received by The Queen when Her Majesty
invested him with the Insignia of a Member of
the Order of Companions of Honour. Senator
George Mitchell was received by The Queen
when Her Majesty invested him with the
Insignia of an Honorary Knight Grand Cross of
the Most Excellent Order of the British Empire.
Mr Harri Holkeri was received by The Queen
when Her Majesty invested him with the
Insignia of an Honorary Knight Commander of
the Most Excellent Order of the British Empire.
12.40 p.m. Mr Justice Elias was received by
the Queen upon his appointment as a Justice
of the High Court when Her Majesty
conferred upon him the honour of
Knighthood and invested him with the
Insignia of a Knight Bachelor.
12.50 p.m. Mr Justice Aikens was received
by the Queen upon his appointment as a
Justice of the High Court when Her Majesty
conferred upon him the honour of
Knighthood and invested him with the
Insignia of a Knight Bachelor.
4.00 p.m. The Queen and The Duke of
Edinburgh gave an Afternoon Party in the
Garden of Buckingham Palace.

The Queen and the Duke of Edinburgh
greeting Virginia and Peter Bottomley, one of
the few husband-and-wife teams in the House
of Commons.

LONDON
BUCKINGHAM PALACE

FRIDAY 16TH JULY. 11.40 a.m. General Sir Charles Guthrie, Chief of the Defence Staff, was received by the Queen.
12 noon. HE Mr Pálsson was received in audience by Her Majesty and Presented the Letters of Recall of his predecessor and his own Letters of Credence as Ambassador from The Republic of Iceland to the Court of St James's.
12.20 p.m. Her Majesty, Colonel-in-Chief, Royal Tank Regiment, received Major General Robert McAfee upon relinquishing his appointment as Colonel Commandant and Major General Andrew Ridgway upon assuming the appointment.
12.40 p.m. HE Dr Ryszard Stemplowski was received in farewell audience by The Queen and took leave upon His Excellency relinquishing his appointment as Ambassador from the Republic of Poland to the Court of St James's.
12.50 p.m. HE Dr Pearlette Louisy, Governor-General of St Lucia, was received in audience by The Queen when Her Majesty invested her with the Insignia of a Dame Grand Cross of the Most Distinguished Order of St Michael and St George.
Afternoon. To Windsor.

MONDAY. Swan Upping begins. Returned to London.

TUESDAY. 11.00 a.m. The Queen held an Investiture.
8.15 p.m. The Queen and The Duke of Edinburgh were entertained to Dinner by Sultan Qaboos bin Said Al Said, Sultan of Oman, at Grove House, London NW1.

THE FIRST BUCKINGHAM PALACE GARDEN PARTY was held in the 1860s, and there are now three a year. The Queen's wish is that as many people as possible from different walks of life should be asked, and about 10,000 people are invited to each with about 8,000 attending. It is not possible to apply for tickets, which are issued either directly, or on recommendation, or through organisations – like the Diplomatic Corps, the armed services or certain charities – that have a regular quota. For those who go alone and know nobody, they can be strangely isolating occasions.

The gates are opened shortly after 3 o'clock. Having crossed the Palace forecourt and inner Quadrangle, guests arrive at the Grand Entrance. From here they go into the Grand Hall and up the red-carpeted stairway to the Bow Room, which leads out onto the terrace and down into the garden.

The Queen and other members of the Royal Family, preceded by a contingent of Yeomen of the Guard, come out onto the terrace at 4 o'clock. The National Anthem is played, and they then move down onto the lawn, making their way slowly along avenues which are opened up through the mass of people. Yeomen are positioned along the route to keep the avenues open. Guests are taken at random out of the crowd to be presented. Eventually the Queen reaches the royal tea tent, where ambassadors, high commissioners and government ministers are waiting. During the afternoon about 27,000 cups of tea, 20,000 sandwiches and 20,000 cakes are served. Those with experience of Garden Parties may decide to take

WEDNESDAY. *12 noon. HE Senhor Silva do Amaral was received in audience by The Queen and presented the Letters of Recall of his predecessor and his own Letters of Credence as Ambassador from the Federative Republic of Brazil to the Court of St James's.*
12.20 p.m. Mrs Justice Hallett was received by The Queen upon her appointment as a Justice of the High Court when Her Majesty invested her with the Insignia of a Dame Commander of the Most Excellent Order of the British Empire.
12.30 p.m. HE Mr Fouad Ayoub was received in farewell audience by The Queen and took leave upon His Excellency relinquishing his appointment as Ambassador from the Hashemite Kingdom of Jordan to the Court of St James's.
12.40 p.m. Meeting of the Privy Council.
4.00 p.m. The Queen and The Duke of Edinburgh gave an Afternoon Party in the Garden of Buckingham Palace.
6.30 p.m. Prime Minister's audience.

a plate of food and a cup of tea down to the lake, where they can sit and watch the ducks – the flamingos that used to live on the lake were killed by a fox in 1990 – and listen to one of the two military bands of the Household Division who take it in turns to play a selection of light music. Others explore the gardens, which are stocked with often rare plants and flowers. On wet days umbrellas are essential, for there is nowhere in the Palace that can accommodate such a large number of people.

At 6 o'clock the Royal Family come back to the terrace, the National Anthem is again played, and the party is over.

WINDSOR

SWAN UPPING

S WAN UPPING is an annual census of swans on the River Thames which dates back to the twelfth century. In the early days this census established how many swans could be slaughtered for the royal table, but now it monitors the birds' numbers and health. The Queen shares ownership of the Thames swans with two of the City Livery Companies, the Worshipful Companies of Vintners and of Dyers.

The Queen's Swan Marker sets off down the river with a flotilla of small boats, flagged and pennanted with the royal crown and cypher. Indignant cygnets are weighed and ringed, and examined for signs of injury. It was Swan Upping that first drew attention to the decline in the swan population in the mid-1980s caused by lead fishing weights. This has now been halted, but the birds still face hazards from anglers and pleasure boats.

LIVERPOOL
CITY CENTRE

WEDNESDAY 21ST JULY. *10.30 p.m. The Queen and the Duke of Edinburgh left Euston Station on the Royal Train to travel to Lancashire.*
THURSDAY. *10.05 a.m. The Queen and The Duke of Edinburgh arrived at Lime Street Station, Liverpool.*
10.15 a.m. Her Majesty and His Royal Highness drove to St. Andrew's Gardens where they toured the Estate, visited Bronte Youth and Community Centre and met representatives from local community organisations.
11.15 a.m. Her Majesty and His Royal Highness visited the Central Library, William Brown Street.
11.50 a.m. The Queen and The Duke of Edinburgh attended a Reception at Liverpool Town Hall and were entertained to Lunch.

LIVERPOOL IS A CITY WITH A VIBRANT IDENTITY and a strong culture. It is also a city that has had huge social problems. The Queen's first venue is St Andrew's Gardens, a tenement block which was built in the 1930s on the site of an old abattoir and which was soon nicknamed 'The Bullring'. When it was opened it offered modern facilities, with running water, baths and electricity, and a strong community spirit grew up. It survived the city's heavy bombing during the war, and in the 1960s new houses were added to the estate. But gradually the City Council could no longer afford to maintain it, and by the mid '80s fewer than a quarter of the homes were occupied, crime rates had soared and life there had become difficult.

For those who remained, the community spirit was undimmed, and they decided to take matters into their own hands. They wanted to re-create the area without breaking up their community. They formed the St Andrew's Residents' Association and began discussions with the City Council and their local MP. They were involved at every stage as plans for its regeneration were drawn up. The Bullring – now a Grade II listed building – was refurbished, new houses built, the community centre modernised, and it is once more a good place to live. During her visit the Queen meets some of the residents who have been involved with the project from the start. She looks at their homes, and joins them for a celebration of their achievement in the refurbished and garlanded Community Centre where a choir of small children sing for her.

Liverpool Central Library is one of a group of fine neoclassical public buildings put up by local worthies during the reign of Queen Victoria. This is National Year of Reading, and the Queen and the Duke have come to the Library to hear about local literacy projects. The Mersey Television soap opera *Brookside* has been carrying literacy storylines throughout the year, with a helpline guiding callers to their local Brookie Basics Centre, where they can drop in for encouragement and advice. By the time of the Queen's visit they have received more than 10,000 calls. She is introduced to some of the actors, and then hears how other local groups are helping adults and children to read.

The Queen visits Liverpool Central Library
(left). Nearby is a statue of Queen Victoria
(above), in whose reign the library was built.

167

LIVERPOOL

SPEKE AND GARSTON

I N THE AFTERNOON the Queen and the Duke of Edinburgh travel out to Speke and Garston on Merseyside, seven miles south of Liverpool. As they do so often, they go to separate venues, the Duke visiting a pharmaceutical factory where 140 new jobs have been created, and the Queen going first to the new Fire Station which she is to open. Here she watches training demonstrations, and sees schoolchildren being taught fire safety. She then meets people from the Speke Harmony Project, set up to build bridges of understanding between the young and old in the community.

From there she goes to Garston Urban Village Hall where the Duke of Edinburgh joins her. Unusually, this project has had a recent royal visit, for in 1998 the Duke saw the work in progress and was so impressed that he arranged to return when it was finished and ready to be opened. It is the focal point for the far-reaching regeneration of the whole neighbourhood, a multimillion-pound development bringing together public, private, voluntary and community sector bodies working in partnership.

As in The Bullring, local residents have been pivotal in the development of the complex, with its day nursery and family centre, its recreational and sports facilities, and its GP surgery and pharmacy. They formed their own company and bid for funds for the project, and now it is they who will run it, building a programme of activities round what the community wants. The people to whom we speak see the Queen's visit as a recognition of the role that they, as local people, have played in the regeneration of their own community.

THE EMPIRE THEATRE

THE FINAL VISIT of the day is to celebrate a different kind of regeneration. The Gala Charity Performance of *The Phantom of the Opera* at the Empire Theatre, in aid of children's and cancer charities, marks the reopening of the theatre at the end of the first stage of a £10.5 million refurbishment. When the curtain comes down after the performance the Queen goes up onto the stage to meet members of the cast.

THURSDAY 22ND JULY. *2.15 p.m. Her Majesty visited Speke and Garston Community Fire Station, where she toured the Station, talked to children using computers to learn about fire safety, and met Fire Station personnel.*
2.50 p.m. The Queen, accompanied by The Duke of Edinburgh, toured and opened Garston Urban Village Hall, and met representatives of local community groups.
6.45 p.m. Her Majesty and His Royal Highness attended a performance of The Phantom of the Opera *at the Empire Theatre. After the performance the Queen officially reopened the Empire Theatre.*
10.40 p.m. The Queen and the Duke of Edinburgh left Lime Street Station on the Royal Train to travel to Morecambe.

LANCASHIRE

MORECAMBE

The Queen talks to Sir Robin Day after unveiling the sculpture to Eric Morecambe on Morecambe sea-front.

CELEBRATION IS THE THEME again next morning when the Queen begins her away day in Lancashire. It is to be one of the happiest, most relaxed days in the whole year. Her first stop is Morecambe Bay, where she has come to unveil a sculpture of the comedian Eric Morecambe who was born here, as John Eric Bartholomew, in 1926. With Ernie Wise, he created one of the most successful comedy duos ever; their 1977 Christmas Show had an audience of 30 million, half the UK population.

On each show a celebrity guest would shed their normal, often serious, persona to become part of the comic act, and the names of the 103 celebrities have been carved into

the granite pavement below the statue. A number of them, including the broadcaster Sir Robin Day, are here for the unveiling. The sculpture by Graham Ibbeson shows Eric Morecambe in mid-dance as he and Ernie disappear off the stage at the end of the show. Birdwatching was one of his hobbies, and, after the unveiling, a group of local school-children perform a dance to the Morecambe and Wise theme tune, 'Bring me sunshine', depicting the flying patterns of the migratory birds that visit Morecambe Bay each year. We talk to them before the Queen arrives. 'Have you been to Buckingham Palace?' they ask. 'Yes.' 'Have you really *really*?'

LANCASTER

FROM MORECAMBE THE QUEEN AND THE DUKE go to Lancaster to celebrate the 600th anniversary of the links between the Monarch and the Duchy. The Queen, like every monarch, is Duke of Lancaster. The original lands were forfeited to Henry III in 1265 and 1266 by the rebellious Earls of Leicester and Derby, and were added to in succeeding centuries. When the Duke of Hereford, soon to be crowned Henry IV, returned from banishment in 1399 he found that his cousin, Richard II, had attempted to confiscate them, and he declared that they were to be held separately from the Crown and would descend personally to his heirs. Because of this the lands of the Duchy were not part of the Crown Estate which was surrendered in 1760 in exchange for the Civil List, and they have remained the source of the personal wealth of monarchs ever since.

After a service in the Priory and Parish Church, and the ceremony of presentation of the Keys of the Castle, the Queen and the Duke go down into Lancaster Market Square for a

FRIDAY 23RD JULY. *9.45 a.m. The Queen and The Duke of Edinburgh arrived at Morecambe Station.*
9.55 a.m. The Queen unveiled a statue to Eric Morecambe on Morecambe sea-front, and subsequently met representatives of Morecambe Voluntary Groups.

FRIDAY 23RD JULY. *11.05 a.m. The Queen, Duke of Lancaster, and The Duke of Edinburgh, attended a service in the Priory and Parish Church, Lancaster, to mark the 600th Anniversary of the link between the Crown and the Duchy.*

11.50 a.m. The Queen and The Duke of Edinburgh were received at Lancaster Castle by the Constable, Mr Eric Jones, who surrendered to The Queen the Keys of the Castle, which Her Majesty returned to him.

12 noon. Her Majesty and His Royal Highness then walked in Market Square, after which they were entertained to Lunch at Lancaster Town Hall.

2.40 p.m. The Queen and The Duke of Edinburgh visited Myerscough College, Bilsborrow, Preston. They toured the College's new facilities, and the Queen opened Fitzherbert-Brockholes Building.

3.30 p.m. Her Majesty and His Royal Highness left Myerscough by helicopter to travel to Windsor.

4.35 p.m. Arrival at Windsor Castle.

walkabout. Happiness is the keynote as she gathers cards and flowers by the armful, listening and laughing, and we see, as we have done many times this year, the delight on the faces of those to whom she talks. At one point Prince Philip lifts a small boy over the barrier so that he too can give his flowers to the Queen.

BILSBORROW

IN THE AFTERNOON the Queen visits Myerscough College, Bilsborrow, near Preston to open its new Learning Resources Centre, which will be available to both students and local rural businesses. The college, with its policy of lifelong learning, trains students in agricultural studies, from forestry and dog grooming to conservation and horse care. These are subjects about which the Queen knows a great deal.

As a centre of practical learning, Myerscough College works closely with local, national and international commercial organisations. As well as talking to students, at the College's Rural Business Centre, the Queen meets some of those involved in the manufacture and distribution of agricultural supplies.

LONDON

MONDAY 26TH JULY. *Returned to London. 7.30 p.m. The Queen took the Salute at the Royal Tournament at Earl's Court.*

TUESDAY. *11.45 a.m. Air Chief Marshal Sir David Evans was received by The Queen upon relinquishing his appointment as King of Arms of the Most Honourable Order of the Bath, and delivered up to Her Majesty the Insignia of Office. General Sir Brian Kenny was received by The Queen upon his appointment as King of Arms of the Most Honourable Order of the Bath, when Her Majesty handed to him the Insignia of Office.*

12 noon. HE Mr Jihad Mortada was received in audience by The Queen and presented the Letters of Recall of his predecessor and his own Letters of Credence as Ambassador from the Lebanese Republic to the Court of St James's.

12.20 p.m. The Queen received the Bishop of Southwell, the Right Revd George Cassidy, who did homage upon his appointment.

12.30 p.m. Mr Patrick Nixon (United Arab Emirates), Mr Roger Hart (Republic of Peru), and Sir John Holmes (Portuguese Republic) were received in audience by The Queen and kissed hands upon their appointment as Her Majesty's Ambassadors. Mr John Wilde (Republic of Botswana) and Mr Edward Clay (Republic of Cyprus) were received in audience by The Queen upon their appointment as British High Commissioners.

6.30 p.m. Prime Minister's audience.

DURING HER SUMMER BREAK the Queen will be away from London for nine weeks, and in the days before she leaves she has a heavier than usual timetable of audiences, with the retirement of a number of her long-standing officers. Her final summer engagement will be at the Royal Institution of Chartered Surveyors, where she is shown a model of the Millennium Dome, the venue for her final engagement of the year.

EARL'S COURT

SINCE 1880 THE ROYAL TOURNAMENT has offered a dramatic and colourful cornucopia of armed services skills, with a nail-biting display of precision riding by Royal Signals Motorcyclists, the Household Cavalry's spectacular Musical Ride, the Royal Air Force display dogs, and massed pipes and drums. For many, the climax of the evening is the Field Gun Competition, for which we saw training in Plymouth a month ago. The Queen is here as Patron to take the final Salute, for this is the last Royal Tournament and the last Field Gun Run; the government sees them as an expensive anachronism. But those

who take part know that the Run is more than a military game. During their rigorous training the teams learn coordination, courage, stamina, self-discipline and teamwork, qualities highly prized in naval life.

ROYAL INSTITUTION OF CHARTERED SURVEYORS

THE VISIT TO THE ROYAL INSTITUTION OF CHARTERED SURVEYORS promises to be rather special. The briefing notes speak of a 'Major Picture Opportunity', for at the end of the visit the Queen and the President of the Institution will stand alone on a roof

Mr Philip Astley subsequently kissed hands upon his appointment as Her Majesty's Ambassador to the Kingdom of Denmark.
12.30 p.m. Mrs Kathryn Colvin was received by Her Majesty and received her Chain of Office upon her appointment as Vice-Marshal of the Diplomatic Corps.
12.40 p.m. Lieutenant Colonel Sir Guy Acland, Bt, was received by The Queen upon relinquishing his appointment as Deputy Master of the Household and Equerry, when Her Majesty invested him with the Insignia of a Lieutenant of the Royal Victorian Order.
12.45 p.m. Lieutenant Colonel Anthony Mather was received by The Queen and took leave upon relinquishing his appointments as Secretary, Central Chancery of the Orders of Knighthood and Assistant Comptroller, Lord Chamberlain's Office.
12.50 p.m. Lieutenant Commander Richard Tarran RN was received by Her Majesty upon relinquishing his appointment as Equerry to The Duke of Edinburgh, when The Queen invested him with the Insignia of a Member of the Royal Victorian Order.
6.00 p.m. The Queen, Patron, visited the Royal Institution of Chartered Surveyors to mark the Centenary of the building and of the Institution's associated charity. The Queen toured the building and presented Diplomas to five new Honorary Members of the Institution.

FRIDAY. 11.00 a.m. Meeting of the Privy Council.
Afternoon. To Sandringham.

terrace looking out across the treetops to Westminster Abbey, the Treasury Building and Big Ben. The notes describe this as a spectacular and little-known London vantage point that takes in a thousand years of national history. It might be something for the cover of the book. The Queen is here to celebrate the centenaries of the Institution's headquarters on the corner of Parliament Square and of the profession's Benevolent Fund. She is greeted in the hall by the RICS Singers, who perform a specially composed humorous and somewhat irreverent Queen's Psalm Chant.

The roof terrace is large enough for forty or more people to gather for a champagne reception after the Queen's visit. When we arrive, though, the Information Officer from the Palace announces that it is dangerous – perched high and small with a low balustrade – and for safety's sake he will allow just one cameraman to be there with the Queen. Everyone else must wait inside. When she has left we can go out onto the terrace, but quite what event we will then be recording is unclear. It is absurd, and we just hope that next time there's a roof-top venue the Palace will send someone with a better head for heights.

AUGUST AND SEPTEMBER
BALMORAL

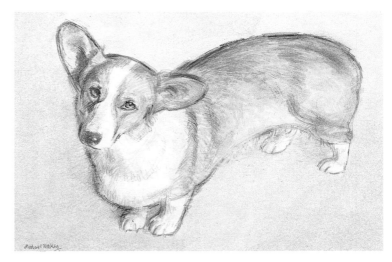

BALMORAL CASTLE, located among the hills and lochs of the Scottish Highlands on Deeside, has been the Royal Family's summer retreat since the mid-nineteenth century. Queen Victoria and Prince Albert first visited the Highlands in 1842, and were so entranced by the wild and hilly country that in 1848 they first leased, and then bought, the estate at Balmoral. The original fifteenth-century castle had been rebuilt in the 1830s, but it was too small for the Queen's family, household and guests, and the present castle, which is still not large, was built in the 1850s. After the Prince's death in 1861 Queen Victoria grew to love the peace and quietness of Balmoral. 'Every year I seem to grow fonder of this dear place,' she wrote, and in 1868 she published her *Leaves from the Journal of Our Life in the Highlands*.

The start of the Queen's visit to Balmoral coincides with the beginning of the parliamentary recess. Before the decommissioning of *HMY Britannia* she would begin her holiday by sailing up to the Western Isles and then down to Aberdeen. She now flies direct to Aberdeen. She stays at Balmoral for about nine weeks, riding, walking, sitting and reading, and enjoying her family who join her there for some of the time. She also works her dogs, which are brought up from Sandringham for the grouse shooting, beginning on the 12th of August.

Each weekday morning at 9 o'clock the Queen's Piper plays beneath her window. The post of Queen's Piper was created by Queen Victoria in 1843; apart from the Royal Family, he is the only person entitled to wear the grey and red Balmoral tartan. Lunch is at 1.15, tea at 4.30, drinks at 7.30 and dinner at 8.15. If the

Close to the River Muick, Inchnabobart is one of the small houses used by the Royal Family on the Balmoral Estate.

weather is good the Royal Family may picnic on the estate, possibly at Inchnabobart in Glen Muick, a small house bought by George VI in 1948 which has a paved terrace with a barbecue. Local bee-keepers keep more than 450 hives on the nearby heather.

The Queen's herd of Highland Cattle was first formed in 1953, and she has had several champions. This hardy breed, with its shaggy coat, is adapted to the harsh northern climate. The cattle are raised for beef, and the land on which they graze is now organically maintained.

During her holiday the daily red boxes continue as usual, she pays a formal visit to at least one local organisation, and although there are no weekly audiences the Prime Minister comes once to talk to the Queen, when he and his wife stay for the weekend.

THE SUMMER
SANDRINGHAM

THE QUEEN, with Queen Elizabeth the Queen Mother, spends a few days at Sandringham for the annual Summer Flower Show. The long-legged foal that we saw in January has grown enormously. He will stay with his mother for another couple of months, and will then move to Polhampton, where he will mature as a yearling before his training begins.

LONDON – CLARENCE HOUSE

THE QUEEN IS BACK IN LONDON in time for the Queen Mother's ninety-ninth birthday. Next year will she receive one of the newly designed cards from the Queen – and will she, like everyone else, have to apply, enclosing her birth certificate?

A set of postage stamps has been issued to mark this birthday. As with new notes and coins, the stamps were seen and approved by the Queen before they went into production. A few years ago it was realised, after the Queen had approved them, that a set of stamps commemorating the centenary of the death of the painter and nonsense poet Edward Lear featured a snail. Since this might suggest slow delivery the design was hastily withdrawn and the Queen was asked to approve its replacement – a bird.

FRIDAY 30TH JULY. *To Sandringham.*

WEDNESDAY. *The Queen returned to London.*

THURSDAY. *The 99th anniversary of the Birthday of Queen Elizabeth The Queen Mother.*

MONDAY 9TH AUGUST. *Afternoon. The Queen flew to Dyce Airport, Aberdeen, and then drove to Balmoral Castle.*

WEDNESDAY 18TH AUGUST. *Morning. Her Majesty visited Ballater Day Centre, Aberdeenshire, on the occasion of its Tenth Anniversary.*

MONDAY 23RD AUGUST. *Gillies' Ball.*

SATURDAY 4TH SEPTEMBER. *Morning. The Rt Hon Tony Blair, MP, and Mrs Blair arrived at Balmoral Castle. Afternoon. The Queen visited The Gathering of the Braemar Royal Highland Society and presented prizes. Evening. The Prime Minister had an audience of the Queen.*

TUESDAY 14TH SEPTEMBER. *Gillies' Ball.*

BRAEMAR

THERE HAVE BEEN Gatherings at Braemar for over 900 years, ever since young Highland Scots competed to become warriors of King Malcolm III. The present Games date back to 1817 when they were re-established to preserve the traditional culture and costume of this part of Scotland. It is both a local, almost family, occasion and an important tourist event. In 1849 Queen Victoria became their first royal Patron.

There is a full day's programme which includes caber-tossing, sword-dancing, stone-putting, tug-o'-war, hammer-throwing, hill-running, Highland flings and reels, and massed pipe bands. The Queen with Prince Philip, and the Prime Minister and his wife on their annual visit to Balmoral, watch the last hour or so of the Games.

Some strange things have happened to us during this year. We have been condescended to, and treated like recalcitrant squaddies. We have been pushed around and told to leave events. This is the first time, though, that we have been physically ejected. It begins well, for we are allowed to wander inside the arena for several hours, watching and drawing the contestants and talking to people. Then, at the end of the afternoon we go, by arrangement, to see the Queen presenting the prizes. Suddenly we are pushed by a Braemar official. 'Out – get out! You've sneaked in here and you've been discovered! Get out immediately!' What gets into people when the Royal Family is around? We've seen so much of it this year. Partly it's panic – they're concerned about security and that things might go wrong – but sometimes it has to do with power. This time we don't wait for the apologies. We have had a good day and we have all we need, so we gather our things and leave.

OCTOBER

THE QUEEN AND THE PRESS

THE MOST DIFFICULT PROBLEM for any Buckingham Palace Press Secretary is establishing a balance between the demands of public interest and those of the public's interest – between the public's right to know, and curiosity. Some people claim that we are entitled to know everything that bears on the Queen's life as Monarch, but how far, if at all, does this right extend to her private life? Is the truth about her marriage or her relationship with her children any of our business, unless they affect her role as Monarch?

The Palace Press Office had its beginnings when George III, weary of inaccurate reports about his movements, appointed a Court Newsman to issue a daily *Court Circular*, listing his previous day's activities. The first full-time Press Secretary was appointed in 1918. The post was abolished in 1931, but in 1944 the Press Office was established with a Press Secretary and one clerk. It is an indication of the public's appetite for royal stories, and of the general development of communications, that there is now a Press Secretary and Deputy Press Secretary, two Assistant Press Secretaries and four Information Officers. Their task is to act as a link between the Royal Family and the world's press, answering queries, briefing correspondents and responding to rumour and speculation. Each day they brief the Court Correspondent – an independent journalist employed by the Press Association – and they oversee books and radio or television projects which the Palace has agreed to support. Any statement from 'a Buckingham Palace spokesman' comes from the Press Office. These are not lies but they are not always the whole truth either, for it is said of Palace spokesmen that they reply to questions but do not always answer them. Away from the Palace their purpose is to act as facilitators, supervising the press during the Queen's engagements and helping them to get good pictures and copy while preventing them from being intrusive.

The press with whom they deal on public engagements must be accredited, and there are different levels of accreditation. Most sought-after are Royal Rota passes. To prevent there being too many press at any event, a limited number of these passes are issued to agencies, newspapers and TV companies on the understanding that they cannot have exclusive use of the material they gather but must share it with others. The number of Rota passes issued depends on the importance of the occasion and the amount of space. They give access to moving positions often very close to the Queen. Whereas the Queen Mother – who was first accustomed to being photographed in the days when film was much slower – will pause momentarily to give an opportunity for the picture to be taken, the Queen to a large extent simply ignores cameras, unlike some other members of the family who loathe photographers. She can, though, be angered by discourtesy and has been known to demand that a photographer who has been officiously removed is brought back. Far less satisfactory than Royal Rota passes are Fixed Positions where the press must stay in one place, sometimes behind a barrier some distance from the Queen, and often outside the place she is visiting so that they see only her arrival and departure.

On foreign tours the Press Office liaises with local press officers and security, and the number of press who can reasonably and safely be accommodated at any venue is agreed between them. These passes are pooled and the press divide them among themselves. The material is then shared. There are occasional absurdities; in an empty stadium designed to hold 110,000 people it was decided that only two reporters would be allowed, a stupidity exacerbated by Palace intransigence. The regular press group are tough, and they do not take kindly to being messed around. They are experienced professionals with a job to do, and each of them represents thousands or even millions of readers or viewers. Grumbles are endemic and often justified, and if the arrangements are bad, or if the person assigned to supervise them is incompetent, they will sometimes take matters into their own hands, although they know that they risk losing accreditation if

Some of the press who specialise in working with the Royal Family. Over the years the family come to know and trust the regulars, many of whom travel all over the world with them.

they do anything foolish or intrusive. On occasion they have downed cameras in protest at bad arrangements, something which pleases neither their editors nor the Palace. Generally, though, the Palace and regular royal photographers and reporters have the measure of one another and work together well.

There is much more openness now than there once was. Richard Colville, Press Secretary in the 1950s and '60s, was both suspicious and contemptuous of the press. His legacy has not entirely disappeared. His successor, William Heseltine, knew that society had changed and that, if it was to retain the people's confidence, the Royal Family must communicate more. With only the *Court Circular* on one hand and gossip columns on the other, he believed that the Palace needed to meet the press on its own terms. The 1969 television film *Royal Family* was a watershed, and although some see it as the beginning of a decline which led to the press free-for-all to which the Princess of Wales was subjected, most feel it was both inevitable and wisely handled.

Yet the relationship between the Palace and the press remains ambivalent, for although they need one another they do so for different reasons. The Palace wishes to present what it sees as the reality of monarchy while protecting the Queen from intrusion, but the press is generally looking for a story that will sell papers. What

that story is depends on its readership; a well-informed piece by Robert Hardman in the *Daily Telegraph* or Alan Hamilton in *The Times* will not satisfy readers of *The Sun,* although a really big royal story will increase the sales of all newspapers. Despite the problems which surrounded the Princess of Wales – and which will return when Prince William moves out into the world – most accredited journalists write straightforward pieces that are not based on scandal or (much) speculation. Reports and photographs from those who are not accredited and over whom they have no control – the paparazzi – are a different matter. Critical, often snide, stories appear which can be outright fabrication, justifying the Palace's wariness of that section of the press.

Most of the time the relationship between the Palace and the press is good, and the Press Office is helpful, courteous and accommodating. They have a difficult job which calls for imaginative engagement, but they cannot always make up their minds as to what they really want. Too often they can be contemptuously dismissive or high-handed, particularly with those, like local papers and freelance journalists, who are not used to dealing with them. They appear then to act on personal whim, the need to be in control even when this is not necessary, seeming to forget whom and what they are there to serve.

LONDON
PADDINGTON

MONDAY 11TH OCTOBER. *11.45 a.m. The Queen left Balmoral Castle.*
1.00 p.m. Left Aberdeen Dyce Airport.
2.30 p.m. Arrival at RAF Northolt.
2.45 p.m. The Queen visited the site of the Paddington railway crash.

TUESDAY. *11.50 a.m. His Excellency Herr Gebhardt von Moltke was received in farewell audience, and took leave upon relinquishing his appointment as Ambassador from the Federal Republic of Germany to the Court of St James's.*
12 noon. His Excellency Signor Luigi Amaduzzi was received in audience by Her Majesty and presented the Letters of Recall of his predecessor and his own Letters of Credence as Ambassador from the Italian Republic to the Court of St James's.
12.20 p.m. The Lord Hunt of King's Heath was received by The Queen and took leave upon relinquishing his appointment as Lord in Waiting to Her Majesty. The Lord Bach was received by The Queen upon his appointment as a Lord in Waiting to Her Majesty.

AT 8.11 A.M. ON MONDAY, 5TH OCTOBER, the 6.03 Intercity train from Cheltenham Spa to London collided with the 8.06 Thames Service train travelling from Paddington to Bedwyn. Thirty-one people were killed. The Queen at once sent a message of sympathy to the families and friends of the dead and injured, and of thanks to those working to help the victims.

Her summer break is over, and on her way from Northolt to Buckingham Palace she has asked to visit the site of the rail crash. Contractors have erected a small wooden platform, from which she can look down onto the railway line below. She talks to police officers and those involved in the rescue work, and looks at the bank of flowers and written tributes. A few days later she visits Ladbroke Hall to meet members of the emergency services who have been working in the aftermath of the disaster.

A visit by the Queen gives encouragement to those involved, but there has been criticism in the past that royal visits to disaster sites, although well intentioned, have interrupted the rescue work. The arrangements which the Royal Family now makes ensure that this does not happen.

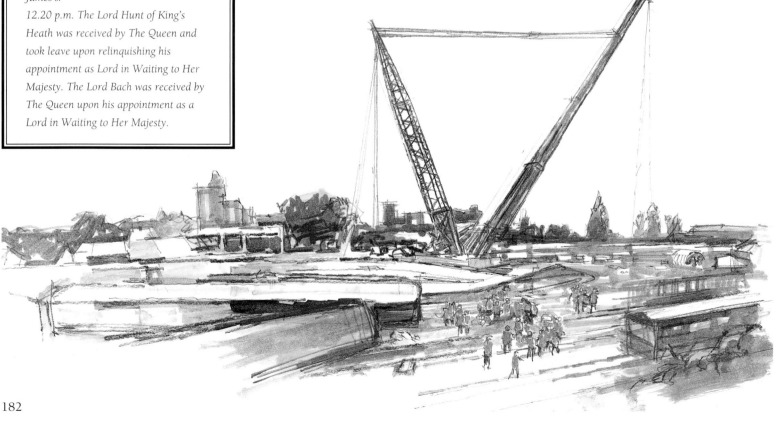

SOUTH KENSINGTON

THE QUEEN IS VISITING the Victoria and Albert Museum to mark the centenary of its renaming by Queen Victoria. The V & A is one of the world's leading museums in art and design. Previously called the South Kensington Museum, it was established in 1852 as part of the huge museum development following the Great Exhibition of 1851, with the idea of inspiring designers and manufacturers in the decorative arts. The exhibition that the Queen has come to see shows how the museum has changed and developed over the century. One of the exhibits is a plaster fig-leaf. The story is that when Queen Victoria visited the museum and saw the cast of Michelangelo's *David*, she was so shocked by its nudity that the fig leaf was cast and kept in readiness for any future royal visit.

BUCKINGHAM PALACE

IT IS VERY UNUSUAL for the Queen to receive any deputation, and the audience she is giving to a group of Aboriginal leaders is a private rather than an official visit. In 1765 the British government made a pledge that land discovered by Captain Cook could be claimed only with the consent of the native people. Australia, though, was declared *terra nullius*, a land belonging to no one, and the pledge was disregarded. The deputation has come to the UK, a month before the Australian referendum on retaining the monarchy, to draw attention to the plight of indigenous Australians, and to press for their ancient rights to be part of the new constitution if their native land should become a republic.

They spend ten minutes with the Queen. When they come out afterwards they say nothing about the substance of their discussion, just that they are delighted with how it went. Five months later, during a visit to Australia, the Queen draws attention to the plight of the indigenous Australians.

12.30 p.m. The Hon David Muirhead was received by the Queen upon his appointment as High Commissioner for Jamaica in London.

12.40 p.m. The Queen held a Council.

3.00 p.m. The Queen, accompanied by The Duke of Edinburgh, opened the Centenary Exhibition 'A Grand Design' at the Victoria and Albert Museum, London SW7.

6.30 p.m. Prime Minister's audience.

WEDNESDAY. *11.40 a.m. Mr David Omand, Permanent Secretary at the Home Office, was received by The Queen.*

12 noon. His Excellency Dr Stanislaw Komorowaki was received in audience by Her Majesty and presented the Letters of Recall of his predecessor and his own Letters of Credence as Ambassador from the Republic of Poland to the Court of St James's.

12.20 p.m. Mr Peter Yu, Executive Director of the Kimberley Land Council, and Mr Gatjii Djerrkura, Dr Lowitja O'Donohue, Mr Patrick Dobson and Professor Marcia Langton, Senior Indigenous Australians, were received by the Queen.

12.30 p.m. Her Majesty held a Council.

THURSDAY. *11.00 a.m. The Queen held an Investiture.*

3.15 p.m.. Her Majesty visited Ladbroke Hall, London W10, and met representatives of the Emergency Services and volunteers involved in the aftermath of the Paddington railway crash.

MANCHESTER
EMERGENCY SERVICES

LAST EVENING THE QUEEN AND THE DUKE OF EDINBURGH hosted a reception at Buckingham Palace for six hundred guests from across the country involved in the emergency services. Today they are in Manchester to see the work of those services at first hand. The Royal Train draws into Manchester Victoria Station at 10 o'clock. Waiting to welcome her on the station concourse is Manchester's Commonwealth Steel Band and a local school choir who sing songs from Nigeria and Swaziland. The waiting crowd is delighted to see that the Queen is wearing red and black, the colours of Manchester United Football Club.

After her car has left, we go outside the station to pick up our taxi. The roads are temporarily closed, and while we are waiting we chat to a group of women about the Queen's visit. 'She's all right but she never comes north,' they say. 'They don't bother about us up here. She's only interested in the south of England.' Very strange!

The Queen's first stop is the Central Ambulance Station, then Manchester Royal Infirmary, and Manchester Central Fire Station, where she has lunch in the canteen. At each stop she is greeted by the Lord Lieutenant, who leaves each venue just ahead of her so that he can be at the next one to greet her and introduce her to her new hosts. In the afternoon she visits West Didsbury Police Station before going to Manchester Airport for a reception for representatives of the Voluntary Emergency Services. Here she speaks of the Paddington rail crash, saying that it was a shocking reminder of the vital role played by the emergency services during times of crisis. These services are to be one of the themes of this year's Christmas Broadcast, and the BBC TV crew is with her for much of the day.

THURSDAY 14TH OCTOBER. *6.00 p.m . The Queen and The Duke of Edinburgh held a Reception at Buckingham Palace to mark the contribution of the Emergency Services in the United Kingdom. 10.50 p.m. Her Majesty and His Royal Highness left Euston Station on the Royal Train to travel to Manchester.*

FRIDAY. *10.00 a.m. The Queen and the Duke of Edinburgh arrived at Manchester Victoria Station.*

10.25 a.m. The Queen and The Duke of
Edinburgh visited Central Manchester
Ambulance Station, where Her Majesty
presented the Ambulance Service
(Emergency Duties) Long Service and
Good Conduct Medal to members of the
Greater Manchester Ambulance Service.

10.55 a.m. The Queen visited
Manchester Royal Infirmary, met
members of the Trust Board and toured
the Infirmary.

11.45 a.m. Her Majesty and His Royal
Highness visited Manchester Central Fire
Station, and Greater Manchester Fire
Service Training Centre where they saw
fire fighting vehicles and equipment and
met Red Cross volunteers before
attending a Reception and being
entertained to Lunch.

2.25 p.m. Her Majesty visited Greater
Manchester Police, West Didsbury,
where she watched presentations on
tackling crime and the millennium, and
met members of emergency services,
voluntary organisations and the public
who have received awards for bravery.

3.10 p.m. The Queen and The Duke of
Edinburgh attended a Reception in
Terminal 2, Manchester Airport, and
met guests representing Voluntary
Emergency Service organisations in
Greater Manchester.

3.50 p.m. Her Majesty and His Royal
Highness left Manchester by helicopter to
travel to Windsor.

4.50 p.m. Arrival at Windsor Castle.

LONDON
THE MALL AND
ST JOHN'S WOOD

The King's Troop Royal Horse Artillery fulfil ceremonial duties, including the firing of 21- and 41-gun salutes using First World War field guns.

THE ROADS AROUND BUCKINGHAM PALACE are closed when we arrive at 4.30 in the morning for the dress rehearsal for tomorrow's State Visit by the President of the People's Republic of China, a visit for which we feel little enthusiasm. There is a strange ghostliness about the soldiers and horses and the carriages lit by small lamps as they make their way in the darkness along the otherwise deserted Mall and Birdcage Walk to Horse Guards. Everything is timed to the minute but is muted and monochromatic. Tomorrow there will be burnished brass and military bands and watching crowds, but in the early morning chill the men are wearing dark great coats, and in the quietness we hear the jangle of harness and the rumble of carriage wheels. Horse Guards, by contrast, is brightly lit. It is here that the Queen will greet the Chinese President as he steps from his car, and the welcoming ceremony is enacted. By the time the last of the procession has returned through the Palace gates it is beginning to get light, and a few people hurrying along with briefcases are overtaken by early morning joggers.

On the morning of the State Visit, we go to the St John's Wood barracks of the King's Troop Royal Horse Artillery. They will be firing a 41-gun salute in St James's Park. The King's Troop is part of the Royal Regiment of Artillery formed in 1793. Mechanised in the 1930s, it was re-formed after the Second World War to carry out State ceremonial duties. It is one of four units that make up the Royal Horse Artillery; the other three are fully operational. As with the Household Cavalry, all members of the King's Troop are fully trained soldiers, but, whereas the Cavalry rotate operational and ceremonial duties, the

King's Troop is a permanent ceremonial unit. Members of the Troop can switch to one of the other units but few of them do.

Reveille is at 6 o'clock, but many of the men and women begin work earlier, mucking out. At 6.30 the officers' horses, which will not be pulling guns, are exercised for about 45 minutes. After breakfast the soldiers are back in the stables to start grooming the Irish-bred Light Draught horses. At 10.15 a Boot and Saddle trumpet call is sounded, and they change into their pre-1914 full-dress uniform and the horses are saddled up. Another trumpet call at 10.45 is a signal for the horses to be led out into the square and hooked into the limbers, 13-pounder First World War field guns, six horses to a gun. Ten minutes later come the first inspections by the Section Commanders, followed at 11.05 by the Commanding Officer's Inspection. At 11.15 the King's Troop leaves barracks.

It takes about 35–40 minutes for them to reach St James's Park. They don't go at a steady pace but with a mixture of trotting, which prevents the horses from being too fresh, and halting, which gives the men a chance to prepare. In the park the guns are brought into action. The salute, timed to coincide with the President setting foot on Horse Guards, is fired at ten-second intervals by each of the six guns in turn.

187

LONDON

BUCKINGHAM PALACE

CHINA'S RECORD IN HUMAN RIGHTS has led to vociferous demonstrations during the State Visit. There is criticism of over-reaction by the police, and questions are being asked about whether a visiting Head of State should be protected from protest in a free country. Chinese officials, for their part, have criticised the British authorities for allowing such demonstrations during the visit.

As we go down to the State Banquet, a large but peaceful group has gathered outside the Palace. They are carrying banners and chanting slogans. Inside, the evening's formalities continue undisturbed. Even though they carry on their protests into the night, the President and his wife, sleeping in the Belgian Suite on the ground floor looking out over the garden, cannot hear them.

The Ballroom at Buckingham Palace has been transformed. A long horseshoe–shaped table is decorated with yellow, red and bronze flower arrangements, and the table and sideboards are laid with exquisite gold plate, glass and china. The guests will eat consommé, fillet of sole, venison and ice-cream bombe, and will listen to music played by the Grenadier Guards.

TUESDAY 19TH OCTOBER. *8.30 p.m. The Queen and The Duke of Edinburgh gave a State Banquet in honour of the President and Madame Wang Yeping at Buckingham Palace.*

WEDNESDAY. *12 noon. The Queen and The Duke of Edinburgh attended a Reception at St James's Palace to mark the 50th Anniversary of the Regimental Association of The 6th Queen Elizabeth's Own Gurkha Rifles.*
3.00 p.m. Way Ahead Meeting.

The Queen and the President process down the East Gallery on their way to the State Banquet in the Ballroom.

At the twice-yearly Way Ahead meetings the senior members of the Royal Family coordinate royal programmes and discuss policy matters, which in recent years have included such major initiatives as tax, Civil List changes, royal travel, the opening of Buckingham Palace and the funding of the restoration of Windsor Castle.

ONE OF THE FIRST ENGAGEMENTS for new Ambassadors to the Court of St James's is a visit to Buckingham Palace to present their credentials, or Letters of Credence, to the Queen. The Marshal of the Diplomatic Corps brings them from their embassy or residence to the Palace in a State Landau. Further State Landaus carry their suites.

As we arrive for the morning audiences, the Chinese President is leaving by the Grand Entrance for lunch at No. 10 Downing Street. The Honduran Ambassador's party waits for a few moments at the side of the Quadrangle until the Rolls-Royce, bearing the Chinese flag rather than its customary Royal Standard, has driven away. He is then met at the Grand Entrance and taken to the Bow Room. In the adjoining 1844 room the Queen is joined by the Permanent Under Secretary of State. The Ambassador is brought in, and presents his Letters of Credence to the Queen in a large envelope. They talk for a few minutes, then his suite is introduced. After they have left the room, the Ambassador's wife is presented. The Queen's Visiting Book is signed, and the audience ends.

When the Queen grants an audience to one of her personal representatives – such as an Ambassador, a Governor-General or a Governor – it is described as having 'kissed hands'. This simply denotes a type of audience. Newly appointed Privy Counsellors or government ministers literally 'kiss hands' when they brush the back of the Queen's hand with their lips.

THURSDAY. 12 noon. HE Señor Hernán Antonio Bermúdez was received in audience by The Queen and presented the Letters of Recall of his predecessor and his own Letters of Credence as Ambassador from the Republic of Honduras to the Court of St James's.
12.20 p.m. HE the Reverend John Ini Lapli, Governor-General of Solomon Islands, was received in audience when Her Majesty invested him with the Insignia of a Knight Grand Cross of the Most Distinguished Order of St Michael and St George.
12.40 p.m. HE Mr Mwanyengela Ngali was received in farewell audience by Her Majesty and took leave upon His Excellency relinquishing his appointment as High Commissioner for Kenya in London.
12.50 p.m. Mr Basil O'Brien was received by The Queen upon his appointment as High Commissioner for the Commonwealth of the Bahamas in London.

The Queen with the Governor-General of the Solomon Islands and Mrs Ini Lapli whom she received in audience at Buckingham Palace.

LONDON
ST JOHN'S AMBULANCE

THURSDAY 21ST OCTOBER. *2.45 p.m. The Queen, Sovereign Head, and The Duke of Edinburgh visited the Order of St John, St John's Gate, London EC1.*

3.50 p.m. The Queen and the President of the People's Republic of China opened and subsequently toured the 'Gilded Dragons, Buried Treasures from China's Golden Ages' Exhibition at the British Museum.

7.20 p.m. The Queen and The Duke of Edinburgh were entertained by the President of the People's Republic of China and Madame Wang Yeping at a Banquet at the Chinese Embassy, Portland Place, London W1.

FRIDAY. *10.00 a.m. The Queen and The Duke of Edinburgh bade farewell to the President and Madame Wang Yeping at the conclusion of the State Visit.*

12 noon. The Queen received Mr Robin Young, Permanent Secretary at the Department for Culture, Media and Sport.

12.20 p.m. Her Majesty received His Honour Dr Neil Conn, Administrator of the Northern Territory, Australia.

12.30 p.m. Mr Iain Kelly (the Republic of Belarus) and Dr John Jenkins (the Union of Myanmar) were received in audience by The Queen and kissed hands upon their appointment as Her Majesty's Ambassadors. Mr Mervyn Jones (Turks and Caicos Islands) and Mr Peter Johnstone (Anguilla) were received in audience by The Queen and kissed hands upon their appointment as Governors. Afternoon. To Highclere.

THE THEME OF EMERGENCY SERVICES is picked up again when the Queen goes to the headquarters of the St John's Ambulance to celebrate the 900th Anniversary of the Order of St John, of which she is Sovereign Head. The Order was set up in the twelfth century by monks in Jerusalem to care for sick crusaders and pilgrims.

The visit gets off to a rather charming hiccough when the band mistakes the Lord Lieutenant's car for the Queen's, and greets him with the National Anthem. Still, it's a useful final rehearsal for when she does arrive, a few minutes later. People are often surprised at the size of the royal retinue. She will be preceded by police outriders, and travelling with her will be a Lady-in-waiting, a Personal Protection Officer, her Equerry-in-waiting, and the Private Secretary who arranged the details of the visit. Someone from the Press Office will be there ahead of her. She will be met by the Lord Lieutenant, and possibly the High Sheriff,

the mayor or the local MP, as well as the president or chairman of the organisation she is visiting, with the wives or husbands of several of these.

When the Duke of Edinburgh is with the Queen, he and her Personal Protection Officer travel with her in the Rolls-Royce. If he is not there, the Lady-in-waiting takes his place in the car beside the Queen. Nowadays the rest of the royal party follow in a dark green people-carrier which is large enough to accommodate them all in a single vehicle.

In most places she goes to, the Queen unveils a tablet as a permanent record of her visit. The form and wording of this is agreed in advance with the Palace.

At the end of her visit to the St John's Ambulance headquarters, the Queen will be coming out onto the pavement to watch a demonstration of heart resuscitation. While they are waiting for her, a group of photographers stage-manage the demonstration by moving the volunteers closer together so that they can get a more compact and dramatic picture. Inevitably, when the Queen comes out she doesn't realise what has been set up and doesn't stand where they are willing her to stand. It is all too spread out, and next morning there are no pictures in the papers.

SUNDAY. *To Windsor.*

MONDAY. *Returned to London.*

TUESDAY. *11.00 a.m. The Queen held an Investiture.*
1.00 p.m. Her Majesty, Duke of Lancaster, was entertained to Lunch at the Savoy Hotel by those who have held the Office of Chancellor of the Duchy of Lancaster to mark the 600th Anniversary of the link between the Crown and the Duchy.
6.30 p.m. Prime Minister's audience.

WEDNESDAY. *11.50 a.m. The Queen, Colonel-in-Chief, Coldstream Guards, received General Sir Michael Rose upon his appointment as Colonel of the Regiment.*
12 noon. HE Mr Simbarashe Mumbengegwi was received in audience by The Queen and presented the Letters of Recall of his predecessor and his own Letters of Commission as High Commissioner for the Republic of Zimbabwe in London.
12.20 p.m. Her Majesty received HE Chief Emeka Anyaoku, Secretary-General of the Commonwealth.
12.40 p.m. The Queen received Mrs Rachel Lomax, Permanent Secretary at the Department of Social Security.
6 p.m. The Queen and the Duke of Edinburgh held a Reception for Common-wealth Non-Governmental Organisations.
11.45 pm The Queen and The Duke of Edinburgh left Euston Station on the Royal Train to travel to Stoke-on-Trent.

The Queen and the Duke of Edinburgh say goodbye to the Chinese President at the Grand Entrance of Buckingham Palace.

191

STOKE-ON-TRENT

HANLEY AND
KEELE UNIVERSITY

SIX TOWNS MAKE UP THE CITY OF STOKE-ON-TRENT, collectively known as the Potteries and for centuries the heart of English ceramics manfacture. Josiah Wedgwood was born in Burslem, one of the six towns, in 1730. With the importation of cheap china the Potteries have faced increasing problems, and many firms have gone out of business. The Queen is here to see something of the regeneration of the city.

Her first visit is to the Dudson Centre in Hanley, a previously derelict Grade II pottery works in a key position in the city centre. This was donated by the thriving Dudson Group of Companies, the oldest family pottery still in business, as a centre for voluntary organisations. The Queen talks to members of various groups, including those giving bereavement care, the Hindu Cultural Society and people helping victims of sexual abuse and incest. She then tours an old bottle kiln in the central courtyard which has been converted into a small museum, and is presented with a replica of a jasper and figure clock produced here for the Great Exhibition of 1851.

After a walkabout in Hanley, she goes to see something of the cultural regeneration of the city, visiting the restored Victoria Hall to hear part of a performance by the City Orchestra and Choir, and the Regent Theatre, re-created from a decayed and abandoned 1929 Art Deco cinema. Here she meets members of the North Staffordshire Amateur Operatic Society, dressed in the costumes of their recent productions, and watches a rehearsal of *42nd Street*.

The Queen, with the Duke who earlier visited local Waterford Wedgwood and Michelin factories, is entertained to a lunch of terrine of salmon, medallions of beef and autumn fruit compote at Stoke Town Hall. They then go to Keele, the first British university to be established after the war, which is celebrating its fiftieth anniversary. Here they attend a service of thanksgiving in the university chapel, and the Queen opens a new entrance road to the university and the Business Innovation Centre, a result of collaboration between the university and local business. They have tea with members of the university and then leave by helicopter from the sports ground.

NOVEMBER

THE QUEEN AND THE COMMONWEALTH

IN 1953 THE QUEEN SAID of the Commonwealth that it 'bears no resemblance to the empires of the past. It is an entirely new conception built on the highest qualities of the spirit of man: friendship, loyalty and the desire for freedom and peace.' It is a voluntary grouping of fifty-four politically independent nations, including some of the world's poorest and smallest countries, who act in equal partnership to build and strengthen democracy, eliminate poverty, oppose racism, advance human rights and develop universal education, while supporting one another and particularly vulnerable members who are under threat. Commonwealth countries were originally linked by the British Empire, but in recent years other countries have applied and been accepted as members. Together they account for 1.7 billion people – over a quarter of the world's population – more than half of whom are under twenty-five and who embrace all the world's major racial groups. They build on a common heritage of language, laws and education yet encompass a huge diversity of races, religions, cultures and traditions drawn from every continent.

Each member country has its own chosen form of constitution. This may be a republic with an elected President (as in South Africa), an indigenous monarchy or sultanate (as in Tonga) or a realm that recognises the Queen as Head of State (as in Canada).

In 1867 Canada became the first self-governing Dominion within the British Empire. In 1901 and 1907, Australia and New Zealand followed, and the Balfour Declaration of 1926 acknowledged their autonomy, saying that they were 'equal in status, in no way subordinate one to another though united by common allegiance to the Crown'. At the moment all three countries have chosen to retain the Queen as Head of State – that is, to remain as realms. When the Queen visits them she does so as Queen of their country, not as Queen of the United Kingdom, and she acts as their Constitutional Monarch on the advice of their ministers.

In the years immediately after the Second World War other countries began to achieve independence. The first was India, who in 1947 expressed a wish to become an independent republic within the Commonwealth. At the meeting of Commonwealth Prime Ministers held in London in 1949, this proposal was accepted, on condition that India accept George VI as 'the symbol of the free association of its independent member nations and as such the Head of the Commonwealth'. The London Declaration of 1949 thus marked the emergence of the modern Commonwealth.

From its inception, therefore, the monarch's role within the Commonwealth has been symbolic; the Queen acts as a figurehead, personally strengthening the links between members. She does this in a number of ways. The first is by visiting Commonwealth countries. Shortly after coming to the throne, between November 1953 and May 1954, she travelled from one Commonwealth country to another. Nowadays, of the two overseas tours that she makes each year, one is always to one or more Commonwealth countries. She is in regular contact with its administrative centre, the Commonwealth Secretariat, based in Marlborough House in London, and with the Secretary-General and the Heads of Government. She is patron of many of its educational, cultural and sporting activities. In March, on Commonwealth Day, she attends the Commonwealth Day Observance in London, and she makes her Commonwealth Day Broadcast which – like her Christmas Broadcast – goes out to all the member countries.

Commonwealth Heads of Government Meetings (CHOGMs) take place every two years enabling leaders to discuss, both formally in the conference hall and informally in numerous private meetings, the issues facing member countries, and to draw up programmes for future development. It is a widespread network for soundings and consultations. Before 1997, when CHOGM was officially opened by the Queen in Edinburgh, she was not present at the conference itself but would always be in the city where it was taking place so that she could have private audiences and discussions with leaders.

Some of these conferences have resulted in important policy statements: most notably in Singapore in 1971 when a Declaration

Children from Little Namaland on the west coast of South Africa resting between dances at the Commonwealth Heads of Government Meeting (see page 208).

of Commonwealth Principles was drawn up; in Harare, Zimbabwe, in 1991, when the principles were reaffirmed in the Harare Commonwealth Declaration; and in 1995 at Millbank, New Zealand, when an action programme was implemented to promote the Harare Principles in practice. The Harare Declaration commits Commonwealth countries to the promotion and protection of democracy, just and honest government, the rule of law and fundamental human rights, the elimination of racial discrimination, equality for women and universal access to education, sustainable development and the alleviation of poverty, environmental protection, combatting drug trafficking, supporting small states, and endorsing the United Nations and other international institutions in the search for peace. These principles place member nations under an obligation to govern themselves according to clearcut rules of behaviour. The Commonwealth must, for example, suspend any military regime that comes to power by force; 1999 saw the suspension of Pakistan from the councils of the Commonwealth after a military coup, but the reinstatement of Nigeria after free democratic elections.

The Queen has for a long time had a personal affection for the Commonwealth. In Cape Town on her twenty-first birthday in 1947 she made a broadcast in which she pledged to devote her whole life to its service, and in her Silver Jubilee speech in 1977 she said that the Commonwealth symbolises 'the transformation of the Crown from an emblem of dominion into a symbol of free and voluntary association. In all history this has no precedent.' Her response depends not only on affection but also on pragmatism. She knows the unique and remarkable function it can perform, for as well as promoting and safeguarding good government in all its meanings, it is also a sharing of peoples at non-governmental levels, encompassing educational, cultural and sporting exchange within a family of nations of which she is the figurehead.

There is much discussion now about the future of the monarch's role within the Commonwealth. An independent think-tank has proposed that the Queen's politically neutral role as Head of the Commonwealth should be downgraded and supplemented by a President who would speak publicly on key issues, that its administration should move from London to Cape Town or Delhi, and that the next British monarch should no longer be Head of the Commonwealth. In November 1999 at CHOGM a high-level group was established, chaired by the President of South Africa and including the Heads of Government of ten other Commonwealth countries, to review the role of the Commonwealth and to advise on how best it could respond to the challenges of the new century.

LONDON

HAMMERSMITH

T HE PRINCE'S TRUST, the largest charitable network in Britain, was set up in 1976 when the Prince of Wales realised the scale of wasted talent, energy and enthusiasm among the disadvantaged young. Beginning with his Royal Navy pension of £3,000, it now has an annual turnover of £55 million and has given life-changing practical support to more than 400,000 young people.

In recognition of its achievement the Queen will this evening grant the Trust a Royal Charter. Such charters, which date back to the thirteenth century and are granted by the Sovereign on the advice of the Privy Council, are the most prestigious way of conferring legal corporate status. But first she has come to see something of the work of the Trust.

MONDAY 1ST NOVEMBER. 11.05 a.m. The Queen left Windsor Castle by car. 11.30 a.m. The Queen, accompanied by The Prince of Wales, visited a Prince's Trust Training Project for Young People in Elgin Avenue, London W12. Her Majesty and His Royal Highness visited houses and flats, were briefed on the aims of the housing project and the training initiative, and met trainees working on the accommodation, others being helped by The Prince's Trust, and trainees from other areas of London.
6.00 p.m. The Queen gave a Reception at Buckingham Palace to mark the granting of a Royal Charter to The Prince's Trust.

During her visit to The Prince's Trust development site, the Queen talks to a number of young trainees who are learning various skills in the building trade.

At a training project in west London, long-term unemployed young people are being trained in the construction industry. On the building site in Hammersmith they learn to be bricklayers, carpenters, painters and decorators, plumbers, electricians – all the building trades are here. The Queen arrives in a Jaguar rather than in her usual Rolls-Royce, for she has come informally as a guest of the Prince rather than of the organisation. He shows his mother round, and she watches the young people working and hears from them what they have achieved.

BUCKINGHAM PALACE

T HE TIMING OF THIS EVENING'S RECEPTION, which is in the Ballroom at the Palace, has been arranged to coincide with the evening television news. It will be broadcast live. We watch from the musicians' balcony as young people tell their own stories of what the Trust has meant in their lives – a former borstal boy who became a BBC producer, a girl who was given the encouragement to defy those who said that because she is deaf she would never be a hairdresser. More than 40,000 have been able to start their own small

businesses under the Trust's Business Start-up scheme, which offers loans, bursaries and volunteer 'Business Mentors' until they are up and running. These businesses in turn have taken on other unemployed young people. Some are in tears as they recall the help they have been given, and through it all runs a thread of real personal gratitude to the Prince himself.

A typical young volunteer has been nominated to receive the Charter from the Queen. He is 23-year-old Alan Scoullar from Cheshire whose life had centred on drugs, crime and the dole queue. He now has a job, a flat and a fiancée. 'They say a leopard can't change its spots,' he says, 'but I'm proof that it can.' In his own speech, the Prince says: 'If I had to sum up what the Trust's message is to the young people who need us, it would be "Yes, You Can". Because we believe in you, we believe that you have talent and ability, and we believe that you have a great deal to offer your community and your country.'

The Ballroom at Buckingam Palace, seen from behind the Musicians' Balcony, is the scene for the granting of a Royal Charter to the Prince's Trust.

2.30 p.m. Her Majesty and His Royal Highness visited Guildhall Art Gallery.
6.30 p.m. Prime Minister's audience.

WEDNESDAY. *12 noon. His Excellency Señor Pablo Cabrera was received in audience by The Queen and presented the Letters of Recall of his predecessor and his own Letters of Credence as Ambassador from the Republic of Chile to the Court of St James's.*
12.20 p.m. Mr Kevin Tebbit, Permanent Secretary at the Ministry of Defence, was received by The Queen.
1.00 p.m. The President of the Federal Republic of Germany and Mrs Rau had Lunch with The Queen.

THURSDAY. *11.00 a.m. The Queen held an Investiture.*
2.30 p.m. Portrait sitting with Mr John Wonnacott.

FRIDAY. *11.40 a.m. The Queen received Colonel Edward York upon relinquishing his appointment as Colonel Commandant, Yeomanry, and Colonel John Hills upon assuming the appointment.*
12 noon. His Excellency Mr Bertrand Rassool was received in audience by Her Majesty and presented the Letters of Recall of his predecessor and his own Letters of Commission as High Commissioner for the Republic of Seychelles in London.

LONDON

THE CITY OF LONDON

I T IS ALMOST EXACTLY a year since the Queen had the first of her themed away days when she visited the City of London, paying tribute to 'the square mile' as one of the leading financial and business centres of the world. She is returning to the City today, but for the first time during our year a proposed visit has had to be cancelled. The new Lloyds Register International Headquarters is not complete, and the Queen will be unable to open it as planned.

Instead she begins her visit with a Millennium Luncheon at Mansion House, the home for over 250 years of the Lord Mayor of London. The Lord Mayor is the holder for one year of an office that goes back to the early twelfth century – his most celebrated predecessor is Dick Whittington. As the Queen's car draws up, the Lady Mayoress realises that they are both wearing blue. There is rarely any previous consultation about dress, and the days are long gone when clashing colours mattered; certainly it doesn't bother the Queen, who is not vain. Sometimes people contact the Palace to find out what colour she will be wearing so that they can give her flowers that will go with her clothes, but they are always told that the Queen has not yet decided.

The lunch, with its menu of foie gras, tournedos, and lemon and chocolate tart, is a celebration of achievement, paid for by the Corporation of London. Most of the three hundred or so guests are household names, but a few are less well-known people who have made a notable contribution to national life. There is, for example, a rural postman. In his speech replying on behalf of the guests, Sir Robin Day proposes his own nomination for achievement, speaking of the Queen's 'exemplary and faultless reign as our Constitutional Monarch'.

After lunch the Queen goes on to open the new Guildhall Art Gallery. The previous gallery was destroyed during the Blitz in 1941. It has taken twelve years to build, for this small area has been inhabited for hundreds of years and archaeological investigations uncovered Roman, Saxon and medieval remains, including an important Roman amphitheatre which had then to be excavated.

12.20 p.m. HE Mr Colding was received in farewell audience by Her Majesty and took leave upon His Excellency relinquishing his appointment as Ambassador from Norway to the Court of St James's.

12.30 p.m. Mr Nicholas Browne (Islamic Republic of Iran), Mr Thomas Young (Republic of Zambia) and Mr Timothy Jones (Republic of Armenia) were received in audience by The Queen and kissed hands upon their appointment as Her Majesty's Ambassadors.

Afternoon. To Windsor.

ACCRA, GHANA
STATE VISIT

WE ARRIVE IN GHANA ahead of the Queen and so miss the Rugby World Cup Final where she presents the cup to the Australian team. Australia will have been much in her thoughts in the last few days, for they have just voted to retain the monarchy. She knows it is only a matter of time before a different decision is made.

A crowd of about 10,000 has gathered at Kotoka Airport in an atmosphere of exuberant festivity. The Ghanaian greeting 'Akwaaba' is spelt out across the airport building in red, yellow and green balloons. The light is beginning to fade as the Queen's plane flies in, and as she comes down the aircraft steps a tribal Elder pours a libation onto the ground to thank the gods for her safe arrival and to bring blessings on her tour.

Her first appointment next day is to visit the President at Castle Osu, but we have not been given passes for this. In fact, it seems that almost no arrangements have been made for us for the whole of this tour; we will be given some positions away from the main action, but we are going to miss other events altogether. We protest, but our protests are dismissed.

At the Parliament Building the Queen is greeted with music, and dancers lead her up the steps. After the President's welcoming speech she addresses the Members, something she cannot do in her own country. Tens of thousands of people bring the city to a standstill as she and the President then drive slowly through Accra in the back of a Range Rover for a twenty-minute State Drive. Meanwhile, people are gathering for a spectacular Durbar of tribal Chiefs and Queen Mothers, some of whom have travelled hundreds of miles with their retinues to be here to greet the Queen. We wander down to where they sit to see their brilliantly coloured ceremonial dress and their heavy gold ornaments, symbols of the power and wealth of their regions. Shortly before the Queen arrives we return to our assigned position several hundred yards from the brilliant ceremony that will be unfolding. This is the most colourful event of the whole African tour and we had planned to spread it across a four-page panorama. Instead, all we can see is a phalanx of pressmen, and beyond them the backs of the Chiefs. We have discovered, though, what has gone wrong: we talked to the wrong person at the Palace about what we hoped to do here. By doing this we have unwittingly become caught in a web of internal politics, and as a result we are to be denied the access that makes a book like this possible. We must find ways round this, but since the Queen has approved and encouraged what we are doing we find it difficult to comprehend.

La Wireless Cluster of Schools is made up of nine different primary schools; there are so many pupils that they come in two daily shifts. Inside the red-earth compound there is an excited bustle, with singing and dancing and tables of colourful craft displays. We leave our useless assigned positions and wander in among the pupils. A group of ten-year-olds standing on a bench indicate that there is space for us to squeeze in, and are highly amused by the eccentric Brits who join them, unnoticed by Palace officials, to watch the Queen as she is shown round the compound.

11.25 p.m. The Queen and The Duke of Edinburgh, with the President and Mrs Rawlings, drove in State to a Durbar of Chiefs where they were received by the President of the National House of Chiefs and watched a cultural display.

3.00 p.m. The Queen, with the President, visited La Wireless Cluster Junior School, Accra.

4.00 p.m. Her Majesty received Commonwealth High Commissioners at the Labadi Beach Hotel.

8.00 p.m. The Queen and The Duke of Edinburgh were entertained at a State Banquet at the State Banqueting Hall.

PRETORIA, SOUTH AFRICA

STATE VISIT

FROM GHANA THE QUEEN GOES TO PRETORIA for a two-day State Visit to South Africa. It is evening when she flies in to the military air base, and her arrival brings omens of good fortune for it is raining as her plane touches down. She goes straight from the airport to the Sheraton Hotel, where the royal party has taken over the two top floors accessible only by special lift. Here she and the Duke have a quiet dinner, the menu chosen from the selection of fifteen sent earlier to Buckingham Palace.

The Queen travels with a small suitcase which is delivered immediately to her hotel. The Travelling Yeoman will oversee the unloading of the rest of the colour-coded luggage, which is taken from the aeroplane once the welcoming ceremony is finished. The Queen's colour is yellow.

Next morning there is a welcoming ceremony led by President Mbeki at the Union Buildings, once the stronghold of the apartheid regime. This is the centenary of the outbreak of the Boer War, and outside her hotel protestors have gathered to demand an apology for the deaths of women and children in British detention camps. After the ceremony, the Queen and the Duke lunch privately with the President and Mrs Mbeke, exchanging presents which include a volume of poems by the new Poet Laureate, and a jewellery box made by the Queen's nephew, Viscount Linley.

Back at her hotel the Queen has had a twenty-minute private meeting with Nelson Mandela. A message has come that we can go to the hotel, and as we wait for them to arrive we hear a peal of laughter from the Queen. They are both smiling happily as they come into the room. 'I can't tell you how nice it is to be back here,' she is saying. 'We are honoured,' replies Mr Mandela. They are here to meet a group of schoolchildren who have won prizes in an essay competition. The subject is 'What I would do if I were Queen for a day'. The prizewinner, Ntsako Mlambo, decided she would hire a plane, let children see any movie they wanted free of charge – and impose the death sentence on anyone raping a girl under the age of twenty-one, for this country has the highest rape rate in the world. The Queen and Mandela spend a long time talking to the children, then they all line up to be photographed. 'This is one of the worse parts of being Queen,' she tells them, somewhat wearily, 'having to pose for photographs.'

In her speech that evening at the State Banquet, the Queen speaks of the sadness of the loss of life and suffering in the Boer War. There is no formal apology: instead she suggests that the war should be commemorated in a spirit of reconciliation.

Alexandra Township is one of the largest in South Africa. It was here, in the jumble of makeshift shacks and brick houses, that Mandela lived when he was working as an articled clerk in nearby Johannesburg in his early twenties. It was known then as 'the Dark City'. The government is working to improve conditions, but life in the townships is still one of hardship and poverty.

The Queen in Alexandra Township near Johannesburg (right). On all her public engagements her Personal Protection Officer is close beside her.

204

TUESDAY 9TH NOVEMBER. *11 a.m. The Queen and The Duke of Edinburgh departed Kotoka International Airport, Accra, for South Africa.*
7.30 p.m. The Queen and The Duke of Edinburgh arrived at Waterkloof Military Airport, Pretoria.

WEDNESDAY. *11.30 a.m. The Queen and The Duke of Edinburgh were welcomed by the President of the Republic of South Africa and Mrs Mbeki at the Union Buildings, Pretoria. Her Majesty and His Royal Highness met Ministers and afterwards attended a meeting with the President and Mrs Mbeki.*
1.00 p.m. The Queen and The Duke of Edinburgh were entertained to Lunch at Oliver Tambo House, Pretoria, by The President of the Republic of South Africa and Mrs Mbeki.
3.15 p.m. Mr Nelson Mandela, OM, and Mrs Garca Machel called upon Her Majesty.
7.15 p.m. The Queen and The Duke of Edinburgh were entertained at a State Banquet at the Presidential Guest House, Pretoria.

The Queen with President Mbeki of South Africa on the steps of the Union Buildings in Pretoria. Thabo Mbeki replaced Nelson Mandela as President earlier in the year.

THURSDAY 11TH NOVEMBER. *2.55 p.m. The Queen and The Duke of Edinburgh arrived at Durban International Airport.*
4.00 p.m. Her Majesty and His Royal Highness drove to the International Conference Centre, Durban, where they toured the main auditorium and the exhibition hall.
6.30 p.m. Her Majesty and His Royal Highness gave a Reception at the Royal Hotel for representatives of the media covering CHOGM.

FRIDAY. *9.25 a.m. The Queen, accompanied by The Duke of Edinburgh, opened the Commonwealth Heads of Government Meeting.*
Morning. Her Majesty received the President of the Republic of Sierra Leone, the Prime Minister of the Kingdom of Lesotho and the President of the Republic of Botswana at the Royal Hotel.
Late morning. The Prime Minister of the Republic of Nauru, the Prime Minister of the Republic of Fiji Islands, the Prime Minister of the Republic of Vanuatu, and the Prime Minister of the Independent State of Samoa were received by the Queen and remained to Lunch.
Afternoon. Her Majesty received the Prime Minister of the Independent State of Papua New Guinea, the Prime Minister of Belize, the President of the Co-operative Republic of Guyana, the Prime Minister of the Republic of India, and the Prime Minister of Australia.
7.45 p.m. The Queen and The Duke of Edinburgh gave a Dinner for Commonwealth Heads of Government.

THURSDAY. 11TH NOVEMBER. *10.35 p.m. The Queen visited the Adult Education Training Centre, Alexandra, where she toured the classrooms and met the schoolchildren.*

11 a.m. The Queen observed the Two Minutes' Silence.

11.20 a.m. Her Majesty visited Alexandra Cricket Oval where she met young players and South African and visiting England Test cricketers.

12.30 p.m. The Queen attended a Reception at the Africa Museum, Johannesburg, given by the British High Commissioner to the Republic of South Africa.

1.35 p.m. The Queen and The Duke of Edinburgh departed from Johannesburg International Airport.

As part of an internationally funded project, the Queen goes first to a school where adults are taught to read and write. It is estimated that ten million South African adults are illiterate, and the government has made it a priority to break the back of illiteracy among adults and young people in five years. She is greeted by a choir of schoolchildren. The television crew filming her Christmas Broadcast has come out here, and the choir will appear in it. She then tours the school, seeing the teaching programme at work. It is Armistice Day, and at 11 o'clock the Queen pauses to observe the two minutes' silence.

From the school she goes to see a huge new cricket oval built on the site of an old refuse tip overlooking the sprawling township, part of a scheme to help South African cricket shed its 'whites only' image. Several games are going on at once, and the nets are busy with bowling practice. Out in the field young boys are being coached by South African cricketers and two of the visiting English team. Our exclusion has been reimposed, and we are put on a hill looking down onto the pitch. We have a panorama of the sports ground with the township beyond, and here we can wander unhindered, talking to the local people and to the children who have gathered with their flags. The Queen, though, is a distant and tiny image.

DURBAN, SOUTH AFRICA

COMMONWEALTH HEADS OF GOVERNMENT MEETING

THE QUEEN HAS MOVED ON TO DURBAN to open the biennial Commonwealth Heads of Government Meeting. Its theme is 'People-Centred Development: The Challenge of Globalisation'. We have no passes for any of the events, and we watch the opening ceremony on television. The Queen and the President are led into the hall by a Xhosa praise singer in a flowing red robe and dramatic porcupine-quill headdress. It is the first time that this has been held in South Africa, and only the second time that the Queen has addressed the conference. In her opening speech she talks of the many strands of a shared past that have been woven together into the Commonwealth in a forward-looking spirit of understanding, tolerance and friendship. 'We are not prisoners of the past, we are reconciled to it. Indeed we build on our history to work together as we face the challenges of the future.' She is followed by the retiring Secretary-General, Emeka Anyaoku. He speaks of the recent successes, and of the challenges still to be faced. 'This is the first time that the Commonwealth is meeting at the summit in a free, democratic South Africa,' he says, but they face the serious problems of deepening world poverty and intolerance. In his valediction he praises the Queen, who has brought 'a special quality of care and inspiration to us all'.

The opening ceremony over, we set about discovering what there is that we can see and do. Parallel to the conference there are various non-governmental organisation events, including a cultural performance programme, exhibitions, workshops and seminars. Many of them are here to draw attention to injustices which they hope the Commonwealth will address. At the Exhibition Centre, which the Queen visited yesterday evening, they are launching the newly formed Commonwealth Association of Indigenous Peoples with a programme of dancing and singing in the Nama language. These people were previously classified as coloured, and they are seeking to rediscover their roots and reclaim their self-respect. We watch a group of their children who perform a slow, quiet dance with a sad seriousness which is very touching. Between dances they sit and wait with scarcely a smile.

All next day the Queen has audiences and meetings with Commonwealth leaders, and she is recording part of her Christmas Broadcast, so we decide to go with the Duke of Edinburgh on his visit of reconciliation to Spionkop, the site of a great British military disaster of the Boer War where the two white armies fought one another for land owned by the Zulus. This is the terrain across which the Naval Brigade pulled their field guns in 1899, the trial of endurance re-enacted in the Royal Tournament Field Gun Competition.

Because the Queen is here she has had to miss two of the most important events in her calendar – the Royal British Legion Festival of Remembrance at the Royal Albert Hall and the Remembrance Sunday ceremony at the Cenotaph in Whitehall. But this is an appropriate place for her to be, for in both world wars the country raised large volunteer armies; Delville Wood on the Somme is for ever linked with South African sacrifice. The

A bugler sounds the Last Post during the Service of Remembrance at the war memorial in Durban.

SATURDAY 13TH NOVEMBER. *Morning. The Queen received The Prime Minister of Malta, The President of the Federal Republic of Nigeria, the Prime Minister of India, and the Prime Minister of Bangladesh.*
King Zwelithini of the Zulus called upon Her Majesty.
6.35 p.m. The Queen and The Duke of Edinburgh gave a Reception for Commonwealth Ministers, Officials and High Commissioners at City Hall, Durban.

SUNDAY. *10.45 a.m. The Queen and The Duke of Edinburgh attended a Service of Remembrance at the War Memorial, Durban, and laid wreaths at the Cenotaph.*
11.25 a.m. Her Majesty and His Royal Highness attended Morning Prayer at St Paul's Church.

Queen will lay a wreath at the fine polychrome Art Deco city war memorial. We have picked up a press pass for this that no one wants. Veterans and servicemen are arriving – but so is one of our friends from the press who has decided that after all he does want the position, and asks if we would mind moving. We do mind, but since he has got this far without being challenged, and as there is plenty of room we suggest that he joins us.

The Queen and the Duke walk the last few hundred yards from their car past the lines of servicemen to the small garden in which the memorial is set. During the short service they sit beneath a white canopy decorated with flowers, a very different setting from Whitehall in November to which the ceremony is being transmitted live. The timing, though, has got out of kilter. The events leading up to the two minutes' silence have been shorter than expected, and it is still only five to eleven. To fill time the band plays, then the bugler sounds the Last Post and the silence begins. After only thirty seconds it is brought to a premature end. Reveille should now be sounded, but instead the Queen is invited to step forward and lay her wreath. As she does so the strokes of 11 o'clock ring out. The Queen herself is quite unfussed by this series of hitches, which do not undermine the point and poignancy of the ceremony, but understandably the higher military command is incandescent.

MOZAMBIQUE
STATE VISIT

THIS IS THE QUEEN'S FIRST VISIT TO MOZAMBIQUE and it lasts just ten hours, her shortest State Visit ever. It is, though, an event of enormous significance to this former Portuguese colony which was admitted to the Commonwealth in 1995 after years of destructive civil war, the first member which was not previously a British colony. The Queen is revered here as a figurehead of stability and continuity, and her visit is seen as an endorsement of its new identity and as encouragement for progress which is still in its early days. As President Chissano, Mozambique's first democratically elected leader, tells her, it is 'further evidence that we are on the right path'.

Many of the press have not come on here, and so we have their spare passes which will give us access to almost everything. In the greeting ceremony at the airport, soldiers march in front of the Queen's dais with a step more familiar in Red Square than in Whitehall, a reminder of recent communist rule. More joyously, musicians and dancing women form a colourful and happy welcoming line. They sing 'Welcome to our mother'. The messages on their T-shirts, urging people to vote for President Chissano in the forthcoming election, are discreetly ignored, for this misuse of a vote-catching opportunity is considered less important than the fact that there are elections at all. At the City Hall the Queen receives the Keys of the City of Maputo before going to the Presidential Palace for lunch.

In the early afternoon she and the President jointly open a UK/Mozambique Partnership Week; Mozambique has the fastest-growing economy in Africa, and Britain is the country's third largest investor. As she arrives, her pathway is lined by children, including some from

a project to help street children, and she is greeted by a choir of local bus drivers and a group of traditional dancers.

After meetings with Commonwealth High Commissioners and the Leader of the Opposition Party, the Queen ends her day at a State Banquet. In the exchange of gifts she presents the President with a Psion 7 Series mobile computer, and in her speech she talks of the partnership between the two countries in combating poverty and improving health and education. Then, as we listen to the President describing the United Kingdom as an ally who is supporting his country in its progress towards democracy and stability, we realise how important this is to a country that has experienced so much fear and change. The floods, which will set back his country's progress so tragically, are still several months away.

From the banquet the Queen goes straight to the airport and her flight home.

MONDAY 15TH NOVEMBER. *10.30 a.m. The Queen and The Duke of Edinburgh departed South Africa for Mozambique.*
12 noon. The Queen and The Duke of Edinburgh arrived at Maputo International Airport and were received by The President of the Republic of Mozambique and Mrs Chissano.
12.40 p.m. Her Majesty and His Royal Highness arrived at City Hall, Maputo, where the Queen received the Keys of the City.
1.15 p.m. The Queen and The Duke of Edinburgh visited The President and Mrs Chissano and remained to Lunch.
3.20 p.m. Her Majesty, accompanied by The President, opened the Trade and Investment Exhibition.
3.50 p.m. The Queen met High Commissioners for the United Republic of Tanzania, the Kingdom of Swaziland, the Republic of Zambia, the Federal Republic of Nigeria, the Republic of India, the Republic of Zimbabwe and the Republic of South Africa resident in Mozambique.
4.05 p.m. Senhor Afonso Dhlakama, President of Renamo, the Opposition Party, called on Her Majesty.
7.50 p.m. The Queen and The Duke of Edinburgh arrived at Ponta Vermelha for a State Banquet.
10.00 p.m. Her Majesty and His Royal Highness drove to Maputo International Airport and boarded British Airways 767 for the United Kingdom.

TUESDAY. *8.15 a.m. The Queen and The Duke of Edinburgh arrived at Heathrow.*
9 a.m. Arrival at Buckingham Palace.

WEDNESDAY 17TH NOVEMBER. *11.10 a.m. The Queen, accompanied by The Duke of Edinburgh, went in State to the Palace of Westminster to open the Session of Parliament. Her Majesty and His Royal Highness drove in a Carriage Procession, escorted by a Sovereign's Escort of the Household Cavalry. Guards of Honour were mounted at Buckingham Palace by The Queen's Guard found by No 7 Company Coldstream Guards, and at the Palace of Westminster by the 1st Battalion Welsh Guards. A staircase party of the Household Cavalry was on duty at Victoria Tower, House of Lords. Gun Salutes were fired in Green Park by the King's Troop Royal Horse Artillery, and from the Tower of London Saluting Battery by the Honourable Artillery Company.*

12.15 p.m. The Queen and The Duke of Edinburgh returned to Buckingham Palace.

Afternoon. Her Majesty and His Royal Highness departed for a private address.

The Queen reads the Speech from the Throne in the Chamber of the House of Lords during the State Opening of Parliament.

LONDON

THE STATE OPENING OF PARLIAMENT

AFTER A SERIES OF NAIL-BITING DELAYS, we arrive back at Heathrow with about two hours to spare before we have to be at Westminster for the State Opening of Parliament. There is just time to nip home to drop off our luggage, have a bath and change, and then into a cab. Black Rod's office has given us wonderful positions – looking down the Royal Gallery, and in the balcony of the House of Lords.

From the day when Charles I entered Parliament and attempted to arrest its members, the Monarch has been banned from entering the House of Commons. When the Queen delivers her Speech from the Throne which formally opens the new session, she does so in the Chamber of the House of Lords. History also plays its part when, early in the morning, the vaults beneath the Chamber are checked by the Yeomen of the Guard to make sure that no modern Guy Fawkes has moved in overnight; it was their Yeoman forebears who uncovered the plot to blow up the Houses of Parliament. More effective security has already been carried out by the Metropolitan Police and sniffer dogs.

The Queen, wearing the Imperial State Crown, processes with the Duke of Edinburgh down the Royal Gallery.

The Queen and the Duke of Edinburgh, travelling in the Irish State Coach and accompanied by an escort of the Household Cavalry, are preceded to Parliament by a carriage bringing the Regalia – the Imperial State Crown, the Cap of Maintenance, and the Great Sword of State – which have earlier been collected from the Tower of London. This coach too has a mounted escort. At the Sovereign's Entrance they are greeted by the Earl Marshal and the Lord Great Chamberlain, who escort them up the Royal Staircase to the Robing Room. Here the Imperial State Crown is placed on the Queen's head, and a train fixed to her shoulders. Then, preceded by the College of Heralds – with names like Rouge Croix Pursuivant and Arundel Herald Extraordinary – the Yeomen of the Guard, the Honourable Corps of Gentlemen at Arms, the Officers of State, and two peers carrying the Great Sword of State and Cap of Maintenance, the Queen and the Duke make their way down the Royal Gallery to the Chamber of the House of Lords.

Meanwhile the members of the House of Commons are summoned by Black Rod. As he approaches the door of the Commons it is slammed in his face, a reminder of Charles I's abuse of privilege. He must now knock three times before it is opened. By convention, members show their lack of awe of the House of Lords by chatting as they make their nonchalant way across the lobby to the bar of the Chamber, where they stand to listen to the Queen.

Her Speech from the Throne, which lays out the plans for legislation for the forthcoming session, is handed to the Queen by the Lord High Chancellor. It has been written by the government of the day; as Constitutional Monarch she speaks their words. When she has finished reading it, she is thanked by two peers, and then she leaves, processing back the way she came. Members of Parliament return to the House of Commons, and the debate begins on the proposals contained in the speech.

LONDON

ROYAL HOMOEOPATHIC HOSPITAL

At the Royal Homoeopathic Hospital the Queen watches a patient receiving acupuncture.

THE QUEEN IS PATRON OF THE ROYAL HOMOEOPATHIC HOSPITAL, and she is here to celebrate the 150th anniversary of its foundation. The Royal Family has had a long association with this alternative, holistic medicine, which uses natural substances to promote the body's own healing mechanisms and restore physical and emotional balance. In 1835 Queen Adelaide was treated with homoeopathy, and the Hospital was founded in 1849 by the physician to Queen Victoria's favourite uncle, Leopold I of Belgium.

Homoeopathy works in conjunction with conventional medicine, and, although some people remain sceptical about its value, patients are referred here from Health Authorities all over the south and east of England. The Queen speaks to cancer patients undergoing Complementary Cancer Care and watches physiotherapy treatment. It is the first time she has seen acupuncture, and as the needles are put in she is anxious to know if it hurts. During her visit she is presented with a posy of homoeopathic flowers from the Royal Physic Garden in Chelsea – marigold, delphinium, monkshood, pomegranate, chili pepper and giant reed.

As we leave, the girl from the Press Office tells us that there will be no Royal Rota passes for us for either the Royal Variety Performance in Birmingham or the reopening of Covent Garden. We can have Fixed Positions on the pavement outside the Opera House to see the Queen arrive, but nothing at all for Birmingham. So a group in the Press Office continues its game of freezing us out. It would achieve nothing to make an issue of it, for once they have made up their minds they are immovable, but why are they making things so difficult?

BUCKINGHAM PALACE

WE HAVE COME to the Palace to watch the floral arrangements being prepared for tonight's Diplomatic Reception. The Florist, Pat Pentney, has arranged the flowers at the Palace and at Windsor Castle for thirty-two years.

For an important reception about sixty arrangements are done, and up to six assistants are brought in to help. Beginning at 7 o'clock each morning, they work for two days. The rooms themselves are so fine and so dominant that the flowers have to be subordinate, blending in with the colour and character of each. The largest arrangements are at the bottom of the stairs facing the Grand Entrance, and there are smaller ones above fireplaces, in front of mirrors, and on the piano and tables, as well as in small buffet bowls. Most of the flowers are now bought at Covent Garden, and the greenery is sent up from Windsor Park.

MONDAY 22ND NOVEMBER. *Returned to London.*

TUESDAY. *11.40 a.m. The Amir of the State of Bahrain visited The Queen. 12 noon. His Excellency Mr Timoor Daghistani was received in audience by Her Majesty and presented the Letters of Recall of his predecessor and his own Letters of Credence as Ambassador from the Hashemite Kingdom of Jordan to the Court of St James's.*

12.20 p.m. Sir Richard Mottram, Permanent Secretary, Department of the Environment, Transport and the Regions, was received by Her Majesty.

12.40 p.m. His Excellency Mr François Nordmann was received in farewell audience by the Queen and took leave upon His Excellency relinquishing his appointment as Ambassador from the Swiss Confederation to the Court of St James's.

12.50 p.m. Mrs Justice Black was received by Her Majesty upon her appointment as a Justice of the High Court when the Queen invested her with the Insignia of a Dame Commander of the Most Excellent Order of the British Empire.

3.00 p.m. Her Majesty, Patron, visited the Royal London Homoeopathic Hospital, London WC1, to celebrate its 150th Anniversary.

6.30 p.m. Prime Minister's audience.

Flowers being arranged for tonight's reception are laid out on drapes on the floor in the State Rooms at the Palace. Smaller arrangements can be done in the Florist's room and brought upstairs on a trolley.

215

LONDON

BUCKINGHAM PALACE

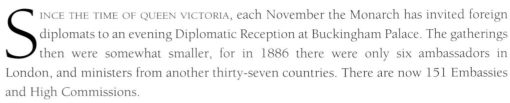

SINCE THE TIME OF QUEEN VICTORIA, each November the Monarch has invited foreign diplomats to an evening Diplomatic Reception at Buckingham Palace. The gatherings then were somewhat smaller, for in 1886 there were only six ambassadors in London, and ministers from another thirty-seven countries. There are now 151 Embassies and High Commissions.

As we arrive, people are laying out tables for the buffet supper and arranging glasses and candles. In a room leading off the State Rooms a temporary kitchen has been set up preparing canapés. The food has been cooked in the kitchens, and is brought up here to be put out on platters before being offered to the guests. Some of those whom we met in the Royal Mews at Windsor on the morning of the Hungarian State Visit, and again in Edinburgh, are here tonight as footmen, their normal role. They are lent to the Royal Mews for carriage duties on special occasions.

We go up onto the musicians' balcony and watch as the guests gather in the State Rooms. Shortly before the Queen comes in, they take up positions in order of precedence according to the length of their diplomatic relations with Britain. As the Queen makes her way down the line of Ambassadors and High Commissioners, the Marshal of the Diplomatic Corps presents each one. Behind them are ranked senior members of their staff, many in national dress. We share our balcony with an orchestra of the Household Cavalry playing light music, and after the Queen and other members of the Royal Family have left there is dancing – one of the rare occasions when the Ballroom is used for its original purpose.

Chefs from the Royal Kitchens prepare canapés. Each year the Queen is hostess to about 40,000 people from all walks of life at lunches, dinners, receptions and garden parties.

WEDNESDAY 24TH NOVEMBER. *11.45 p.m. Mr Justice McLaughlin was received by The Queen upon his appointment as a Justice of the High Court in Northern Ireland when Her Majesty conferred upon him the honour of Knighthood and invested him with the Insignia of a Knight Bachelor.*

11.55 a.m. Mr Mark Cunliffe-Lister was received by The Queen and delivered up the Insignia of the Order of the Thistle worn by his grandfather, the last Viscount Whitelaw.

12 noon. His Excellency Mr Jonathas Niyungeko was received in audience by Her Majesty and presented the Letters of Recall of his predecessor and his own Letters of Credence as Ambassador from the Republic of Burundi to the Court of St James's.

12.20 p.m. General Sir Charles Guthrie, Chief of Defence Staff, was received by Her Majesty.

12.40 p.m. The Queen held a Council.

9.30 p.m. The Queen and The Duke of Edinburgh held an Evening Reception at Buckingham Palace for the Diplomatic Corps.

A footman wearing semi-State livery. Normally they wear black tail coats, but when serving at State Banquets footmen wear full State livery of scarlet tail coats and knee breeches, pink stockings and black buckle shoes.

LUTON

PLANS FOR THE QUEEN'S VISIT TO LUTON began when she accepted an invitation to open the new £40 million extension to London's third airport, and she travels on the 10.28 Thames-link train from Moorgate to Luton Airport Parkway, a new station which she will also open. It is not the first time the Queen has been on an ordinary public train, but there is tight security, with the usual dungaree-clad police and eager sniffer dogs.

The Palace never discloses details about security,
which is the combined responsibility of the
Metropolitan Police and the local police force in the
district or country the Queen is visiting.

From there she goes to open the secure mental health Orchard Unit, and then on to the New Opportunities and Horizons – NOAH – training centre. Housed in a once-derelict building, the centre is open 365 days a year. It was established by two nuns, in conjunction with the local welfare services and with the support of local business, to give a chance in life to homeless, unemployed people. They show the Queen their new practical skills of joinery and upholstery, for it is said of NOAH that people come in with a bottle and go out with a certificate. Inside a few months, the lives of those with little hope – not all of them young – can be turned around as they find work, independence and self-esteem.

From NOAH she crosses the road to the Welbeck Youth Centre. As well as a playgroup, it offers IT training, work placements and job-search facilities for young people. Then, after a private lunch at the University of Luton, the Queen and the Duke go on to the airport. This development has a particular appeal to the Queen, for the surrounding grassland is maintained as a haven for wildlife. Orchids and insects, the rare marbled white butterfly, linnets, skylarks, yellowhammers, and the besieged brown hare all thrive here. In opening this new building, though, she has unwittingly become involved in a dispute between the airport authorities and easyJet, whose low-cost flying operation is responsible for nearly

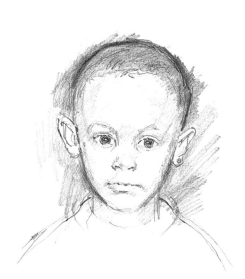

At the NOAH centre the Queen talks to some of those who are learning to make and upholster furniture.

half the flights out of here. They are protesting about the expense of what they see as an unnecessary development whose cost they will have to pass on to their customers. The Queen, whose own travel arrangements do not involve the tedium of queuing at check-in counters, watches as two passengers go through the formalities. As their bag is whisked away through a hole in the wall onto the new robot baggage-handling system, she says with a grin, 'I hope you see your suitcase again.' The passengers are flying with easyJet.

11.50 a.m. Her Majesty visited New Opportunities and Horizons, NOAH, where she toured the workshops, and the Welbeck Youth Centre.
12.10 p.m. The Queen and The Duke of Edinburgh visited the University of Luton where they attended a Reception and were entertained to Lunch.
2.45 p.m. Her Majesty, accompanied by His Royal Highness, toured and opened the new terminal at London Luton Airport.
3.15 p.m. Left Luton by car for a private address.

219

MONDAY 29ᵀᴴ NOVEMBER. Afternoon. Returned to London.

4.30 p.m. The Queen, and The Duke of Edinburgh left Euston Station on the Royal Train to travel to Birmingham.

6.55 p.m. Her Majesty and His Royal Highness arrived at Birmingham New Street Station.

7.00 p.m. The Queen, Patron, and The Duke of Edinburgh attended a Royal Variety Performance in aid of the Entertainment Artistes' Benevolent Fund at the Birmingham Hippodrome.

10.35 p.m. The Queen and The Duke of Edinburgh left Birmingham International Station on the Royal Train to travel to Stirling.

BIRMINGHAM
ROYAL VARIETY PERFORMANCE

FROM NEWSPAPER PHOTOGRAPHS, the multicoloured sequinned evening dress that the Queen wore in Birmingham looks wonderful – especially for something as jolly as a Royal Variety Performance. The Queen frequently wears bright colours so that she can be more easily seen, but recently she seems to have been wearing even more colourful clothes, which suit her well. They must be practical – the hats not too large nor the skirts too tight. Her outfits reappear many times, for there is no sense that she must not wear something which people have seen before. For many years her clothes were designed by Norman Hartnell and Ian Thomas, but since their deaths she has used Hardy Amies, and Karl-Ludwig Rehse who designed this particular dress.

SCOTLAND
STIRLING CASTLE

THE QUEEN ARRIVES at Stirling Station at 11.15, having travelled overnight from Birmingham, the second year running that she has come to Scotland for St Andrew's Day. Originally her train had been expected five minutes earlier, but that would have meant altering the schedule of a local commuter train, so her arrival time was put back.

The Royal Train has a normal diesel locomotive which is used for general duties when not needed for the Royal Train. The specially designed carriages, which were built in 1972, have modern office and communication facilities. The Queen can sleep overnight, hold meetings and do routine paperwork as she travels, and arrive into the city centre the following morning ready to begin her away day.

She is here to reopen the restored Great Hall in Stirling Castle, the centre of James IV's brilliant court. The Great Hall was completed in about 1503. During the Napoleonic Wars it became a military barracks, and, in order to make three floors, the original hammer-beam roof was removed. It remained a barracks until the mid-1960s, and then the painstaking work of restoring its medieval features began. Using surviving drawings and descriptions, and evidence from buildings of a similar age, the five fireplaces, four spiral staircases, stained glass windows, gallery, trumpeters' loft and stonework have been re-created. Three hundred and fifty oak trees were used in the new hammer-beam roof, which is constructed without nails or screws.

TUESDAY. *11.15 a.m. The Queen and The Duke of Edinburgh arrived at Stirling Station. Her Majesty and His Royal Highness drove to Stirling Castle and were received by the Rt Hon Donald Dewar, MP MSP, Mr Graeme Munro, Director and Chief Executive, Historic Scotland, and the Earl of Mar and Kellie, Hereditary Keeper of Stirling Castle, who surrendered to The Queen the Keys of the Castle which Her Majesty returned to him. The Queen, accompanied by The Duke of Edinburgh, unveiled the Cloth of Estate, reopening the Great Hall of Stirling Castle. Her Majesty and His Royal Highness subsequently attended a Reception and were entertained to Lunch by the First Minister of the Scottish Executive in The Queen's Outer Presence Chamber.*

3.30 p.m. The Queen and The Duke of Edinburgh visited The Scotsman headquarters, Edinburgh. Her Majesty and His Royal Highness toured, and The Queen subsequently officially opened, the new building.

6.00 p.m. Her Majesty and His Royal Highness gave a Reception at the Palace of Holyroodhouse for Scottish Young Achievers.

Having received the Keys of the Castle, the Queen is greeted in the Great Hall by a fanfare of trumpets. To mark its reopening she unveils a magnificent new Cloth of Estate, a re-creation of the embroidered wallhanging used by medieval monarchs as a sign of royal presence. The design is based on James IV's original Cloth of Estate.

EDINBURGH

FROM STIRLING THE QUEEN TRAVELS to Edinburgh, where her first engagement is to open the new headquarters of *The Scotsman* newspaper near Holyroodhouse. In the evening she holds a reception in Holyroodhouse for 350 of Scotland's young achievers. With its theme of youth and looking to the future, part of the reception is filmed in preparation for her Christmas Broadcast.

DECEMBER:
THE QUEEN AND THE CHURCH

As with so much to do with the monarchy, the relationship between the Queen and the Church has developed out of historical circumstance. At crucial times in the country's history, Acts of Parliament were passed that established power or curbed what were seen as dangerous influences. Many of these laws remain unchanged, resulting in what some now see as unacceptable anomalies.

Until Henry VIII's break with Rome in 1534, England was a Catholic country which acknowledged the universal authority of the papacy. In 1521, after the King had published a pamphlet defending the Church against Protestant attack, Pope Leo X had invested him with the title of Defender of the Faith. But with the Pope's refusal to allow him to marry Ann Boleyn, Henry broke with Rome and was declared by Parliament to be Supreme Head of the new Church of England. He retained the title Defender of the Faith, although he was no longer defending the authority of the Pope.

Under Henry's son, Edward VI, England became officially a Protestant country. Shortly before he died, Edward named the Protestant Lady Jane Grey as his successor, but within days the throne was claimed by Mary, Henry's daughter by his first wife, and a Catholic. During her five-year reign Mary restored the old religion and England returned to the papal fold, but when she died without an heir in 1558 the throne passed to the Protestant Elizabeth. In 1559, by virtue of the new Act of Supremacy, Elizabeth was declared Supreme Governor of the Church of England and thus vested with virtually the same ecclesiastical authority as her father had exercised. On the accession of James II in 1685, Protestant supremacy was once more challenged, for in the late 1660s he had become a Catholic. Parliament wished to block his succession but was unable to do so. When he was forced to flee to the Continent in 1688, the crown was offered to his Protestant daughter Mary and her husband, William of Orange, and this time Parliament took steps to prevent any further Catholic claims to the throne. In 1701 the Act of Settlement required the

Monarch to profess the Protestant reformed religion, and the Act of Union of 1707, in which Scotland lost not only its Parliament but also its right to choose its own monarch, formally excluded all 'Papists and persons marrying Papists'. This law still stands, although followers of other faiths are not excluded.

By these historical steps the Queen assumed the roles of Defender of the Faith and Supreme Governor of the Church of England. Since the time of Henry VIII, the jurisdiction exercised by bishops is conferred on them by the Crown by virtue of the Royal Supremacy. When a bishopric becomes vacant, the General Synod's Crown Appointments Commission submits two names to the Prime Minister, who advises the Queen on which of the two is to be offered the bishopric. Since the bishop is dependent upon the Monarch for the right to exercise the spiritual powers that have been invested in him by Christ through the Church, he is required, after his consecration but before his enthronement, to do homage to the Queen. In a private audience he kneels before her, and she places her hands around his. The Home Secretary, representing Parliament, then administers an oath in which the bishop recognises the Queen as Supreme Governor. As in so much relating to the monarchy, absolute power is given to no one.

The Church of England is the established Church in England; that is, it is recognised by law as the country's official Church. As Supreme Governor, every five years the Queen opens its General Synod in which current Church matters are discussed and measures passed. The Church of Scotland is the established Church in Scotland. Historically it was not part of the Church over which Henry VIII was appointed Supreme Head – indeed, it recognises only Christ as its Supreme Governor. The Queen is Christ's subject, and as such she is an ordinary member. The Churches in Wales and in Northern Ireland were disestablished in 1869 and 1920.

Bishops have jurisdiction over the churches and chapels within their dioceses, with the exception of Royal Peculiars. These, which

go back to Anglo-Saxon times, not only owe allegiance directly to the Sovereign but also are not subject to episcopal visitation. They include Westminster Abbey and St George's, Windsor, and a number of private chapels within present or previous royal residences at St James's Palace, Hampton Court and the Queen's Chapel of the Savoy, the only remaining part of a royal palace which once stood on that site. Because of the Queen's relationship with the Royal Peculiars, she is personally involved in any dispute affecting them. After the sacking in 1998 of the Abbey organist, and the resulting feud, the Queen ordered a commission to examine the organisation, management and accountability of all Royal Peculiars.

The Chapels Royal is an establishment rather than a building. Since Anglo-Saxon times there have been personal chaplains serving the spiritual needs of the Sovereign. The Keeper of the Chapel oversaw the vestments, relics, plate and books which were carried in panniers on two packhorses that travelled with the King. The Chapel accompanied Henry V to France, and Mass was sung before the Battle of Agincourt. By the time of Henry VIII, permanent chapels had been established at St James's, Whitehall, Hampton Court and Greenwich, employing the finest church musicians. From these choral foundations grew the present

Chapels Royal, with its choir of six Gentlemen and ten Children who sing each year at the Royal Maundy Service and at the Cenotaph.

Wherever she is, the Queen attends church each Sunday. That is her regular commitment to the Anglican faith, but her most intense and personal moment of involvement with the Church came during her Coronation when she was anointed, blessed and consecrated by the Archbishop of Canterbury. This, based on the anointing of Solomon by Zadok, was for her a moment of deep religious significance. This spiritual element of monarchy, in its broadest sense the religious dimension of royalty, is a complex aspect of its role and, subconsciously perhaps, of its appeal. The decline in the perceived significance of the monarch comes in part from a decline in spiritual acknowledgement by the people.

Because of its Old Testament and Christian derivation, this part of the Coronation is now being questioned by other faiths within the United Kingdom. The monarch's roles as Supreme Governor of the Church of England and Defender of the Faith are also perceived by many as divisive and inappropriate in a multi-faith society. Addressing these concerns, the Prince of Wales has spoken of his wish to be the 'defender of faith'. It is a profound and complex issue in which matters of moment once again challenge the role and definition of the monarchy.

LONDON
COVENT GARDEN

WEDNESDAY 1ST DECEMBER. *10.15 p.m. The Queen left Holyroodhouse by car.*
10.35 a.m. Arrival at Edinburgh Airport to fly to Northolt.
12.20 p.m. Arrival at Buckingham Palace.
12.40 p.m. The Queen held a Council.
7.10 p.m. the Queen and The Duke of Edinburgh attended the reopening of the Royal Opera House, Covent Garden.

THURSDAY. *11.00 a.m. The Queen held an Investiture, televised for the first time.*
1.00 p.m. The President of Ireland, Mary McAleese, and Dr Martin McAleese, visited Her Majesty and remained to Lunch.

FRIDAY. *11.30 a.m. The Lord Carter, Captain of Her Majesty's Body Guard of the Honourable Corps of Gentlemen at Arms, had an audience of The Queen and presented an Address from the House of Lords to which Her Majesty was graciously pleased to make reply.*

I N OUR FIXED POSITION outside the Royal Opera House, Covent Garden, on the night of its Gala Opening, we join celebrated photographer friends – Tim Graham, Arthur Edwards and Mark Stewart – who are here with their step-ladders and cameras. Happily, they suggest that we might like to have a foot on their ladders so that we can see what is going on.

This is one of the great opera houses of the world, and the part-old, part-new Floral Hall – a reminder of the days when Covent Garden Market was the centre of London's flower, fruit and vegetable trade – looks bold and dramatic, its white cast-iron tracery reminiscent of an albino Victorian railway station. The refit has cost £214 million. Two and a half years ago Darcey Bussell extinguished the lights one by one at the end of a performance of *Sleeping Beauty*; tonight she will relight them. It is a family party, for the Queen, Queen Elizabeth and Princess Margaret have all come. Princess Margaret is President of the Royal Ballet. They have been here together many times, most notably in 1938 when they came to see the pantomime *Little Red Riding Hood*, and for the last gala reopening in 1946.

THE ROYAL INSTITUTION

THE ROYAL INSTITUTION was set up, among other things, to share the excitement of scientific phenomena with the public. At lectures in its steeply raked lecture theatre, nineteenth-century London society would gather to see demonstrations of weird and exciting phenomena. The first member of the Royal Family to visit it was Prince Albert, who in 1849 heard a lecture by Faraday 'On Magnetic and Diamagnetic Bodies'. In 1855 he brought the Prince of Wales and Prince Alfred, then aged thirteen and ten, to the first of a series of six lectures for young people which are still held every Christmas.

This is the bicentenary of the granting of its Royal Charter by George III. Today the Queen listens in that same theatre to three five-minute illustrated talks, and then she is asked to press a button in the lecture theatre to unveil a tablet in the entrance hall commemorating her visit. With amusement she watches the remote-controlled unveiling on closed-circuit television, and then young scientists explain some of their latest work to her.

11.40 a.m. Major General Evelyn Webb-Carter, Major General Commanding Household Division, was received by The Queen.

12 noon. His Excellency Dr Hans-Friedrich von Ploetz was received in audience by Her Majesty and presented the Letters of Recall of his predecessor and his own Letters of Credence as Ambassador from the Federal Republic of Germany to the Court of St James's.

12.20 p.m. Sir Alistair Goodlad was received in audience by Her Majesty upon his appointment as British High Commissioner to the Commonwealth of Australia.

12.40 p.m. General Sir Samuel Cowan, Chief of Defence Logistics, was received by Her Majesty.

12.50 p.m. Dr Humayun Khan was received by The Queen upon relinquishing his appointment as Director of the Commonwealth Foundation.

12.55 p.m. Mr Alfred Oates was received by The Queen when Her Majesty decorated him with a Bar to the Royal Victorian Medal (Silver).

Afternoon. Left for a private address.

MONDAY. Afternoon. Returned to London.

TUESDAY. 11 a.m. The Queen held an Investiture.

3.00 p.m. The Queen, Patron, and The Duke of Edinburgh, Honorary Member, visited the Royal Institution of Great Britain, London W1, to mark its Bicentenary Year.

6.30 p.m. Prime Minister's Audience.

NOTTINGHAM

WEDNESDAY 8TH DECEMBER. *11.35 a.m. Mr Graham Allen, MP, Vice-Chamberlain of the Household, was received in audience by The Queen and presented an Address from the House of Commons to which Her Majesty was graciously pleased to make reply.*

11.40 a.m. Sir Michael Bichard, Permanent Secretary at the Department for Education and Employment, was received by The Queen.

12 noon. His Excellency Dato Haji Yusof Hamid was received in audience by Her Majesty and presented the Letters of recall of his predecessor and his own Letters of Commission as High Commissioner from Brunei Darussalam in London.

12.20 p.m. Her Majesty received the Bishop of Norwich, the Rt Revd Graham Jones, who did homage upon his appointment. The Rt Hon Jack Straw, Secretary of State for the Home Department, administered the Oath.

12.30 p.m. Admiral Sir Michael Boyce, Chief of Naval Staff and First Sea Lord, was received by The Queen.

1.00 p.m. The Queen and The Duke of Edinburgh gave a Luncheon Party at Buckingham Palace.

10.50 p.m. The Queen and The Duke of Edinburgh left Euston Station on the Royal Train to travel to Nottingham.

I N THE BROADMARSH SHOPPING CENTRE IN NOTTINGHAM, seven-year-old Kayne Riley is waiting to give a posy to the Queen. As with so many people who meet her, it's all over too quickly. 'It was fun meeting her, not scary,' he tells us. 'I'd like to meet her again. I just said "Good morning Your Majesty", and she said I was very kind and thanked me for the flowers.' Posies and flowers that are still in good condition at the end of the day are kept by the Queen, or passed on to others on her staff, or to local hospitals, hospices or old people to be enjoyed.

In the Beeston Ward of the City Hospital the Queen meets patients who are receiving stroke rehabilitation treatment, one of a number of visits she has paid to stroke patients as Patron during the centenary year of the Stroke Association.

At Nottingham University the Queen is coming to see the new Jubilee Centre, an exciting development on a former 30-acre industrial site, with a waterside walkway beside an artificial lake and a dramatic glass atrium. To mark her visit, ten new scholarships are to be given to Commonwealth students.

As we wait for her to arrive, one of their officials comes up to us and asks us who we are. We tell him about the book, and what we are doing. '*I think not,*' he says. There's a moment's silence, then, 'What don't you think?' we ask. '*I think not,*' he repeats. '*You are not on my list.*

Kayne Riley waits to present flowers to the Queen. Many of the children chosen to do this have struggled against illness or disadvantage.

In an atmosphere of early millennium celebration, local shopkeepers prepare for the Queen's walkabout in the Broadmarsh Shopping Centre.

THURSDAY. *9.55 a.m. The Queen and the Duke of Edinburgh arrived at Nottingham Station.*

10.05 a.m. Her Majesty and His Royal Highness arrived at Broadmarsh Shopping Centre and walked through the renovated Centre.

10.25 a.m. The Queen, Patron of the Stroke Association, visited Beeston Ward, the stroke rehabilitation ward, at Nottingham City Hospital where she toured the ward area and met patients, staff and representatives from other stroke associations.

11.10 a.m. The Queen and the Duke of Edinburgh visited Nottingham University where The Queen opened the new Jubilee Campus and they were entertained to Lunch.

2.25 p.m. Her Majesty and His Royal Highness visited the Reserves Training and Mobilisation Centre, Chetwynd Barracks, Chilwell, where the Queen saw the Quartermaster's Department and watched reservists undergoing training by the United Nations Training Advisory Team.

3.50 p.m. The Queen and The Duke of Edinburgh left East Midlands Airport for Heathrow and Windsor.

Will you please leave.' Not again! At least this time we're not pushed. 'Well, no, we won't actually. We have Royal Rota passes.' They are hanging prominently from our buttonholes. 'The Palace knows we're here.' *'You may have Royal Rota passes, but you're not on my list. I would ask you to leave immediately.'* We suggest he goes and rings the Palace. A few minutes later he is back. *'You can stay,'* he says. *'I just wish they'd told me you were coming.'* We can see his point.

Here there is one of the few student protests of the year. 'What do we want?' *'No Queen!'* 'What do we want?' *'Guillotine!'* they chant, and are treated with good-humoured banter by those around. There are also banners about student grants, possibly aimed at the Secretary of State for Education who is here with his guide dog.

The Reserves Training and Mobilisation Centre at Chetwynd Barracks is a new unit of the British Army. It was set up earlier this year to prepare reservist volunteers, from both the Territorial Army and the Individual Reserve, to take their place on attachment to the Regular Army. It is a response to the financial cutbacks by making maximum use of trained men. The Queen tours the Quartermaster's Department to see the equipment issued to the reservists, and she watches a group preparing for posting to Bosnia. In a United Nations Training Advisory Team session, she sees a soldier working with an interpreter as he learns how to interview a refugee.

LONDON
THE PRESS ASSOCIATION

Morning. The Queen presented the Windsor Staff presents.
Evening. Staff Dance at Windsor Castle. Returned to Buckingham Palace.

TUESDAY. *Morning. The Queen presented the Buckingham Palace Staff presents.*
12.30 p.m. The Queen held a Council.
2.30 p.m. Christmas Broadcast preparation.
6.30 p.m. Prime Minister's audience.

WEDNESDAY. *11.00 a.m. The Queen held an Investiture.*
12.15 p.m. Her Majesty received a spray of the Holy Thorn of Glastonbury as a Christmas gift from the Church and people of Glastonbury.
4.00 p.m. The Queen and the Duke of Edinburgh visited the Press Association, London SW1, to mark the Centenary of the appointment of the first Court Correspondent. Her Majesty and His Royal Highness toured the building, met present and past Court Correspondents and photographers, and subsequently attended a Reception and met regional newspaper editors.

SINCE 1899 THERE HAVE BEEN ONLY EIGHT COURT CORRESPONDENTS. It is obviously an agreeable job, for three of its holders served for more than twenty years. The post was set up by the Press Association, an international news-gathering agency, and is held by one of their staff. The present incumbent, since 1994, is Peter Archer. Each morning he goes to the Palace to be briefed and to be brought up to date with royal news. He accompanies members of the Royal Family on many of their engagements in and around London, and on overseas tours. Royal visits out of London are generally covered by local Press Association staff.

There is no Court photographer, but in the Queen's Silver Jubilee Year in 1977 the Press Association was asked to send a photographer to cover every event to ensure the media had access to pictures of all these. Since then, one of their photographers has been regularly present at audiences, receptions and other events within the Royal Palaces, although, unlike the American President, the Queen is not photographed with all those who come to see her. The photographer is not part of the Royal Household, and the Press Association retains editorial and storage control of all the images.

Since this is the centenary of the first Court Correspondent, the Queen has come to the Press Association to see something of the way in which it currently functions. She visits the newsdesk, sees demonstrations of digital photography, teletext and racing coverage, and uses a computer mouse to transmit the story of her own visit.

Peter Wilkinson, one of the most experienced and delightful of the royal press group, is the accredited Royal Television Cameraman. He is not part of the Press Association but has been with Independent Television News for thirty-six years, and is the only cameraman allowed at routine royal engagements in and around London, although others are accredited for special events and away days. His film is distributed to ITV, BBC and Sky.

Peter Wilkinson (above) records the Queen's visit to the Press Association.

LORD CHARTERIS OF AMISFIELD

DURING HIS FINAL ILLNESS, the Queen goes to visit Lord Charteris of Amisfield. As Martin Charteris, he was Private Secretary to Princess Elizabeth, and on her accession he became her Assistant Private Secretary, and then Private Secretary from 1972 to 1977. He was a man of enthusiasm and energy, a hugely influential Private Secretary who brought a relaxed and humorous touch to his work, and who has been described as the person who breached the old walls standing between royalty within and the people without. On his retirement he became an expansive and popular Provost of Eton. He died on 23rd December at the age of eighty-six.

CHRISTMAS BROADCAST

LONDON AND WINDSOR

THE FIRST CHRISTMAS BROADCAST was made in 1932 when George V spoke live on radio from Sandringham. Since 1960 the Queen's message has been pre-recorded so that it can be sent to Commonwealth countries in advance, and can go out at times that are convenient for each country. Since 1957 it has also been televised.

In this broadcast the Queen shares her own thoughts without consultation with ministers, although her Private Secretary will have an input into its preparation. Plans begin several months in advance. Once she has chosen her theme and drafted the shape of what she wishes to say, relevant film is shot during her engagements and away days. This footage is then cut into the Queen talking direct to camera. It is often observed that, however easy and jolly she is immediately before the cameras start to roll, she becomes stilted and formal when filming begins. In the more spontaneously shot film of her engagements she is seen laughing and relaxed.

A camera crew preparing the Christmas Broadcast was with the Queen at engagements earlier in the year, including her away day in October when she visited emergency services in Manchester.

The filming is not without its problems. One year, at the time when the broadcast was directed by Sir David Attenborough, the Queen decided to speak from the Royal Mews – a stable seemed appropriate for Christmas. Standing with one of the horses behind her, she solemnly spoke to her people. Unfortunately the horse, enjoying the attention, raised its upper lip into a broad and toothy grin. The piece had to be reshot, but the Queen was much amused and asked to keep a video of the first and failed attempt.

This year the pieces to camera have been filmed in her hotel in Durban, South Africa, in Holyroodhouse, and in St George's Chapel, Windsor. She speaks about the millennium, and about the lessons of the past that we can carry forward into the future. Within this framework she ranges widely over Scottish young achievers, Africa and the Commonwealth, and the selflessness of those who work in the emergency services – all aspects of her working life during this past year. Having begun by speaking about the rate of change which sweeps away so much that is familiar and comforting, she finishes by pondering on the constant and unchanging values that have stood the test of time and experience – fairness and compassion, justice and tolerance – and suggests that the message of caring for others, which is at the heart of Christianity and all the great religions, can give guidance and reassurance as we step into the twenty-first century. 'I, for one, am looking forward to the new millennium,' she says.

THURSDAY 16TH DECEMBER. *11.40 a.m. The Archbishop of Canterbury was received in audience by The Queen.*
12 noon. Mr Barney Smith (the Kingdom of Thailand) and Mr Ian Gerken (the Republic of Ecuador) were received in audience by The Queen and kissed hands upon their appointment as Her Majesty's Ambassadors. Mr David Carter was received in audience by The Queen upon his appointment as British High Commissioner to the People's Republic of Bangladesh.
1.00 p.m. Royal Family Christmas Luncheon.
6.30 p.m. Royal Mews Christmas Carols.

FRIDAY. *Morning. The Queen recorded her Christmas Broadcast.*
Afternoon. To Windsor.

SATURDAY. *6.30 p.m. Windsor Carol Singers.*

MONDAY. *To Sandringham.*

This year's Christmas Broadcast begins and ends inside St George's Chapel, Windsor, as the Queen looks back on its antiquity and forward to the dawn of a new millennium.

LONDON

THE MALL

Over the New Year the Mall is closed to traffic and transformed into a funfair.

For two days over the new year the Mall is closed to traffic, and there is a funfair. It is strange, and rather merry, to see the solemnity of Buckingham Palace through a foreground of roundabouts and swings.

The Queen has come from Sandringham for tonight's millennium celebrations. She has asked that the first visit of the evening should be to the Crisis shelter in Southwark where, during the winter, beds, food and clothing are provided for up to forty people, including drug addicts. She meets and talks to some of the people here, but there is no red-carpet treatment. Interestingly, in view of public perception, while she is at the shelter the Prime Minister is hosting a cocktail party in the House of Lords. Also interestingly, there is no attempt to exploit this low-key visit for its obvious PR potential. That is not why she is here.

SOUTHWARK AND GREENWICH

HER NEXT STOP IS SOUTHWARK CATHEDRAL, where she lights a millennium candle to mark the beginning of an all-night vigil of prayer; she has been anxious that the spiritual aspect of this commemoration of Christ's birth should not be forgotten. From here she is driven to Bankside Pier, where she boards *Millennium of Peace*, the boat that will take her down the river to Greenwich. Ships' horns sound all around her, and huge crowds are gathered along the embankment; it seems as though the whole of London is *en fête*. As her boat reaches Tower Bridge there is a fanfare of State Trumpeters. Here she is handed a torch with which she lights the fuse that triggers a laser which fires the National Millennium Beacon, the first of a chain of beacons across the United Kingdom.

A 21-gun salute, fired from the Tower of London, booms out over the water when her boat crosses the meridian line. As it reaches Greenwich Pier she is again greeted by a fanfare. At 11.15 she takes her seat in the Dome for the celebration concert. It is nearly 11.50 when, assisted by a group of eight children from the Meridian School in Greenwich, she formally opens the Dome, and huge curtains drop away to an extravaganza of light and colour and music. John Tavener's 'A New Beginning' runs dangerously close to midnight, and by the time its last haunting strains die, there is already the sound of soaring fireworks outside, along the Thames. Big Ben, projected onto a huge television screen, rumbles into its midnight chimes, and the Queen raises her champagne glass to toast the new millennium. Into the noise of celebration comes the sound of a piper playing 'Auld Lang Syne', and she takes the hands of the Duke of Edinburgh on one side and the Prime Minister on the other. As the Prime Minister's wife sings along, one television commentator reports that the Queen is standing close to the First Lady.

FRIDAY 31ST DECEMBER. *4.00 p.m. Left Sandringham by car.*
6.30 p.m. Arrival at Buckingham Palace.
8.15 p.m. The Queen and The Duke of Edinburgh visited the Crisis Shelter, Southwark, London SE1.
8.40 p.m. Her Majesty and His Royal Highness visited Southwark Cathedral, where they attended a short service at the start of a Vigil of Prayer for the new Millennium and Her Majesty lit the Millennium Candle.
9.20 p.m. The Queen and The Duke of Edinburgh drove to Bankside Pier where they embarked in the City Cruises 'Millennium of Peace' and proceeded downstream towards Tower Bridge.
9.45 p.m. The Queen lit the National Millennium Beacon on the River Thames before crossing the Meridian Line.
10.35 p.m. Her Majesty and His Royal Highness disembarked at Queen Elizabeth II Pier, Greenwich, before going to the Millennium Dome. Just before midnight The Queen opened the Millennium Dome, and then watched the Opening Winter Carnival.

SANDRINGHAM

SATURDAY 1ST JANUARY 2000. *12.30 a.m. The Queen and The Duke of Edinburgh left the Dome by car.*
3.15 am Arrival at Sandringham.

Michael Noake
1999

AFTERWORD

As we have come to the end of our royal year, how do we now feel about what we have seen, about the Queen's daily life as working monarch?

To begin with, we have been surprised at the heavy workload that a woman now well into her seventies continues to bear. She is helped by her advisers and her supporting staff, but there remains a large amount which only she can do. Not only does the Queen work far harder than we imagined, but the work she does is more relevant to national life than we had expected.

Then, we have been struck by the breadth of the canvas of her working life, how much more variety there is than we anticipated. The range of events and the diversity of the people whom she meets build into a kaleidoscope of British life. We have been at grand State occasions and we have watched as she listened to the problems of people struggling to re-create their lives after suffering strokes. We have seen formal, glittering receptions in Buckingham Palace and low-key tea-parties on inner-city housing estates. We have stood by during international conferences and as she talked to a dying cardinal, and we have gone to race meetings in high summer and to the wet and muddy Norfolk countryside in winter.

Wherever she goes, the Queen is shown the success stories, the prize-winners, the best rather than the worst. There is logic in this, for it gives encouragement and endorsement to those who have succeeded, whether this is a personal battle to overcome pain or the achievement of a country that has struggled to establish democratic government. In Africa she sees the dancing, the singing, the celebration. From her red boxes and her talks with its leaders she knows well its darker, destructive side, but it is the success which she publicly endorses. At least one person we spoke to wished that she could sometimes be shown a run-down, no-hope prison instead of cutting the tape for yet another sparkling new police station. She herself expressed a wish to visit the Crisis shelter on New Year's Eve, and perhaps in time her advisers will suggest that this kind of thing happen more often.

It has all been far jollier than we expected. The Queen is sometimes portrayed as uptight and joyless, but she is neither. She has, though, two basic expressions. When she is concentrating or listening she appears glum, almost dour, but this can suddenly dissolve into smiles and laughter – and we have seen a great deal of laughter, both from the Queen herself and from those she is with. Queen Victoria once remarked that a monarch can give pleasure by doing very little, and the happiness on the faces of those she has met and talked to is something we will not easily forget. Of course, we do not pretend that everyone responds to her in this way. Those who wait to see her, sometimes in the cold and rain, are likely to be excited by her visit and to support what she represents; but others stay away, either from indifference or from hostility, possibly cursing the inevitable disruption to normal life that such a visit creates. And there have been protests – though surprisingly few.

We had heard that the Queen is unable to respond to children or old people, a criticism that has particularly been levelled at her since the change in expectation created by the Princess of Wales. Certainly she does not have the Princess's immediate, tactile response to the very young, but she is a different person with a different background and upbringing, and she is from another generation. When she is out and about working, she doesn't pick children up or cuddle them – in fact, she sometimes stands back and looks on, missing obvious opportunities to move closer to them. But there were many times when we saw her talking happily and imaginatively to small children who presented her with posies or who wanted to show her their drawings or models. With young people, teenagers and students, she seems to have an easy rapport. Nor did we see any evidence that she is unable to respond to the old. Indeed, she appears to enjoy their company and to be considerate of their problems. We have seen old men struggle to their feet as she approached. 'I am not going to sit in the presence of my Monarch', said one old soldier. She appreciated his wish to stand as much as she respected the needs of others who had to remain in their wheelchairs, and she would lean forward to speak to them, on occasion discouraging them from attempting to get up. We saw in her the reserve that is inseparable from high office, but we saw also the warmth.

One problem she has is that there is never enough time. She must move on to the next person, and the next, and it is difficult for her to be more than superficial in what she says. On occasion, especially towards the end of a tiring day, there were short, aching silences, but these would be broken by a question from her, then concentrated listening and finally a smile or a laugh. 'She really seemed to care,' one person after another said to us after she had talked to them. Yet the people to whom she speaks are rarely at their best. They are often nervous and talk too much, or tongue-tied so that they scarcely talk at all. Some of those to whom we spoke wished that they could do the whole thing again, only better.

As the year went by we realised increasingly how misinformed many people are about aspects of her life. The belief that she does not work hard, and does little to justify her privilege, is one. The perceived remoteness of her personality is another. Money is a third. Of course she is rich, as anyone with centuries of inheritance will be. But she is anxious to keep the costs of running the monarchy as low as they can be, consistent with the dignity of the office and the expectations of the people. Cuts in expenditure are made wherever possible. Clothes are well looked after so that they can be worn many times. Not only is she aware of the dangers of personal extravagance, but the running of all the royal estates on ecologically sound principles is based on both responsible stewardship and her understanding of the vulnerability of natural resources.

We did not fully appreciate, when we began the year, the value of the Queen as emissary abroad. In the countries we visited she personifies a stability we had always taken for granted. As we watched how people in uncertain democracies responded to what she represents, we were reminded of Solzhenitsyn's anger, after he moved to the West, at the way in which freedoms undreamt of in Soviet Russia were so often undermined by the complacency of those who easily possess them.

But to balance this praise there is also criticism, and this centres on some of those around the Queen. We have touched on these difficulties in this book, but we experienced and witnessed many more. Problems arising from arrogance can be found in any large and important organisation where employees ride on the back of its status. Many of those with whom we dealt were consistently helpful and polite, but some were not, and our experience of discourtesy and unhappiness in dealing with the Palace is too widely shared with others – from cub reporters to bishops – to be ignored. We were affected by the petty internal politics found in any community, and there was a sense that we must not expect to take things for granted, that we were privileged but must not think ourselves too privileged, that we must be pulled back from demanding too much. Part of this rose from the shadow of Bagehot and his often quoted phrase about the danger of letting the daylight in on the magic. It is an idea that we grew increasingly to mistrust. To relate magic to monarchy is to undermine its reality. There is a spiritual element in monarchy, but that has nothing to do with magic either. We have no wish to see the monarchy become commonplace, but that is not the alternative. In practice, this belief in the need to hold onto the magic is too often an excuse for an unnecessary and damaging secrecy. Society is different from how it was in Bagehot's day. The public now wishes to know, and by increasing our understanding of what the Queen does we can more readily see how extraordinary her role is, and how important it is to the people of this country. The more the monarchy is understood, the more it will be trusted, and the people's trust is essential to its survival. But if it is to be fully understood, it must be fully open, more prepared willingly to share its way of life with the people who sustain it. In recent years it has gone a long way down this road, but it needs to go further. There is, after all, nothing to hide in the monarch's working life. Suspicion by the Palace of those who wish to exploit the monarchy for scandal and profit is one thing; suspicion of those who wish to explain its role is another.

As the year ends we have moved from our position of sixty-forty in favour of constitutional monarchy. We now see it as one of the most delicately tuned and enviable forms of government there is. It not only offers stability and continuity, and prevents overall power from falling into the hands of any one person or political group, but it also gives human form to a disembodied state. Throughout centuries of change, the British monarchy has adapted, sometimes unwillingly, to the demands of the people. It is a living system that has moved with the circumstances of time. This ability to respond has secured both its own survival and the vitality of the constitution it represents. For constitutional monarchy exists not for the benefit of the Monarch and the Royal Family, however privileged their lives are, but for the people of the country. In the end the monarchy is not to do with any individual sovereign but with the way we, all of us, choose to be governed. It is not the only system that secures the freedom of its people, but it is one that has both grown from, and helped to form, our national character, and it has stood the test of time and circumstance.

Some people believe that the abolition of the House of Lords in its traditional form has weakened the hereditary principle, and with it the monarchy. We do not agree. However ill-thought out the reforms have been, they have removed the dead wood of heredity from our constitution, allow its more living aspects to flourish. The very arbitrariness of succession is part of the monarchy's strength. Our Head of State neither seeks nor competes for the position. The Queen is not drawn by ambition and she offers no personal manifesto. She carries no political baggage and has no need to pursue short-term compromise in a search for votes.

The danger is that the monarchy is under threat for the wrong reasons. One is that it is not open to all-comers. In a society that promotes equality, an unacceptable spectre of privilege is evoked by the automatic right of succession, and the advantages that go with it. Another is its antiquity. The long history of our monarchy sits uncomfortably in an age where vitality and relevance are seen as qualities associated only with the new. A third is the decline in national identity which is tied to shame about our imperial and world-leading past. As we have shared during the year in the entertainments arranged for the Queen, we have observed an almost complete lack of interest in the English – though not Scottish or Welsh – heritage. We have watched exciting multicultural dance and song performed by British people whose roots are in Commonwealth countries and who are justifiably proud of their inheritance and determined that it will not disappear. Yet only once – when they were rehearsing Shakespeare at the Young Vic – was the Queen invited to see English children performing anything of their own culture. While other groups are encouraged to be proud of their inheritance, it would seem that the English are not.

The monarchy is part of that inheritance, and it too is suffering from this sense of later-generation shame. As we have lost faith in ourselves, so we have lost faith in our monarchy. The irrelevancies of media revelation have become centre-stage in the discussion of its future. Alongside this there is the drip, drip of slow erosion as its purpose is calculatedly whittled away by those who would prefer leadership, and its accompanying power, to rest unchallenged in the hands of elected politicians and unelected bureaucrats. Perhaps, in the end, it will be the as yet unresolved power of the European Union that will be the unstoppable and deciding factor in its future.

INDEX